"*Practical Pedagogy* is a timely and beautifully crafted book that accurately describes what good pedagogy should be. Practical suggestions for teaching and learning link to theoretical perspectives, with evidence of impact on learners. It is essential reading for educators starting out on their career and also for experienced professionals in need of a gentle reminder of what is possible in modern day classrooms, schools and education systems."

Ollie Bray, *Principal at Kingussie High School, Scotland*

"It's remarkable to find such clear yet comprehensive writing about the future of teaching and learning. With this guide in hand, educators will be able to discover and explore a collection of powerful, research-based approaches like epistemic education, computational thinking, embodied learning, among many other recent innovations."

Jeremy Roschelle, *Executive Director,*
Learning Sciences at Digital Promise, California, USA

"This is a great book, born out of the great series of *Innovating Pedagogy* reports published by The Open University. It is a clearly written compendium of evidence-informed practical guidance about how to learn, teach and assess. This will be an invaluable tool in any teacher's toolkit."

Rose Luckin, *Professor of Learner Centred*
Design at UCL Knowledge Lab, London, England

"Oftentimes, teachers and policy makers are enthusiastic and passionate to seek improvements and innovations in teaching and learning, but are not very well informed about what can work and how it works. *Practical Pedagogy* fills in this gap. Its lucid presentations provide novel and valuable insights for education stakeholders to understand, improve and innovate with the latest developments of emerging pedagogies."

Chee-Kit Looi, *Professor of Education at*
National Institute of Education, Singapore

Practical Pedagogy

Practical Pedagogy expands the universe of teaching and learning. It is an accessible guide to new and emerging innovations in education, with insights into how to become more effective as a teacher and learner. New teachers will find a comprehensive introduction to innovative ways of teaching and learning. Experienced educators will be surprised by the range of useful pedagogies, such as translanguaging, crossover learning, teachback, bricolage and rhizomatic learning. Policy makers will gain evidence of how new teaching methods work in practice, with resources for curriculum design and course development.

Drawing on material from the hugely influential *Innovating Pedagogy* series of reports, this book is a compilation of the 40 most relevant pedagogies, covering:

- innovative ways to teach and learn;
- how pedagogies are adopted in new ways for a digital age;
- evidence on how and why different methods of teaching work, including case studies set in classrooms, informal settings and online learning spaces;
- practical implications of the latest research into the science of learning, combining psychology, education, social sciences and neuroscience.

Organised around six themes – Personalization, Connectivity, Reflection, Extension, Embodiment and Scale – *Practical Pedagogy* is a comprehensive source for teachers, policy makers, educational researchers and anyone interested in new ways to teach and learn.

Mike Sharples is Emeritus Professor of Educational Technology at The Open University, UK. He is Honorary Visiting Professor at Anglia Ruskin University, Centre for Innovation in Higher Education. His research involves pedagogy-informed design of new technologies and environments for learning. He is author of over 300 publications in pedagogy, science education, educational technology and the learning sciences.

Practical Pedagogy

40 New Ways to Teach and Learn

MIKE SHARPLES

Routledge
Taylor & Francis Group

LONDON AND NEW YORK

First published 2019
by Routledge
2 Park Square, Milton Park, Abingdon, Oxon OX14 4RN

and by Routledge
52 Vanderbilt Avenue, New York, NY 10017

Routledge is an imprint of the Taylor & Francis Group, an informa business

British Library Cataloguing-in-Publication Data
A catalogue record for this book is available from the British Library

Library of Congress Cataloging-in-Publication Data
Names: Sharples, Mike, 1952- author.
Title: Practical pedagogy: 40 new ways to teach and learn / Mike Sharples.
Description: Abingdon, Oxon; New York, NY: Routledge, 2019. | Includes bibliographical references.
Identifiers: LCCN 2018057063 (print) | LCCN 2019005057 (ebook) | ISBN 9780429485534 (Ebook) | ISBN 9781138599802 (hbk) | ISBN 9781138599819 (pbk) | ISBN 9780429485534 (ebk)
Subjects: LCSH: Effective teaching. | Individualized instruction. | Curriculum planning.
Classification: LCC LB1025.3 (ebook) | LCC LB1025.3 .S5266 2019 (print) | DDC 371.102–dc23
LC record available at https://lccn.loc.gov/2018057063

ISBN: 9781138599802 (hbk)
ISBN: 9781138599819 (pbk)
ISBN: 9780429485534 (ebk)

Typeset in Dante and Avenir
by Deanta Global Publishing Services, Chennai, India

Contents

Preface

The Open University (OU) is a great British institution. It was founded in 1969, with the radical aim of being a full university carrying out high-quality research and teaching that is open to everyone. Most of the undergraduate courses have no formal entry requirements – any person can apply to start a course of study towards a degree. Yet graduates of the OU have have knowledge and skills equal to those leaving a traditional university. Many companies like to employ OU graduates because they have the motivation that comes from fitting part-time study around a busy life.

How has the OU taught over two million people at university level through distance education? The answer is good pedagogy. Pedagogy[1] is the theory and practice of teaching, learning and assessment. Some pedagogies, such as lecturing, are well known to everyone. Others, like inquiry learning, will be familiar to teachers and educational researchers. Many more pedagogies are practised in schools, colleges and universities, but have no name and have gone largely unrecognized. How can this be? How can something so important be so ignored?

I think the answer is that pedagogy is something teachers do, but don't generally talk about. There are many books on how to teach. These cover topics such as managing students, lesson planning, cultivating passion in young learners and dealing with problems in the classroom. Other books discuss theories of learning or summarize research into effective teaching. But there are no recent books on practical pedagogy. The author Stephen Melville Barrett did write a book on just that topic in 1908, but we've learned so much more about how to teach and learn since then.

In 2011, I was appointed Professor of Educational Technology at The Open University. It was a time for exciting new technologies, such as mobile learning and virtual reality. The annual NMC/EDUCAUSE Horizon Reports discussed how new technologies may influence education[2]. There was also an emerging new science of learning that combines insights from neuroscience, education, psychology and machine learning. I decided there was a need to understand and promote innovations in pedagogy alongside technology. Each year since then, colleagues from the OU, and later other centres of innovation in teaching and learning, have produced annual reports on *Innovating Pedagogy*[3]. The reports explore new forms of teaching, learning and assessment to guide educators and policy makers. They have been successful, with up to 80,000 copies accessed each year.

The *Innovating Pedagogy* reports are free and published under a Creative Commons licence that allows anyone freely to copy, redistribute, remix, transform and build upon the content, provided they acknowledge the original reports. That's what I am doing in this book. I have selected 40 pedagogies from the reports, then rewritten and extended them to provide a comprehensive practical guide. As a teacher, student, researcher or policy maker, you may be familiar with some pedagogies such as 'learning to learn' or 'learning through storytelling'. You may have heard of others such as 'assessment for learning' or 'threshold concepts'. But I'm pretty sure that however much you know about theories of learning or classroom teaching, you will not be familiar with all 40 pedagogies. Even if you are, I hope that this book will offer new insight into how they have been developed and adopted by teachers and learners worldwide.

This book builds on the ideas and writings from the authors of the *Innovating Pedagogy* reports: Anne Adams, Sarit Barzilai, Dani Ben-Zvi, Clark A. Chinn, Roberto de Roock, Rebecca Ferguson, Elizabeth FitzGerald, Mark Gaved, Christothea Herodotou, Tony Hirst, Yotam Hod, Yael Kali, Elizabeth Koh, Agnes Kukulska-Hulme, Haggai Kupermintz, Chee-Kit Looi, Patrick McAndrew, Barbara Means, Yishay Mor, Julie Remold, Bart Rienties, Jeremy Roschelle, Ornit Sagy, Kea Vogt, Martin Weller, Denise Whitelock, Lung Hsiang Wong and Louise Yarnall. They are inspiring colleagues. I could not have written this book without their contributions.

I give my deepest thanks to Minji Xu, Evelyn Sharples and Jennifer Taylor who in their differing ways are putting pedagogy into practice.

Notes

1 The word 'pedagogy' can be pronounced either with a soft or a hard final 'g'.
2 www.nmc.org/publication-type/horizon-report/
3 www.open.ac.uk/blogs/innovating/

Innovative pedagogy 1

In July 1913, the *New York Dramatic Mirror*, a theatrical trade newspaper, reported an interview with the inventor Thomas Edison. The newspaper asked Edison for his views on the future of the motion picture. Like many entrepreneurs, Edison couldn't resist the opportunity to speculate on how his invention would improve society. Here is how the newspaper reported his words:

> "Books," declared the inventor with decision, "will soon be obsolete in the public schools. Scholars will be instructed through the eye. It will be possible to teach every branch of human knowledge with the motion picture. Our school system will be completely changed inside of ten years."

Even at the time, this prediction was treated with scepticism and derision. One commentator remarked "O joy! Books in the public school will soon be obsolete, Edison predicts". In recent years, Edison's remarks have been resurrected to show how 100 years of technology have not transformed classroom teaching, nor made books obsolete.

The power of pedagogy

However, Edison was not only trying to promote a new educational technology (the classroom movie projector) but also a new method of teaching "through the eye". His quoted words continue:

> We have been working for some time on the school pictures. We have been studying and reproducing the life of the fly, mosquito, silk weaving moth, brown moth, gypsy moth, butterflies, scale and various other

insects, as well as chemical chrystallization [sic]. It proves conclusively the worth of motion pictures in chemistry, physics and other branches of study, making the scientific truths, difficult to understand from text books, plain and clear to children.

Learning from short animated movies is still a hot topic of research. Animations can help students understand complex dynamic processes, such as how the heart pumps blood or chemicals crystallize. New interactive software apps, such as an animated periodic table, a simulation of animal breeding and a virtual planetarium offer ways to learn "through the eye" that would have delighted Edison. This book covers these in Chapter 19. Edison got the technology wrong, but the pedagogy right.

If we focus on how new technology may or may not change education, we are missing the more important and enduring transformations brought by pedagogy – the theory and practice of teaching, learning and assessment. New pedagogies may well involve technology, but the emphasis is on improving how people learn, not just introducing devices into classrooms.

Here are two examples of how new pedagogies are changing education. Until the 1970s, almost all research in educational innovation was about individualized instruction – how to match teaching content to the needs and activities of individual students. Then, findings from social psychology began to show the value of working together. When students cooperate in small groups of between four and eight people, they are more creative and have better outcomes than when they work alone. For many students, learning in groups is not a natural process, so they need to learn how to cooperate by arguing constructively and resolving conflicts. Schools and colleges now make time for group learning activities. New methods of learning through conversation and teamwork have been developed for online distance education.

Another educational success story is constructive feedback, where students learn by getting immediate responses to their actions and answers. These can come from a teacher, another learner or from a computer. Giving feedback is most successful when it helps a learner to improve, by finding out how to correct a misunderstanding or to build new knowledge in reaching a goal. A student learns something and thinks she understands it, she is tested on that learning and finds some missing or faulty knowledge, then she is helped to correct it.

The science of learning

By emphasizing pedagogy rather than technology, we get to the core of how people learn and how to make teaching more effective. In a paper for the journal *Science,* Andrew Meltzoff, Patricia Kuhl, Javier Movellan and Terrence Sejnowski laid foundations for an interdisciplinary science of human learning that brings together findings from psychology, education, social sciences, neuroscience and artificial intelligence.

They started by pointing out that humans are the only species to have developed formal ways to enhance learning, through teachers, schools and curricula. Every human being from birth is equipped with a powerful mechanism for learning. Meltzoff and colleagues describe human learning from three perspectives: computational, social and neural.

As **computational** beings, we learn from experience by forming structured models of our environment. For example, we learn the difference between a dog and a cat, the taste of an apple or a pear, or the voice of mother or a stranger. This process can be simulated on computers through methods of 'machine learning' that show how learning can happen without direct teaching, through observation and inference. New computer models of 'deep learning' are starting to show how our brains are able to recognize scenes or concepts. They also provide powerful tools for computer-based face recognition or automated car driving.

As **social** beings, we learn by copying others, starting with our parents. Young babies can match gestures that are shown to them, such as opening their mouths or sticking out their tongues. This imitation game is particularly remarkable because babies can do it even before they have seen their own faces in a mirror. It is a foundation for learning through apprenticeship – following other people and gaining their skills – and for empathy, in regulating emotions and sympathizing with other people. Imitation is also the basis for learning language. Experiments with young children have shown that they are able to pick up a foreign language quickly when interacting with other humans, but not by just watching TV or listening to the radio.

As **neural** beings, we possess brains of great complexity. Each human brain has around 85 billion brain cells, or neurons, each connected with up to 10,000 other neurons. Learning happens in the brain by modifying the connections, called synapses, between neurons, so that the links are strengthened or weakened. Each new word, fact or skill we learn causes a change in the circuitry of the brain. Young children's learning may seem effortless as they pick up language through games and conversation, but it is accompanied by high brain activity.

The paradox of pedagogy

Humans are remarkable learning systems. We learn by imitation, instruction, conversation, self-reflection and exploration. Our learning starts at birth and continues throughout our lives. On average, adults engage in 13–17 hours per week of active learning, with around eight major learning projects a year, such as learning a foreign language, a sport or a new skill. Bookshops and TV schedules are filled with advice on gardening, cooking and home repair.

Table 1.1 Types of learning

Learning is ...	Specialisms	Educational methods
Changing behaviour	Behavioural sciences	Behaviour modification
Making connections	Neuroscience	Drill and practice
	Cognitive science	Tuition
Enhancing skills	Cognitive development	Apprenticeship
		Collaboration
Gaining knowledge	Epistemology	Inquiry
		Problem solving
Making sense of the world	Social sciences	Exploration
Personal change	Psychology and psychoanalysis	Reflection
		Conversation

The paradox of pedagogy is that humans can't stop learning – yet we often find it hardest to learn what other people want to teach us. The education system of schools, colleges and universities has evolved over centuries to provide a foundation of knowledge and skills that are needed in society and the workplace. But sitting young people in classrooms, instructing them in times tables or chemical elements, then examining them on their recall of this knowledge, is a highly inefficient way of preparing them for life. So, what are the alternatives?

There is no single answer to that question. As Table 1.1 shows, there are many ways to learn. As those who try to study learning or improve education have found, each type of learning has its own research area and educational methods, often separated or at loggerheads. Cognitive scientists clashed with behavioural scientists in the 1970s over whether learning is about modifying behaviour or developing minds. Researchers who study collaborative learning have little in common with those who investigate cognitive neuroscience. Even instruction by drill and practice has its place for learning the basics of arithmetic or history.

Innovative pedagogies

Rather than trying to split learning and teaching into separate compartments, the focus here is on pedagogy as a unifying theme – a process that binds together all the different strands of education. In particular, this book looks at new pedagogies that link different educational methods, such as reflection and exploration, or conversation and inquiry. Some pedagogies work best in a classroom, with a teacher to guide the learning. Others are designed for learning outdoors, in museums or online. This book puts pedagogy centre stage, as the way to explore new methods of teaching and learning, in formal and informal education, within and outside classrooms, for young and old.

In the book you will find descriptions of new pedagogies, accounts of how they are being applied in practice, evidence of their success and discussion of their scope and limitations. Some may be familiar, but the book will show how they are being adopted in new ways for a digital age. Each pedagogy has practical suggestions on how to apply it within or outside the classroom, or online. I have organized them around six themes, shown in Table 1.2: Personalization, Connectivity, Reflection, Extension, Embodiment and Scale.

Table 1.2 Themes and pedagogies

Themes	Pedagogies
Personalization	Adaptive teaching
	Spaced learning
	Personal inquiry
	Dynamic assessment
	Stealth assessment
	Translanguaging
Connectivity	Crossover learning
	Seamless learning
	Incidental learning
	Learning from gaming
	Geo-learning
	Learning through social media
	Navigating knowledge
Reflection	Explore first
	Teachback
	Learning through argumentation
	Computational thinking
	Learning from animations
	Learning to learn
	Assessment for learning
	Formative analytics
Extension	Threshold concepts
	Learning through storytelling
	Learning through wonder
	Learning in remote science labs
	Context-based learning
	Event-based learning
	Learning for the future
Embodiment	Embodied learning
	Immersive learning
	Maker culture
	Bricolage
	Design thinking
Scale	Massive open social learning
	Crowd learning
	Citizen inquiry
	Rhizomatic learning
	Reputation management
	Open pedagogy
	Humanistic knowledge-building communities

Personalization

Imagine if each student could have a personal tutor, always available, attentive to the student's needs, sensitive to weaknesses and gaps in knowledge, and with a fund of knowledge to impart. Personalized instruction has been a dream of educational technologists since the early 20th century. They have developed increasingly sophisticated teaching machines that respond to the behaviour of each student or infer a student's mental states and correct misunderstandings. So far, this has only been successful for limited topics in mathematics or science. **Adaptive teaching** now offers the promise of using data about each learner's previous and current learning to create a personalized path through educational content. Techniques of **spaced learning** draw on new findings from neuroscience to work out the optimum time to teach.

Personal inquiry provides opportunities for investigations based on a learner's own questions and interests. Personalized learning is a wider process of understanding and developing the aptitudes and skills of each learner through methods, such as **dynamic assessment** and **stealth assessment**. **Translanguaging** recognizes the language abilities of each student and helps the student to understand and express knowledge in their own terms.

If teaching is adapted to the needs and abilities of each learner, with a personalized curriculum and pathway, what will be its effect on the student's motivation? Learning is inherently social. From an early age, children learn about the world by imitating their parents, holding conversations and playing with friends. Personalized learning threatens to replace this social experience with a dance between child and computer. To enrich and engage, personalized learning needs to be combined with pedagogies that connect learners and encourage them to learn from each other.

Connectivity

Connectivity covers learning among people and across locations. In **crossover learning**, students may start an investigation in class, initiated by a teacher, then continue it outdoors or at home, using mobile devices, such as smartphones, to collect data and evidence that are then shared and presented back in class. These are specific kinds of **seamless learning**, connecting learning experiences across locations, times, devices and social settings.

Another goal is to connect the productive **incidental learning** that goes on in homes, workplaces, museums and the outdoors, with formal classroom education. This connection could be made using **learning from gaming** (an approach that enables students or employees to gain occupational skills of decision-making, strategy and negotiation through playing online strategy games) or **geo-learning** (students explore their local environment with the support of interactive maps and guides while connecting with other learners investigating the same environment online).

Learning online offers opportunities for connectivity between learners from different nations, cultures and perspectives. **Learning through social media** makes use of Twitter and Facebook to share ideas and engage in productive conversations. The challenge for educators is to create friendly and supportive spaces for learning, where differing views are respected and there is productive discussion on controversial topics, but knowledge and expertise come to the fore and teachers have a strong role in guiding the conversations. **Navigating knowledge** addresses this challenge by helping students understand the nature of knowledge, to distinguish truth from falsehood, evidence from fakery.

Reflection

All this activity online and in the physical world could suggest a future for education that is hugely dynamic and mobile. That may be one vision. But knowledge also comes from reflection and contemplation. The engine of learning is a continuous cycle of engagement and reflection. Our activity in the world – as we explore an environment, perform an experiment or read a book – produces new information that must be linked to existing knowledge. This provides both the enrichment and the mental conflict that are sources for reflection and understanding, perhaps leading to discussion and plans for further investigation. This cycle of productive learning appears in school classrooms (where teachers encourage reading, reflection and discussion), the science lab (through experiment, note taking and synthesis of data) and field or museum trips (where students form an inquiry question, collect data in the field, then reflect on the findings at home or in the classroom). A pedagogy of **explore first** encourages students to start a new topic by exploring its scope, trying to solve problems and reflecting on failure and success, before getting formal teaching.

Learning from animations involves watching an animated presentation of a dynamic process (such as how the heart pumps blood), or a problem being solved (such as how to solve quadratic equations). Learners are encouraged to reflect on each step of the process and explain it in their own words.

Teachback encourages reflection by having one person explain their knowledge to another, then that person tries to teach it back. Teachback can be extended to groups through structured **argumentation**, where students explain their reflective processes to others, in a collaborative process of experimentation and discussion.

Computational thinking offers a powerful approach to solving problems using structured techniques derived from computing, including iteration, debugging and problem decomposition. It forms part of **learning to learn** – developing the high-level knowledge and skills needed to become an effective learner.

Assessment for learning can help each learner to reflect on current learning difficulties, find relevant resources and overcome difficulties. At its most effective, this kind of formative assessment fits into the cycle of learning, providing feedback on how well new information has been learned and giving pointers to new learning activities that will fill gaps in knowledge.

Formative analytics enable data from processes and outcomes of learning to be harnessed to improve the quality of teaching and learning. Visualizing data from learning offers educators a means to reflect on how they teach and how to design more effective methods. It gives students insight into how they learn. Extending that idea of designs for learning, schools and universities can introduce a process of institutional learning, where everyone, including students and parents, can reflect on successes and failures, and propose ideas to improve the quality of education.

Extension

Some innovative pedagogies form part of this process of institutional improvement not by offering radically different ways of teaching, but by extending the scope of current teaching methods and overcoming their weaknesses. **Threshold concepts** are ideas that open up new ways of thinking about a problem. If a threshold concept, such as 'heat transfer' or 'centre of gravity', is taught well, it can inform everyday activities, such as cooking or sports coaching. **Learning through storytelling** offers new perspectives on an ancient tradition through techniques that blend classroom and online storytelling, with teachers and students creating shared stories. **Learning through wonder** begins by seeing wonder in an object or event that provokes a journey of investigation, discovery and celebration.

Technologies enable us to extend the settings in which learning takes place. Students can now **learn in remote science labs**, operating expensive equipment that is not available on site but can be controlled remotely at distant locations. A variety of technologies, such as augmented reality, also provide opportunities for **context-based learning** and **event-based learning**, bringing the learning process to where it is most immediately relevant.

Good management is essential to ensure that students are learning productively. Educators, researchers and policy makers need to move beyond assumptions that playing games and chatting online with friends is necessarily bad. Instead, we should look for ways to integrate the worlds of social media, gaming and formal education. We should be developing the knowledge and skills needed for jobs that don't yet exist through **learning for the future**. This will not be easy and it can't be done in a naïve way, by adding a layer of game playing or social chat onto traditional schooling.

Embodiment

School, university and online learning all promote the importance of abstract academic knowledge. Yet **embodied learning** recognizes that we are creatures with bodies that we use to explore, create, craft and construct. **Immersive learning** suggests that a sense of being and acting in the world can be intensified through immersion, even when that world is created through virtual reality. Immersive learning integrates the senses of vision, sound, movement, spatial awareness and sometimes touch.

A renewed interest in **maker culture** has seen people gathering for maker faires, jamborees and craft days. Enthusiasts use modern tools, such as hobbyist computers or 3D printers, to carry out environmental surveys, create soccer-playing robots or design intricate jewellery. **Bricolage** is a practice of learning by tinkering with materials, transforming products or materials that are ready to hand into new constructions. It is a fundamental process of playful learning, from building sandcastles to creating improvised art and fashionable clothing. **Design thinking** combines bricolage and reflection into a creative process of proposing, designing, testing and redesigning.

Scale

Delivering education at massive scale has been a headline innovation in recent years. Massive Open Online Courses (MOOCs) now engage millions of people in learning online. MOOCs have demonstrated that it is possible to produce methods of learning that improve with scale. If the pedagogy of a MOOC can be based on **massive open social learning**, then the more people who take part, the richer the interactions, with people around the world exchanging ideas and sharing perspectives. To manage this level of engagement requires techniques from social networks, of 'liking' comments, 'following' learners and educators, and rewarding popular learners and their contributions, so the most successful contributions are highlighted.

Other pedagogies that are being explored at massive scale include **crowd learning** (participants post questions, stories, images, videos and computer programs for other learners to answer or review), **citizen inquiry** (members of the public propose and engage in investigations and science projects) and **rhizomatic learning** (learners work together in dynamic ways to determine their own curriculum and modes of learning). **Reputation management** is a way to draw on the power of the crowd to assess and enhance people's reputation and so learn from their expertise.

Is personalization compatible with learning at scale? Will we be able to develop new pedagogies that offer thousands of learners the opportunity to pursue their personal pathways to knowledge, at the same time as they engage in shared discussion and collaborative inquiry? **Open pedagogy** may be one solution, where teachers and learners collectively create, annotate, extend, mix and share teaching materials. Another may be to create **humanistic knowledge-building communities** where each person's knowledge and interests is prized and developed within a supportive community.

Amongst all this innovation in teaching, learning and assessment, some principles endure. The teacher still performs a central function, but that is changing from delivery of educational content to facilitating discussion and reflection. Structure is still important, perhaps even more so, as we discover effective ways to initiate, embed and extend learning. Learners still need appropriate goals and support. And most important, learning is a collegiate process. It only works when people want to learn, enjoy the process and support each other. The next decade of innovating pedagogy may focus less on the elements of instruction and more on how to merge the new pedagogies into an effective process of lifelong learning.

In a report written in 1993 to the UK National Commission on Education, Professor David Wood offers a scenario of 'A Day in School: 2015 AD'. It is remarkably prescient with regard to technologies for education, including fieldwork projects supported by mobile wireless devices, learning with pen tablet computers, collaboration through computer networks and tools for teachers to analyze the progress and outcomes of learning. Then, having offered a picture of a bright technology-enhanced future for education, the report states

> If the recent past can be taken as a reliable guide to the near future, then one can have little confidence that (even if considered desirable) the kinds of developments in education that have been described will come about.

The reasons for such pessimism back in the early 1990s are revealing. The main obstacle indicated in that report, of providing each learner with a personal computer, is being overcome. New smartphones and tablets are powerful affordable tools for learning. Professor Wood's second obstacle, of developing more user-friendly and useful technology for learning, is also being addressed, through an increased awareness of the importance of good design and usability. But the final impediments relate to pedagogy rather than technology. They are as important now as they were then: that schools, colleges and universities are attempting to teach knowledge and skills for jobs that no longer exist, and that teachers are not fully involved in educational innovation and curriculum development. *Practical Pedagogy* explores current and emerging innovations in education for the 21st century, to offer teachers a greater range of methods, to guide educational policy makers in making informed decisions about curriculum design, course development and teaching strategies, and to help everyone improve their learning.

Resources

Interview with Thomas Edison:
Smith, F. J. (1913). The evolution of the motion picture: VI – Looking into the future with Thomas A. Edison. *New York Dramatic Mirror*, July 9, 1913. New York, p. 24.
http://bit.ly/1MysBpR

Contemporary comment on the article:
Oregonian (1913). *Section Four: The Sunday Oregonian*, Photo-Play Notes, p. 2, column 5. Portland Oregon. Quoted in Quote investigator.
https://quoteinvestigator.com/2012/02/15/books-obsolete/

Conditions for effective group work:
Johnson, D. W., & Johnson, R. T. (2009). An educational psychology success story: Social interdependence theory and cooperative learning. *Educational Researcher*, 38(5), 365–379.
https://bit.ly/2PDsiz6

For a review of research on feedback, with advice on how to design effective feedback see:
Shute, V. J. (2008). Focus on formative feedback. *Review of Educational Research*, 78(1), 153–189.
https://fla.st/2KVx9ZC

New science of learning:
Meltzoff, A. N., Kuhl, P. K., Movellan, J., & Sejnowski, T. J. (2009). Foundations for a new science of learning. *Science*, 325(5938), 284–288.
www.ncbi.nlm.nih.gov/pmc/articles/PMC2776823/

Introduction to deep learning, with a reading list:
http://deeplearning.net/

Research into whether children can learn vocabulary from watching television:
Krcmar, M., Grela, B., & Lin, K. (2007). Can toddlers learn vocabulary from television? An experimental approach. *Media Psychology*, 10, 41–63.

Estimate of the number of neurons in the human brain:
Azevedo, F. A., Carvalho, L. R., Grinberg, L. T., Farfel, J. M., Ferretti, R. E., Leite, R. E., ... & Herculano-Houzel, S. (2009). Equal numbers of neuronal and nonneuronal cells make the human brain an isometrically scaled-up primate brain. *Journal of Comparative Neurology*, 513(5), 532–541.
https://bit.ly/2P7pwEZ

Research into adults' informal learning activities:
Livingstone, D. W. (2001). *Adults' Informal Learning: Definitions, Findings, Gaps and Future Research* (Working paper 21). Toronto: NALL (New Approaches to Lifelong Learning). https://bit.ly/2AiKLvE

Research into adults' informal learning projects:
Tough, A. (1971). *The Adult's Learning Projects: A Fresh Approach to Theory and Practice in Adult Learning.* Toronto, Canada: Ontario Institute for Studies in Education. https://eric.ed.gov/?id=ED054428

Report written in 1993 by David Wood on a day in school, 2015:
Wood, D. (1993). The classroom of 2015. *National Commission on Education Briefing No. 20,* October 1993. London: National Commission on Education.

Part I

Personalization

Adaptive teaching

2

Adapt teaching to the learner's knowledge and actions

Overview

Adaptive teaching uses data about a student's previous and current learning to create a personalized path through educational content. No human teacher can track the actions of each student in a class, so adaptive teaching is usually done by students logging onto a computer system that provides the customized instruction. The computer sets a quiz at the start of the lesson to test knowledge of the topic. Then, it sends each student down a different route based on how that person responds to questions, asks for help or makes a choice of teaching material. Some adaptive systems provide tools for the student to monitor progress. They can also help teachers choose classroom activities or teaching content based on responses from students. Products for adaptive teaching have been developed for use in classrooms, in workplaces and at home.

A vision of adaptive teaching

A student on a college mathematics course is learning with adaptive teaching software. She chooses a sequence in which to study the material and after each section, she is given a diagnostic test. If she is stuck on a problem the software offers hints. When she understands easier problems, she is given more difficult ones. The computer suggests areas of weakness she should review. At the end of the day, the teacher views the performance of each student. The system shows that a large group of students had trouble answering specific questions, so the teacher plans either to re-teach those concepts in class the next day or to split the students into small groups to discuss their problems, as suggested by the software.

Adaptive teaching technologies

Some educators see adaptive teaching systems as providing flexible study options to students, particularly those struggling in remedial and general education courses, or students taking fully online classes. Adaptive teaching products have their roots in 1980s research into 'intelligent tutoring systems'. These were developed primarily to support mathematics teaching, but new products address a broad range of subjects including languages, psychology, economics and biology.

Adaptive products are designed and sequenced by professional software designers and educational technologists. Pearson's MyLab & Mastering products include many subjects: biology, chemistry, engineering, psychology, writing, culinary sciences, oceanography and accounting. Knewton uses psychometric tools to analyze student ability, probabilistic models to recommend the learning activities to complete next, clustering to group students by proficiency and 'forgetting curves' to trigger reminders. Knewton, and others, such as Smart Sparrow, allow a teacher to select the lesson design and to set the range of adaptability.

Smart Sparrow provides tools to create simulations and interactive content. CogBooks enables educators either to select from previously created courses or to create their own. Its adaptive course sequence is neither a pre-set path, nor one based on test results, but it employs algorithms and machine learning methods that continuously tailor a learning sequence for each learner. It also adds learner interests to standard educational content, for example producing mathematics problems that appeal to the learner.

The Cognitive Tutor® systems from Carnegie Learning trace changes in a student's knowledge. They try to act like a good human tutor, asking the students to explain their reasoning, making inferences about the student's knowledge and offering hints and explanations.

Some recent research into adaptive technologies goes beyond cognitive learner data by responding to learners' moods, such as whether the students are paying attention. An interactive companion to the MathSpring math tutoring game sends encouraging messages to students and adapts the game difficulty depending on learner confidence, interest, frustration or excitement.

Adapting adaptive teaching

Despite much progress, adaptive teaching faces barriers. A study of research into intelligent tutoring systems found strong positive outcomes compared to traditional teaching. But when adaptive teaching is taken into classrooms, the results are less promising. A systematic review of Cognitive Tutors® in secondary schools found mixed effects on algebra and no discernible effects on general mathematics. For geometry, there were potentially negative effects with secondary students.

The difference between the promising research and the disappointing practice seems to lie with the need for teacher development to manage the new technology and pedagogy, integration into classroom teaching, finding suitable educational content and pressure in the school system to move all students on, whether they have mastered the material or not.

The cost of developing adaptive teaching systems can be high if teaching material must be produced to match the needs and interests of different learners. To create an adaptive lesson, an instructional designer must plan sequences of content, with branches for remedial teaching and hints to give the right level of challenge and support. Design of these tutoring systems can involve years of research into learners' misconceptions. Recent work on efficient ways to analyze and select content, including content provided by teachers or other learners, may help the growth of adaptive teaching.

Adaptive teaching without computers

Some educators suggest that adaptive teaching can be carried out by teachers without the need for software to log the activity of every student. A paper by Allen, Webb and Matthews claims that a good teacher can adapt to students in a class, through well-developed knowledge of how students think and learn, strategies for engaging students in inquiry processes and ability to connect classroom teaching to everyday life. They give a case study of Amelia, a novice science teacher who engaged in adaptive teaching by encouraging students to work together on science problems. She watched for learning to emerge as they tinkered with materials and ideas. She encouraged the students to discuss their thinking processes and helped students to see how their experiments connect to everyday science. Then, she highlighted these connections for the entire class. It could be argued that Amelia was just developing the qualities expected of an experienced classroom teacher, but the authors make a case that her focus was on adapting her teaching to ideas, activities and questions as they arose from the students.

Adaptive teaching in practice

The Global Freshman Academy of Arizona State University is an online program for students to try out first-year college courses for free. The aim is to teach students how to solve problems and to increase their confidence in mathematics. It has adopted ALEKS adaptive software from McGraw-Hill Education.

The BioBeyond adaptive biology course from Smart Sparrow has been adopted by 70 colleges and universities in the United States. It starts with a motivating big question, such as 'What is life?', then takes students through projects, with adaptive pathways and assessments as they go. An independent evaluation by SRI International at four of the colleges found significant positive impact on grades in three out of the four.

Conclusions

Adaptive teaching is one way to provide a learning experience that is more personalized than listening to a lecture or reading a book. It is also a way to check that the student has mastered the content, by giving regular tests and providing extra remedial material for students who are struggling.

It is an experience where the teacher (usually, a computer-based system) is in charge, though the learner may have some choice over the order of studying the materials and at what level to start. It works best where the content is well-structured and can be broken down into small teachable chunks, the teacher can see how each student is progressing and the students can discuss their progress.

Resources

Knewton system for teachers to create adaptive learning content:
www.knewton.com
www.knewton.com/wp-content/uploads/knewton-adaptive-learning-whitepaper.pdf

CogBooks: adaptive learning books:
pub.cogbooks.com/~cogbooks/product/

Adaptive flashcards:
https://www.brainscape.com/

Pearson MyLab & Mastering adaptive tutoring products:
www.pearsonmylabandmastering.com

Smart Sparrow adaptive e-learning platform:
www.smartsparrow.com

MathSpring adaptive mathematics practice software:
mathspring.org/

Global Freshman Academy of Arizona State University:
https://gfa.asu.edu/courses

Article on the BioBeyond adaptive courseware:
SmartSparrow (2017, September 28). *New Research Finds Digital Courseware Increases Student Success in Critical Introductory Science College Courses.* San Francisco: CISION PR newswire.
https://prn.to/2ysmba2

158 schools across Ireland have used the Build Up adaptive teaching system for mathematics:
https://www.irishexaminer.com/business/irish-tech-teaches-world-a-lesson-458260.html

The Cognitive Tutor® system and its successor MATHia have been adopted in schools across the United States:
https://www.carnegielearning.com/login/index.html

Introduction to adaptive web-based systems for education:
Brusilovsky, P., & Peylo, C. (2003). Adaptive and intelligent web-based educational systems. *International Journal of Artificial Intelligence in Education* (IJAIED), 13, 159–172.
telearn.archives-ouvertes.fr/hal-00197315/document

Meta-study of research into the effectiveness of intelligent tutoring systems:
Kulik, J. A., & Fletcher, J. D. (2016). Effectiveness of intelligent tutoring systems: A meta-analytic review. *Review of Educational Research*, 86(1), 42–78.

Systematic review of Cognitive Tutors® in secondary schools:
What Works Clearinghouse™ (2016). *WWC Intervention Report: Cognitive Tutor®.* US Department of Education.
https://ies.ed.gov/ncee/wwc/Docs/InterventionReports/wwc_cognitivetutor_062116.pdf

Paper proposing teacher-led adaptive teaching:
Allen, M., Webb, A. W., & Matthews, C. E. (2016). Adaptive teaching in STEM: Characteristics for effectiveness. *Theory Into Practice*, 55(3), 217–224.
https://bit.ly/2R2DuWl

Crowdsourced adaptive social learning, where learners contribute mini-lessons:
Karataev, E., & Zadorozhny, V. (2017). Adaptive social learning based on crowdsourcing. *IEEE Transactions on Learning Technologies*, 10(2), 128–139.
https://ieeexplore.ieee.org/abstract/document/7373654

This chapter draws on material from *Innovating Pedagogy 2015*, published under a Creative Commons Attribution Licence:
Sharples, M., Adams, A., Alozie, N., Ferguson, R., FitzGerald, E., Gaved, M., McAndrew, P., Means, B., Remold, J., Rienties, B., Roschelle, J., Vogt, K., Whitelock, D., & Yarnall, L. (2015). *Innovating Pedagogy 2015: Open University Innovation Report 4.* Milton Keynes: The Open University.

Spaced learning

3

Build long-term memories in minutes

Overview

It has long been known that we learn facts better in a series of short chunks with gaps between, rather than by a long teaching session, such as a lecture. Recent research in neuroscience has uncovered the detail of how we produce long-term memories. This has led to the teaching method of spaced learning where: (1) a teacher gives information for 20 minutes; (2) students take a break of 10 minutes to participate in an unconnected practical activity, such as aerobics or clay modelling; (3) students are asked to recall key information for 20 minutes followed by a 10-minute break; and (4) students apply their new knowledge for a final 20 minutes. A study of spaced learning shows a significant increase in learning compared to a typical lesson. The method has been tested successfully in schools, but a larger scale trial is needed to show whether it can be deeply implemented into practice.

Making memories

Studies of human memory have shown that we remember more when learning is spaced over time rather than crammed together in a single session. Typically, these studies have focused on learning short items, such as words or phrases in a foreign language, with increasing spaces between attempts to recall the items. For example, a person trying to learn the Spanish for 'What time is it?' might read the phrase (*¿Qué hora es?*), then try to recall it after five minutes, an hour, a day, three days and a week. Software, such as Anki, Cerego and Memrise, use this method of spaced repetition to teach foreign-language vocabulary and other associations, such as the names of national flags and their pictures.

The way this is thought to work is that each recall session stimulates the learner's short-term memory for the item and its new association until these become fixed in long-term memory. The method is generally successful, providing the student is willing to stick with it. However, the learning takes place over days and has been limited to building connections between words, phrases or images.

New research into the neuroscience of learning has now identified how long-term memories can be made in minutes rather than days and for complex topics, not just basic associations. In brief, the human brain contains around 85 billion cells, or neurons. Each can connect with up to 10,000 other neurons through synapses – tiny gaps that transmit electrical or chemical impulses. As well as being briefly activated by stimuli, such as sights and sounds, connections between synapses can be strengthened by persistent chemical changes. These connections are the basis of long-term memories.

Experiments with animal cells have shown that the chemical strengthening between neurons happens while learning and again later, including during sleep. In one study, brain cells removed from a rat hippocampus (the part of the brain used to consolidate short-term to long-term memories) were stimulated with electricity. The researchers found that three bursts of stimulation, with 10-minute spaces between them, produced more active connections between synapses than one long period of stimulation. The spaced bursts also produced a protein in the cells that is observed when long-term memories are being made.

A few studies of human brain activity while learning have been carried out. One of these examined Magnetic Resonance Imaging (MRI) brain scans of adult volunteers after they had tried to memorize 120 novel pictures of faces. In the 'massed learning' condition, each face was presented to adults multiple times, followed by the next face. In the 'spaced learning' condition, the faces were presented in sequence, one after the other. The study showed that spacing out the faces, by showing a sequence of different ones, produced more activity in the part of the brain linked to face recognition than the massed presentation. There have not yet been any attempts to study effects on the brain of longer spaces (such as ten minutes) between periods of learning.

The evidence so far, mainly from experiments with animal brain cells, suggests that a period of learning stimulates connections between brain cells. It takes time for the chemical bonds between synapses to strengthen. Trying to learn too much in one session may not give the brain time to embed the knowledge in long-term memory. The animal cell experiments suggest a space of ten minutes between learning episodes.

Spaced teaching of curriculum topics

This is early research and more studies are needed to understand the relations between brain activity and human learning. Based on this work, former head teacher now researcher Paul Kelley and brain scientist Terry Whatson have designed a method for spaced teaching of curriculum topics. The teaching consists of three 20-minute sessions, with 10-minute breaks between them.

- **Session 1** (20 minutes) The teacher gives a rapid presentation of a new topic.
- **Break** (10 minutes) Students engage in physical activity, such as origami or clay modelling.
- **Session 2** (20 minutes) Students actively recall key concepts from the presentation.
- **Break** (10 minutes) Students engage in physical activity, such as origami or clay modelling.
- **Session 3** (20 minutes) Students apply their new knowledge through problem exercises.

Kelley and Whatson ran trials of their teaching method with students aged 13–15 who were learning biology in a UK school. In one trial, students studied an entire first biology course through spaced learning over a period of 90 minutes. Their exam performance was compared to a control group of students who studied the course in standard lessons over four months. There was no significant difference in exam scores between students who had done spaced learning in a single day and those who studied over four months.

In another trial, students aged 14–15 used spaced learning to review material for a biology exam. The same students also used traditional intensive review for a physics exam. Their exam scores after biology spaced review were significantly higher than the national average for similar students. Their exams scores for physics did not differ from the national average.

Spaced learning in practice

These studies, suggesting that 90 minutes of spaced learning could have the same outcomes as months of study, led to national press coverage. The UK's Educational Endowment Foundation (EEF) has carried out a further randomized trial in schools of three different types of spaced learning: 10-minute spaces between teaching sessions; 24-hour spaces; and a combination of 10-minute and 24-hour spaces.

In the combined method, teachers taught biology, chemistry and physics in three 12-minute lessons with 10-minute spaces between each topic. This process was repeated on three consecutive days to give the additional 24-hour spaces. The EEF trial found that this method, combining 10-minute and 24-hour spaces between lessons, brought the best results. Teachers and students appeared to enjoy the program. This study was only intended to give preliminary evidence and the EEF has recommended a larger trial before drawing firm conclusions about the success of spaced learning.

Conclusions

We still have much to discover about spaced learning. Is it a 'miracle education' method for teaching school subjects, or a slightly more efficient way of reviewing material for exams, or something in between? Is it as successful for learning new material as for consolidating previous knowledge? Most important, does it lead to deep learning, where students retain the new concepts, integrate them with previous knowledge and gain long-term understanding and skill?

Resources

Report by the Education Endowment Foundation on a pilot evaluation in schools of a sequence of lessons based on spaced learning:
https://educationendowmentfoundation.org.uk/our-work/projects/spaced-learning

Review of research literature on spaced repetition:
https://www.gwern.net/Spaced-repetition

Anki spaced repetition flashcard software:
https://apps.ankiweb.net/

Cerego adaptive learning using spaced repetition:
https://www.cerego.com/

Memrise language learning using spaced repetition:
https://www.memrise.com/

Report of study to stimulate rat brain cells:
Fields, R. D. (2005). Making memories stick. *Scientific American*, 292(2), 74–81.
http://bit.ly/2heDemH

The main study of spaced learning by Kelley and Whatson. It covers the neuroscience that informs the method and describes three classroom studies and their results:
Kelley, P., & Whatson, T. (2013). Making long-term memories in minutes: A spaced learning pattern from memory research in education. *Frontiers in Human Neuroscience, 7*, 589.
http://bit.ly/2yv6kYB

Study in which adults memorized 120 novel faces through massed or spaced learning. Brain activity was recorded using functional MRI scans:

Xue, G., Mei, L., Chen, C., Lu, Z.-L., Poldrack, R., & Dong, Q. (2011). Spaced learning enhances subsequent recognition memory by reducing neural repetition suppression. *Journal of Cognitive Neuroscience*, 23(7), 1624–1633.
http://bit.ly/2PPK5TA

This chapter draws on material from *Innovating Pedagogy 2017*, published under a Creative Commons Attribution Licence:

Ferguson, R., Barzilai, S., Ben-Zvi, D., Chinn, C. A., Herodotou, C., Hod, Y., Kali, Y., Kukulska-Hulme, A., Kupermintz, H., McAndrew, P., Rienties, B., Sagy, O., Scanlon, E., Sharples, M., Weller, M., & Whitelock, D. (2017). *Innovating Pedagogy 2017: Open University Innovation Report 6*. Milton Keynes: The Open University.

Personal inquiry

4

Learn through collaborative inquiry and active investigation

Overview

Personal inquiry builds on our natural curiosity about ourselves and the world around us. It runs as a series of investigations where students, individually and collectively, take ownership of the inquiry process. A typical personal inquiry might start in the classroom, with students proposing questions that have personal meaning to which they genuinely want to know the answer. The teacher guides them to discover what kinds of questions can be answered through investigation, how these can be framed as valid inquiries, who they can find and trust as scientific informants, what kind of studies are appropriate, why it is important to collect reliable data, how this can be analyzed and presented as valid evidence and how the results of an inquiry can be shared and discussed. Then, the students continue the investigations at home or outdoors by collecting and analyzing data. Lastly, they come back to the classroom to share and present results.

Personally meaningful inquiry

There are two fundamental reasons for encouraging students to engage in personally meaningful inquiry. The first is to give them the experience of acting like scientists. By taking part in scientific practices within and outside the classroom, students can experience shared scientific investigation and discover the value of building their investigations on the findings of others. Scientific practices include generating their own research questions, selecting from many possible variables to investigate, designing procedures to explore questions, employing multiple measures, holding reasoned arguments about findings and coordinating results from multiple studies.

The second reason is that by carrying out investigations about themselves and their surrounding world, young people can feel the surprise and unease that are foundations of scientific curiosity. Eighty years ago, the educator and philosopher John Dewey referred to inquiry arising from a "felt difficulty", a vague feeling that something is out of place or an experience of unexpected response to a habitual action. This provokes a need for resolution through reasoned investigation. Inquiry can also arise from a sense of wonder that leads to curiosity and a desire for explanation. It is this aspect of personal commitment to an inquiry that is often missing from school science.

An example of personal inquiry

The Personal Inquiry Project was a three-year study of personally meaningful inquiry learning with children aged 11–16 in classrooms, at home and outdoors. The most successful investigation came from a group discussion with students aged 12–13 on the broad theme of 'ecology'. Their teacher asked the students to say words related to ecology (they came up with 'environment', 'habitats', 'animals') and to propose questions they would like to investigate.

The students' questions were: 'How does noise pollution affect the way birds eat and live?', 'Would we find the same organisms in a pond in winter compared to summer?' and 'What do chickens eat; what do they survive on?'. Further discussion led them to agree on the question: 'What is the effect of noise pollution on how birds feed?'. To investigate this, the teacher took the class on a trip to a local nature reserve to observe whether birds were nesting in noisy areas (such as next to a railway line).

Then they designed an experiment in the school grounds to measure whether bird feeding is affected by noise and made predictions about the results. First, they used a sound sensor to measure noise levels at different parts of the school grounds. Next, they put up bird feeders at the same height in the quietest and noisiest areas. Then, they put a measured amount of bird feed into each feeder and then after two days, they weighed how much food was eaten at each location. Last, they shared and discussed their results in class.

The results were exactly the opposite to their predictions! They found that more food was being eaten from containers in noisy areas. After further observations, including setting up web cameras, they found that a greedy pigeon was eating most of the food and, unlike the smaller birds, it preferred the noisy parts of the ground. The students had learned for themselves a basic principle of science, that facts don't always support predictions. Later, they carried out a 'fair test' experiment, in a garden with bird feeders on two trees and a radio playing music under one of the trees and found what they had predicted, that small birds are scared away from noisy areas.

Challenges of personal inquiry

The two biggest challenges of personal inquiry are helping students to frame good questions and for the teacher to manage the 'integration' lesson when the students bring their findings back into the classroom. Some questions can be engaging, but too difficult for young people to investigate. One investigation proposed for the Personal Inquiry Project was: 'What is the relation between fitness and heart rate?'. Apart from the technical difficulties of equipping each child with a heart-rate monitor, there are problems of how to measure a person's 'fitness' and a complex relationship between health and heart rate. Other questions can be more easily studied but bring ethical issues. For example, a study of 'healthy eating' involved students taking photos of their daily meals and calculating the nutritional content (calories, salt, etc). Some of the children were understandably embarrassed about sharing photos of their unhealthy food – even when the teacher had said the images and data would be anonymous. Some personal inquiries can be too personal!

The other main problem is the burden placed on the teacher to run a lesson that integrates the findings and presents them to the class. Personal inquiry is not like traditional homework, where students hand in set work and the teacher can check the answers later. In a personal inquiry activity, the students arrive with results that need to be checked, shared and discussed. The classroom teacher must improvise a lesson around these fragments of data and help the students to reach a satisfying, scientific conclusion.

The teacher may decide to hold back a scientific answer to the question until the students have processed and discussed their own results. This has been called the 'teacher's dilemma' – should a teacher give the correct (or generally accepted) answer to a scientific question, or let the students struggle with their own findings? A study by Erin Furtak of middle school teachers guiding inquiry learning found that teachers who pretended not to know the answer "did not fool their students". Students went along for a while with collecting and analyzing their data, but eventually gave up and asked for answers. If there is no 'right answer' to a personal inquiry question, then the teacher has the hard task to explain to students that they will learn better if they persevere and develop the knowledge themselves.

These difficulties make personal inquiry a daunting prospect compared to running a traditional classroom experiment or lab class. But becoming a scientist does involve grappling with difficult questions and struggling to find good answers.

Personal inquiry in practice

WISE is a free inquiry science environment from the University of Berkeley where students can examine real-world evidence and engage in scientific debate. Web-based software guides students to gather evidence, collaborate and reflect, with tools for data visualization, modelling, simulation and assessment. Its project library includes projects on motion in amusement parks and how detergents can be used to clean up oil spills. A study in Northern California of how to guide understanding with WISE involved over 4,000 middle school students.

The Personal Inquiry Project engaged two schools over three years in developing and testing the nQuire platform for personal inquiry learning. The teachers followed an 'inquiry cycle' (see Figure 4.1) to guide students through the process of scientific inquiry. The same inquiry cycle was also the interface to a computer system, called nQuire, which students took home and outdoors to carry out investigations.

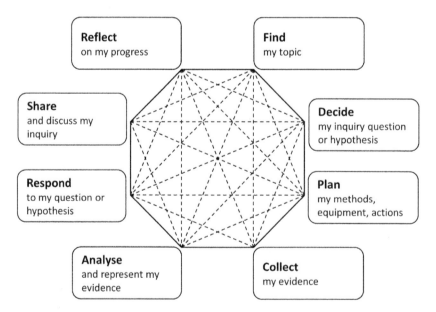

Figure 4.1 Representation of the personal inquiry process (from Anastopolou et al., 2012[1])

Conclusions

Personal inquiry takes the idea of inquiry-led learning propounded by Dewey and makes it personal. The inquiry has personal meaning and relevance to the student. It could be related to a hobby, or a local issue, such as air or water pollution, or a nagging question that calls to be answered. The teacher assists the students, individually or in groups, to carry out a scientific investigation. Since the teacher doesn't know the specific topic in advance, then the teacher may be improvising the method and equipment alongside the students. That can take courage and resources, so personal inquiry may work best in an after-school club or summer school with plenty of time to plan the investigation and analyze the results.

Note

1 Anastopoulou, A., Sharples, M., Ainsworth, S., Crook, C., O'Malley, C. & Wright, M. (2012). Creating personal meaning through technology-supported science learning across formal and informal settings. *International Journal of Science Education*, 34(2), 251–273.

Resources

WISE Web-based inquiry science environment, a free online science learning environment for students in grades 4–12 created by a large team around Marcia Linn at the University of California, Berkeley:
http://wise.berkeley.edu

Overview of the Personal Inquiry Project:
Sharples, M., Scanlon, E., Ainsworth, S., Anastopoulou, S., Collins, T., Crook, C., Jones, A., Kerawalla, L., Littleton, K., Mulholland, P., & O'Malley, C. (2015). Personal inquiry: Orchestrating science investigations within and beyond the classroom. *Journal of the Learning Sciences*, 24(2), 308–341.
http://oro.open.ac.uk/41623/

Edited book on how to support inquiry learning within and beyond the classroom.
Littleton, K., Scanlon, E., & Sharples, M. (Eds.) (2012). *Orchestrating Inquiry Learning*. Abingdon, Oxon and New York: Routledge
https://bit.ly/2J7Fjyk

John Dewey on 'felt difficulty' in practical thinking and reasoning:
Dewey, J. (1910). The analysis of a complete act of thought. *How We Think*, pp. 68–78. Lexington, Mass.: D.C. Heath.
https://bit.ly/2PMqLH4

Study of teachers guiding inquiry learning:

Furtak, E. M. (2006). The problem with answers: An exploration of guided scientific inquiry teaching. *Science Education*, 90(3), 453–467.

https://bit.ly/2CwwWez

This chapter draws on material from *Innovating Pedagogy 2012*, published under a Creative Commons Attribution Licence:

Sharples, M., McAndrew, P., Weller, M., Ferguson, R., FitzGerald, E., Hirst, T., Mor, Y., Gaved, M., & Whitelock, D. (2012). *Innovating Pedagogy 2012: Open University Innovation Report 1*. Milton Keynes: The Open University.

Dynamic assessment   5
Give learners personalized assessment to support learning

Overview

The central idea of dynamic assessment is to assess students' *potential* to learn rather than measure what they have just done. Dynamic assessment focuses on the progress of the student. Testing acts as a diagnostic tool for a teacher to guide the student to successful learning, finding ways to overcome each person's current learning difficulties. Assessment and intervention combine in the process of dynamic assessment.

As well as being a way to guide and support learners, dynamic assessment can inform the teacher about topics and skills that many students are finding difficult and so help to re-design and improve the teaching. It can also motivate students to reflect on their learning journeys and decide which skills they need to improve.

Bridging the gap

At any point during learning, a student can demonstrate some skills and knowledge unaided. With the help of a teacher, or knowledgeable expert, the student can perform better. The psychologist Lev Vygotsky called the gap between what a student can do without help and what can be done with some personal assistance, the Zone of Proximal Development (ZPD). This is the 'zone of opportunity', where a teacher can have the most success in improving the student's learning. If the gap between the student's ability and the teacher's intervention is too narrow, then the student will learn too little. If the gap is too wide, then

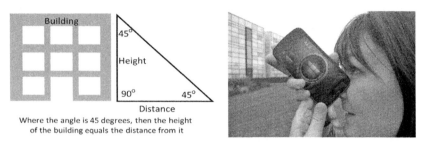

Figure 5.1 Measuring the height of a building using a tilt sensor on a mobile phone

the student will fail to understand. In dynamic assessment, the teacher continually probes the ZPD and offers appropriate teaching that bridges the gap. The same approach can be applied to individual students or groups.

Consider a group of college science students who are set a problem to measure the height of the school building. One student proposes to lower a weight on a string from a window on the upper floor and measure the length of the string. That would find the height to the window, but not to the top of the building. Another student suggests throwing a ball from the window up to the height of the building, timing how long it takes to fall to the ground and using a formula for the ball's acceleration to calculate the height. But that all seems too complicated. The students are ready to give up.

The teacher is listening to the discussion and decides to intervene. The teacher helps some of the students to bridge the gap by offering the scientific formula[1] for calculating the distance, given the time it takes for the ball to drop. For others, the teacher prompts them to think about angles and shows a right-angled triangle placed against a drawing of the building (see Figure 5.1). The students discuss this and decide to use a mobile phone tool to measure the angle from the ground to the top of the building. When the angle is 45 degrees, then the distance to the building is the same as the height of the building.

When and how the teacher decides to intervene will depend on the teacher's judgment of the students' knowledge and whether giving some guidance will help them to progress. That is dynamic assessment.

Methods of dynamic assessment

For a small tutorial group, the teacher may be able to assess how the students' knowledge and skills develop from minute to minute, but that would not work for a large class. Instead, the teacher may need to set a pre-test of each student's knowledge or skill, followed by a teaching intervention and then a post-test to see how the knowledge or skill has changed. The 'pre-test, intervention, post-test' method resembles a traditional research design, but the aim is not to carry out a research study on a class of students, rather to use this information to guide the learners and inform the teacher.

Let's say the teacher in the previous example is teaching an entire class about scientific measurement. The pre-test could ask each student individually to write down a way to measure the height of the building. Then, the teacher asks some students to present their solutions and the class discusses the accuracy of each solution and how easy it is to perform. If no student proposes a solution based on angles, then the teacher might give a hint. If a student gives a solution that involves complicated trigonometry, the teacher could show how the height can be calculated more simply with 45-degree angles. All the students could be taken outside to measure the height of the school building, then they could be individually re-tested to see if they are able to apply their knowledge to a similar problem.

There is also an interactionist method that takes more account of the student's ZPD. In this method, teacher and student work together to solve a problem, with the teacher providing continual appropriate guidance.

Dynamic or static assessment?

The differences between dynamic assessment and conventional or static assessment are that:

- the focus of dynamic assessment is on guiding future development, whereas static assessment measures past achievement;
- the assessor and student relationship is different, since the assessor intervenes during the dynamic process;
- with dynamic assessment there is feedback to the student during the process.

Dynamic assessment in practice

An example of dynamic assessment at university level was the placing of students on undergraduate Spanish courses by finding a good match between the level of development for each student and appropriate Spanish teaching. The students gave spoken answers to a question and the assessor prompted them to amend their answers if they had made mistakes. Some students were able to improve with prompting, while others were not. The ones who struggled were enrolled in a course to improve their conversation.

A second example comes from a school science lesson with children aged eight and nine years who were learning about magnetism. The teacher discussed the topic with the children and was sensitive to each child's ZPD, helping the class to move from everyday language, such as 'hold' and 'push', to the use of scientific terms, such as 'attract' and 'repel'.

A third study was designed to support young immigrant adults learning English as a Foreign Language in Israel. The students were given a reading and comprehension pre-test. Assessors then went through the test with the students, building strategies with them to address each test item and, more importantly, showing them how these strategies could be transferred from one example to another. A learning potential score was devised by the assessors and the students were then designated as high, medium or low performers. The dynamic assessment led to recommendations that helped these students improve their English-language skills.

Conclusions

Dynamic assessment has been criticized on the grounds of its reliability. To construct a reliable test, the test items need to be stable, but the dynamic assessment procedure is deliberately associated with change, not stability. However, the main value of any assessment lies in the inferences that can be made from it about how well the student is progressing. With dynamic assessment these inferences are sound, since they are tightly connected to administration of its test procedure. Although dynamic assessment takes time and puts new demands on teachers, test instruments have been constructed for use in the classroom. It should be considered as part of a range of assessment tools that can support individual students to reach their full learning potential.

Note

1   The formula is: Distance $= \frac{1}{2} * G * time^2$, where G is the acceleration due to gravity (a constant 9.8) and the distance is measured in meters.

Resources

Classic paper on the Zone of Proximal Development:
Vygotsky, L. S. (1978). Interaction between learning and development. In M. Cole, V. John-Steiner, S. Scribner, & E. Souberman (Eds.), *Mind in Society: The Development of Higher Psychological Processes*, pp. 79–91. Cambridge, MA: Harvard University Press.
http://www.psy.cmu.edu/~siegler/vygotsky78.pdf

Three studies of dynamic assessment in practice:
Lantolf, J. P., & Poehner, M. E. (2004). Dynamic assessment of L2 development: Bringing the past into the future. *Journal of Applied Linguistics*, 1(1) 49–72.
https://bit.ly/2S5QifS

Overview of Dynamic Assessment, including the school science example:
Haywood, H., & Lidz, C. S. (2006). *Dynamic Assessment in Practice: Clinical and Educational Applications*. New York, NY: Cambridge University Press.
https://bit.ly/2yUUFSi

Ways to measure the height of a tall building:
https://bit.ly/2S5tpJi

This chapter draws on material from *Innovating Pedagogy 2014*, published under a Creative Commons Attribution Licence:
Sharples, M., Adams, A., Ferguson, R., Gaved, M., McAndrew, P., Rienties, B., Weller, M., & Whitelock, D. (2014). *Innovating Pedagogy 2014: Open University Innovation Report 3*. Milton Keynes: The Open University.

Stealth assessment
6
Assess learning processes unobtrusively

Overview

As people play computer games – to explore simulated worlds, combat foes and overcome challenges – the computer software monitors their progress. It continually collects data about players' actions, making inferences about their goals and strategies to set appropriate new challenges. This approach of continually tracking a person's progress while providing immediate automated responses has been termed 'stealth assessment' and it is starting to be applied to educational games and simulations.

The claim is that stealth assessment can test hard-to-measure aspects of learning, such as perseverance, creativity and strategic thinking. It can also collect information about students' learning states and processes without asking them to stop and take a test. In principle, stealth assessment techniques could provide teachers with continual data on how each learner is progressing. However, much research remains to be done, both to identify the measures of the student learning process that predict learning outcomes for different learning systems and to understand what data are useful to teachers. Concerns have been raised about the collection of vast amounts of student learning data and the ethics of using computers to monitor a person's every action.

Stealth assessment and inquiry learning

The term was first used by Valerie Shute in 2005 to describe the automated assessment process in a system named Smithtown to teach principles of microeconomics (for example, the laws of supply and demand). Students explored the Smithtown simulated world and altered variables, such as the price of coffee and the incomes of inhabitants. They engaged in inquiry learning by forming hypotheses and testing predictions. The software employed methods from artificial intelligence to monitor and analyze the students' actions, giving them feedback to support their inquiry skills without disrupting the game.

Stealth assessment extends adaptive teaching (see Chapter 2) by making continual adjustments to a simulated environment rather than selecting a path or exercise based on the diagnosis of a learner's knowledge and misconceptions. The adjustments are based on the learner's actions while playing the game, such as what evidence the learner collects in the simulated world before making a prediction, or which game characters the learner asks for help. The assessment is embedded within the flow of the game and the student may not be aware that this dynamic process of monitoring and response is taking place.

Principles of stealth assessment

The key principles of stealth assessment are that:

- the software analyzes the activities of students within a computer game or simulation;
- the system continually adjusts the structure of the game to support learning, for example by offering new challenges matched to the student's performance;
- the system maintains the flow of the game, so that teaching and assessment are part of the game and not separate tests or exams;
- the system builds a dynamic model of the learners to indicate their abilities and competencies;
- it is intended to reduce learners' anxiety about taking tests by blurring the distinction between assessment and learning while carrying out accurate diagnosis.

This can be complex when carried out by computer but is just what a good human sports coach would do in teaching tennis or soccer. The coach watches the students as they practise the game and gives new challenges for each student matched to the level of ability. These are part of the game play (such as a serve in tennis or a penalty kick in soccer) rather than a separate test. All the time, the coach is forming an understanding of each student's skills and weaknesses.

How to design stealth assessment

The pedagogy that underlies stealth assessment is competency learning. The teacher (in the case of stealth learning, the computer) estimates what the student knows and can do, continually providing tasks and assessment that are matched to the student's competency. To do this the teacher, or teaching system, must diagnose how the student is performing on specific problems and then infer levels of competency across a network of skills. The objective is to detect the student's problem-solving skills involving knowledge, comprehension and application while also uncovering the higher level abilities of creativity and critical thinking.

A successful method of developing stealth assessment games is through 'evidence-centred design'. First, the educational game designer needs to determine what knowledge, skills and competencies will be assessed so that they can be built into the gameplay. These attributes cannot be assessed directly (since the game has no direct way of knowing what the student is thinking and the stealth approach does not set explicit tests of knowledge), so the designer has to work out which behaviours and interactions will provide evidence of a player's knowledge, skills and competencies.

Then the games designer chooses actions that are appropriate to the player's abilities: setting goals to be achieved, managing conflict, introducing challenges. The designer builds measures of success and failure into the game as the learner undertakes a mission or solves a game problem. These measures link together to form a network of probabilities that the learner has gained the desired skill or reached the required level of competency.

Opportunities and challenges

Stealth assessment works best when the assessment strategies, the game and the simulated world are all developed together through a process of evidence-centred design that applies not only to the assessment but also the gameplay (so that the game elements are included to stimulate engagement and learning). A less successful approach is to add dynamic assessment to an existing game or simulation.

Stealth assessment techniques can give learners immediate feedback on their actions and provide teachers with information on how each learner is developing skills of inquiry, critical thinking, decision-making and creativity. This work is at an early stage and it is not yet clear whether the methods of stealth assessment need to be developed afresh for each game and topic, or whether general methods of design can be adopted.

Stealth assessment in practice

An example of a computer game that employs stealth assessment is *Portal 2*, developed by Valve Corporation. The player takes the role of Chell, who has to explore an advanced science laboratory, realized as a complex mechanized maze and find an exit door by using a set of tools. Educational aims are for the user to learn aspects of physics, gain visual-spatial skills and develop critical thinking abilities.

Another, very different, example is TAALES. This analyzes the lexical properties of students' essays (such as word frequency and use of academic language) to assess the students' vocabulary knowledge. Stealth assessment of student essays with TAALES is being coupled to a system that helps the students to improve their essay-writing skills.

Shute and colleagues embedded stealth assessment in the educational game *Use Your Brainz*, for middle-school students to learn skills of problem solving. A study with 55 school students over three days (an hour a day) showed that the stealth assessment by the computer matched standard measures of problem-solving ability. But there still needs to be a large-scale trial to validate the approach.

Conclusions

The term 'stealth assessment' provokes debate. Is it ethical to design a computer system that monitors students' actions, assessing their skills of problem solving or creativity while purporting to give them an entertaining game? Would it be more acceptable if the students know they are being continually monitored and assessed – which, after all, is exactly what a good human coach does?

For research projects, these systems can, and should, be developed within strict ethical guidelines that include telling the learners how they are being monitored, how the information will be used and gaining informed and willing consent from the participants. But stealth assessment is already being embedded into commercial games and might, for example, be used without players' knowledge to assess insurance risks.

Stealth assessment offers engaging ways to teach competencies, such as creativity, problem solving, persistence and collaboration, by incorporating dynamic assessment and feedback into computer games. The methods need to be introduced with care and sensitivity, but early results show promise in combining the engagement of simulation games with the diagnostic power of dynamic assessment.

Resources

Portal 2 game:
www.thinkwithportals.com

Study of TAALES for essay assessment:
Allen, L. K. & McNamara, D. S. (2015). You are your words: Modeling students' vocabulary knowledge with natural language processing tools. In *Proceedings of the 8th International Conference on Educational Data Mining*, 26–29 June 2015, pp. 258–265. Madrid, Spain. https://bit.ly/2EDiaVT

Evidence-centred design:
Messick, S. (1994). The interplay of evidence and consequences in the validation of performance assessments. *Educational Researcher*, 23(2), 13–23. https://bit.ly/2q4n6c4

Introduction to stealth assessment:
Shute, V. J. (2011). Stealth assessment in computer-based games to support learning. In S. Tobias & J. D. Fletcher (Eds.), *Computer Games and Instruction*, pp. 503–524. Charlotte: Information Age Publishing. https://fla.st/2SbaEo2

Study of problem-solving skills with stealth assessment for *Use Your Brainz*:
Shute, V. J., Wang, L., Greiff, S., Zhao, W., & Moore, G. (2016). Measuring problem solving skills via stealth assessment in an engaging video game. *Computers in Human Behavior*, 63, 106–117. https://bit.ly/2ysxT4N

This chapter draws on material from *Innovating Pedagogy 2015*, published under a Creative Commons Attribution Licence:
Sharples, M., Adams, A., Alozie, N., Ferguson, R., FitzGerald, E., Gaved, M., McAndrew, P., Means, B., Remold, J., Rienties, B., Roschelle, J., Vogt, K., Whitelock, D., & Yarnall, L. (2015). *Innovating Pedagogy 2015: Open University Innovation Report 4*. Milton Keynes: The Open University.

Translanguaging   7
Enrich learning through use of multiple languages

Overview

Many learners study in and speak a language that is not their mother tongue. Translanguaging refers to moving fluidly between languages. Teachers can support bilingual students to speak with bilingual partners, search the internet in multiple languages and access a wide range of online communities and resources. They can also organize international online discussions in two or more languages. Translanguaging can expand and deepen students' understanding and help them to gain broader perspectives. It can also enrich the cultural experience and worldviews of other learners as they listen to a variety of languages. But a bilingual or multilingual classroom may exclude monolingual learners or take for granted the ability of bilinguals to use their languages for effective learning.

Moving between languages

The word 'languaging' describes a dynamic process of using or producing language to make meaning. Languaging refers primarily to verbal communication, but can also include gesturing, body language, drawing or media production. Moving flexibly and fluidly between familiar languages is known as 'translanguaging'. It can be thought of as the interweaving of multiple linguistic resources or using more than one language during a conversation or self-expression. For example, in a family or with friends, one person may say something in one language then a second person elaborates on it in another. Or a student may find and compare information through web searches in multiple languages to answer a question. These everyday practices already occur in some conversations and exchanges on social media and they can help informal learning.

Mobility and language

With the growth of the World Wide Web and international travel, an increasing number of learners are studying in a language that is not the one they spoke in early childhood or learned at school or university. A move to a different country for work or education often means that learning will have to be done in another language. Many learners already belong to bilingual or multilingual families, where the languages spoken at home differ from the ones used in school or college. Furthermore, large numbers of learners are joining online courses, or taking part in discussions on social media, in languages where they may not be fluent. In many parts of the world, including India, Philippines, South Africa and Ethiopia, International English is the language of formal education in secondary schools and universities, although learners come from different language backgrounds. It is still unusual for these other languages to be welcomed into the educational experience and for learners to be able to use them to share their ideas with others or to demonstrate achievement.

A fluid pattern of language education and interaction brings challenges and opportunities. Studying in an unfamiliar language presents learners with challenges they would not face otherwise, which may result in inequality. Learners not only need to understand and respond to educational content, but also join in the social interactions and informal support that come from being able to communicate comfortably in a common language with teachers and fellow students. It may also be more difficult for learners to express their creativity or unique perspective if they are denied the full range of expression that is often taken for granted by those who are proficient in the required language.

On the positive side, bilingual learners are sometimes able to draw on mental resources and skills that are less available to monolingual students. Other learners may benefit from bilingual students' increased awareness of cultural and linguistic differences if they have opportunities to share that knowledge and experience. This requires a pedagogy that acknowledges the value of supporting speakers of other languages. It encourages them to take a full part in the educational experience and to use their languages in ways that help them and may also benefit others.

Translanguaging, pedagogy and technology

Translanguaging usually applies to bilingual students, but it can be extended to students who speak just a single language. Some examples are:

- identify bilingual partners who can help each other;
- design group work with individuals' language backgrounds in mind;
- allow learners to discuss some topics and issues in their preferred language;
- find multilingual resources and tools, then demonstrate to learners the advantages compared to resources in one language;
- set tasks to search for information or access communities in multiple languages;
- allow learners to use preferred languages when working together to create digital artefacts such as annotated pictures or videos while ensuring the products are understandable to others;
- co-teach with teachers from a different language background;
- make use of multilingual chatbots (conversational computer programs) or virtual assistants.

Technology, such as translation software, online dictionaries, cross-cultural social networks, web resources in other languages and virtual assistants, can contribute to translanguaging among teachers and learners. Automated translation tools can become learning resources, with bilingual students exploring and discussing how the software translates everyday sentences. These resources can expand and deepen students' thinking and understanding, so they gain more diverse perspectives. Teachers can also benefit from this experience, by listening to students speak more confidently in their home language.

Translanguaging in practice

A teacher in a rural school in India has many students who are not first-language speakers of Hindi. She started including translanguaging practices in her classes. These included encouraging the students to translate Hindi vocabulary into their home language, or to read a page of a Hindi textbook aloud in pairs or groups, then to discuss the text in their home language to understand the meaning of unfamiliar words and make sense of the text. She found a short story that was printed in multiple languages and asked groups of students to read the stories in parallel, then discuss the different versions. The children's confidence in using Hindi increased and monolingual Hindi speakers began to pick up words and phrases from the other languages.

In a school in Wales, students aged 10–11 watched a video presented in English, then discussed and wrote about the contents in Welsh. The teacher was using translanguaging to help the students gain fluency in both English and Welsh. In other Welsh schools, teachers allowed the students to access English-language internet resources when searching for information for a Welsh-language assignment.

Conclusions

Translanguaging considers the language practices of bilingual people to be normal rather than strange. It extends educational practices for understanding and using standard national languages, to support diversity and encourage integration of mobile and social technologies into everyday communication and learning.

There are risks involved. A pedagogy for supporting bilingual speakers may exclude monolingual learners. Or it may take for granted the ability of bilinguals to use their first language effectively in learning. If we consider languages to be flexible resources for meaning-making, then traditional boundaries between languages become softer. Learners and teachers have opportunities to draw on all their linguistic resources instead of being confined to one language. The versatility of mobile and online tools supports this permeability and additional tools to support translanguaging could be developed.

Resources

Example of the teacher in a classroom in India, part of the TESS-India project:
http://bit.ly/2dYA86g

Examples of translanguaging in Welsh classrooms:
Lewis, G., Jones, B., & Baker, C. (2013). 100 bilingual lessons: Distributing two languages in classrooms. In C. Abello-Contesse, P. M. Chandler, M. D. López-Jiménez, R. Chacón-Beltrán (Eds.), *Bilingual and Multilingual Education in the 21st Century*. Multilingual Matters. http://bit.ly/2v3eg3M

Educator's viewpoint on translanguaging:
Jiménez, R. (2015). Translanguaging to bridge the gap with English learners. *Literacy Daily*, October 29, 2015.
https://bit.ly/2CV028l

Systematic review of research literature on bilingualism:
Adesope, O. O., Lavin, T., Thompson, T., & Ungerleider, C. (2010). A systematic review and meta-analysis of the cognitive correlates of bilingualism. *Review of Educational Research*, 80(2), 207–245.
https://bit.ly/2AljGI3

Evidence of intercultural learning in comments on YouTube videos:

Benson, P. (2015). Commenting to learn: Evidence of language and intercultural learning in comments on YouTube videos. *Language Learning and Technology*, 19(3), 88–105. https://bit.ly/2nfD7uB

Translanguaging as a pedagogy:

Creese, A., & Blackledge, A. (2010). Translanguaging in the bilingual classroom: A pedagogy for learning and teaching? *The Modern Language Journal*, 94(1), 103–115. https://bit.ly/2S38EhD

Introduction to a special issue on digital literacies and language learning:

Hafner, C. A., Chik, A., & Jones, R. H. (2015). Digital literacies and language learning. *Language Learning and Technology*, 19(3), 1–7. https://bit.ly/2Akbyro

Analysis of a Serbian student's multilingual practices on Facebook:

Schreiber, B. R. (2015). "I am what I am": Multilingual identity and digital translanguaging. *Language Learning and Technology*, 19(3), 69–87. https://bit.ly/2q2CqGc

This chapter draws on material from *Innovating Pedagogy 2016*, published under a Creative Commons Attribution Licence:

Sharples, M., de Roock, R., Ferguson, R., Gaved, M., Herodotou, C., Koh, E., Kukulska-Hulme, A., Looi, C.-K., McAndrew, P., Rienties, B., Weller, M., Wong, L. H. (2016). *Innovating Pedagogy 2016: Open University Innovation Report 5*. Milton Keynes: The Open University.

Part II

Connectivity

Crossover learning   **8**
Connect formal and informal learning

Overview

Learning in informal settings – at home, outdoors, in museums and in after-school clubs – can link educational content with issues that matter to learners in their lives. These connections work in both directions. Learning in schools and colleges can be enriched by experiences from everyday life; informal learning can be deepened by adding questions and knowledge from the class-room. These connected experiences spark further interest and motivation to learn. A school 'nature trip' is a time-honoured form of crossover learning, where the teacher takes students on a walk to collect leaves, water samples or tree rubbings that they bring back into the classroom to analyze or display. Alternatively, the teacher could expand on objects or experiences that students bring into school, from old postcards through YouTube videos to dance rou-tines. Crossover learning experiences exploit the strengths of both environ-ments and can give learners authentic and engaging opportunities for learning. Learning occurs over a lifetime. It links experiences across multiple settings. A broad opportunity is to support learners in recording, connecting, recalling and sharing their diverse learning events.

Connecting learning

We spend our lives learning, yet we label particular periods with terms, such as 'kindergarten', 'school', 'university', 'qualifying' or 'professional development'. Such distinctions are becoming less useful, as formal aspects of learning are

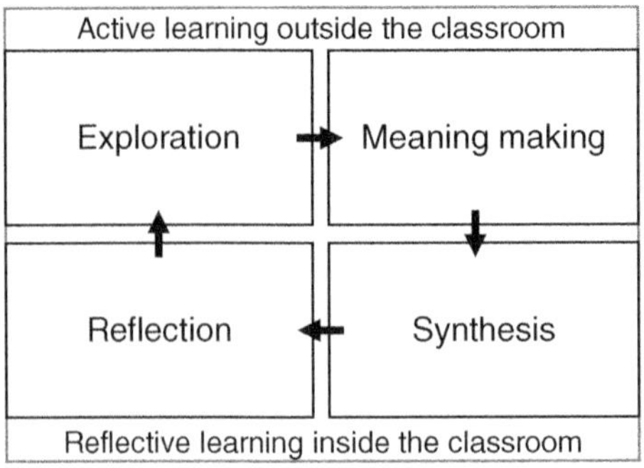

```
┌─────────────────────────────────────────┐
│      Active learning outside the classroom │
│  ┌──────────────┐  ┌──────────────┐       │
│  │ Exploration  │─▶│ Meaning making│      │
│  │       ▲      │  │       │       │       │
│  │       │      │  │       ▼       │       │
│  │ Reflection   │◀─│  Synthesis   │       │
│  └──────────────┘  └──────────────┘       │
│     Reflective learning inside the classroom │
└─────────────────────────────────────────┘
```

Figure 8.1 Connecting learning within and outside the classroom

interlinked with the informal learning experiences that occur during museum visits, after-school and hobby clubs, or internships. Networked technologies, new approaches to assessing and recognizing learning and new insights into the value of informal learning are combining to blur the familiar distinction. Crossover learning refers to ways we can connect formal and informal learning experiences, benefiting from the relations between them (see Figure 8.1). At its most successful, crossover learning is a cycle that involves exploring the world, creating meaning from experience, synthesizing that understanding, reflecting on the new knowledge and using that enhanced knowledge to guide new explorations.

Learning outside school supports the development of skills and dispositions that help students do better within school. By creating space in the formal curriculum for students to pursue individual themes based on their interests, a school can allow informal experiences to influence curriculum topics and tasks.

The concept of crossover learning can be applied to how we think about learning as a whole. Educators, policymakers and researchers increasingly view learning as an 'ecosystem' with formal and informal elements. This perspective has coincided with a rise of interest in, and opportunities for, crossover learning. The emphasis is on helping learners to connect experiences gained in different settings. For example, a school topic of 'sustainability' might include students bringing examples of food packaging from home into the classroom, carrying out a home experiment into how different vegetables decay and monitoring the school's use of electricity.

Recognizing achievement

A shift towards crossover learning requires adjustments to the ways in which we assess and recognize achievement. For example, using badges (a more general version of Scout and Guide badges) to record less-formal achievements recognizes activities that come from different sources. Software that allows students to gather resources, such as Tumblr or Pinterest, can allow learners to develop transferable skills, such as curation, evidence building and reflective commenting. As students use these tools, they provide records of their interactions and paths through information, so one item or a single collection can act as an entry point for a deeper exploration of a subject.

Teachers and informal educators now have more opportunities for professional development related to crossover learning. Education officers working in museums and community centres can help teachers make connections to local collections or activities. For example, the Teacher Institute at the Exploratorium, a museum that emphasizes hands-on activities in San Francisco, California, helps teachers facilitate activities based on the principles behind the interactive exhibits at the museum. Partnerships between formal and non-formal education can ensure that staff strategies for encouraging crossover learning are sustained over time.

Crossover learning in practice

MyArtSpace was a UK project to connect learning in classrooms and museums. In their classrooms, teachers worked with the students to propose 'big questions' to investigate in a museum. For example, a teacher and class planned a visit to the D-Day museum which commemorates the Allied landings in Normandy, France during the Second World War. They decided on two questions: 'Was D-Day a triumph or disaster for Britain?' and 'What was the role of women during D-Day?'. In the museum, the children were asked to collect evidence to answer one of the questions. They were given mobile phones with specially designed software to take photos, make voice recordings and write notes as they toured the museum galleries. They could also watch video presentations at some exhibits and were prompted to note how the display related to the 'big question'. The students worked in pairs as 'media reporters', collecting evidence and interviewing each other. Each piece of evidence was transmitted to a personal web space. Back in the classroom, the children worked in small groups to review and organize the evidence they had collected, to make presentations that answered the questions. Three museums and around 3,000 school children took part in the project over two years.

The Da Vinci Schools network in California has pioneered a form of crossover learning that they call Real World Learning. This connects learning on and off campus, in partnership with companies and community organizations. An article written by a former student describes missing out on traditional high school activities, including learning from textbooks and taking exams. In their place were a safe space for creativity, strong relationships with educators and locally based projects, including one to re-house dogs from a shelter into caring homes which had a lasting effect on the local community.

Conclusions

Finding space to bring informal learning into formal education has the potential to enrich knowledge with experience. Adding formal direction to informal activities can enhance motivation and increase the impact of informal experiences on school learning and in the workplace. The challenge is to design this crossover so that it retains the coherence of the established curriculum while embracing some of the creativity and freedom of informal exploration.

Resources

Partnerships between art museums and schools:
https://bit.ly/2AlHyvk

The Exploratorium Teacher Institute, San Francisco:
exploratorium.edu/education/teacher-institute

Example of crossover learning between an elementary school and local museums:
Amos, D. S. (2015). Museum magnet creates little 'curators' and 'docents' with cross-over learning. *The Florida Times Union*, May 10, 2015.
https://bit.ly/2CW4x2h

Report exploring the relationships between science education in formal and informal settings:
Bevan, B., Dillon, J., Hein, G. E., Macdonald, M., Michalchik, V., Miller, D., ... & Yoon, S. (2010). *Making Science Matter: Collaborations Between Informal Science Education Organizations and Schools*. Washington DC: Center for Advancement of Informal Science Education.
https://bit.ly/2ymXJXG

Report on after-school, summer and informal STEM programs:
National Research Council (2015). *Identifying and Supporting Productive STEM Programs in Out-of-School Settings*. Washington, DC: National Academies Press.
https://bit.ly/1dHNU9m

An article by a former student at Da Vinci Schools on Real World Learning:
Sierra, R., & Avallone, A. (2018). *Practitioner's Guide to Next Gen Learning*. Next Generation Learning Challenges, January 29, 2018. EDUCAUSE.
https://bit.ly/2CvPCuP

Paper on the MyArtSpace project:

Vavoula, G., Sharples, M., Rudman, P., Meek, J., & Lonsdale, P. (2009). Myartspace: Design and evaluation of support for learning with multimedia phones between classrooms and museums. *Computers & Education, 53*(2), 286–299.
https://bit.ly/2yp9zAE

This chapter draws on material from *Innovating Pedagogy 2015*, published under a Creative Commons Attribution Licence:

Sharples, M., Adams, A., Alozie, N., Ferguson, R., FitzGerald, E., Gaved, M., McAndrew, P., Means, B., Remold, J., Rienties, B., Roschelle, J., Vogt, K., Whitelock, D., & Yarnall, L. (2015). *Innovating Pedagogy 2015: Open University Innovation Report 4*. Milton Keynes: The Open University.

Seamless learning

9

Continue learning across locations, technologies and activities

Overview

Seamless learning is where learning activities continue across times, locations, devices and social groups. A college student might wake up and check for messages on her mobile phone, find a message from a friend about a team assignment, open her laptop and set up a shared document for the team, send a calendar notification to hold an online meeting, meet one of the team members for an informal chat in a café, continue the chat online with the other team members, and so on. The student keeps a focus on the assignment across changes in location (bedroom, café, online), device (phone, laptop) and group (alone, with one person, in a group). For those with skills to manage a continuity of learning, the benefits come from keeping the learning in mind despite a changing environment and combining information from many sources.

Continuous experience

In 1996, George Kuh introduced the idea of seamless learning. He proposed that distinct experiences of learning (in-class and out-of-class; academic and non-academic; curricular and co-curricular; on-campus and off-campus) should be bound together to appear continuous. Seamless learning may be intentional, such as a teacher starting an activity in the classroom, then asking students to complete it as homework. It can also be accidental, for example when an interesting piece of information from a newspaper or television program sets off a learning journey that leads to exploration, discussion or formal learning. The learner may be aware of crossing boundaries when exploring a topic, but the overall experience is of carrying out a single piece of learning, abstracted away from specific times and locations.

Lifelogging

Seamless learning is emerging from research projects to become part of mainstream technology and education. Technology companies, including Microsoft and Google, are developing 'lifelogging' devices to learn from everyday memories. Our memories have an episodic component where we capture a sequence of events, and a semantic component to build abstract knowledge. Wearable cameras and sound recorders can make these aspects of human memory external, so people can capture the flow of everyday life as they see and hear it, then link these experiences to web pages or information sources. They offer opportunities for pedagogy. How do we create 'teachable moments' from a technology-supported flow of experience? How can incidents in daily life become resources for learning, so people can create links to personally meaningful moments? How can groups of people create shared lifelogs, so they can scroll back in time to recall and discuss previous activities?

Lifelogging may seem futuristic, but it's the principle behind web tools and social networks, such as Google and Facebook. Each interaction with these tools is logged and sophisticated algorithms give the illusion of a seamless experience across times and devices. When we search the internet, the responses are based on our previous searches. If we click an advert, it pops up again in many places online. Our online contacts are sources of news and conversation. These inter-connected experiences are manipulated by social media companies to make it seem that we are in a small online world of our own making. This has the benefit that personally relevant information may be ready to hand, but the danger is that we may come to believe that our views, preferences and connections are not just the most relevant, but all there is.

A way out of this rabbit hole is to create breaks in the flow of learning experience, spaces to stop and reflect, spot the gaps in our understanding, take into account the perspectives of others and try to gain a genuinely new experience. The school classroom has traditionally been a place for reflection and that now needs to include reflecting on online experiences. Classroom discussion can include which experiences should be shared and whether we should move towards a world where we record the entire flow of experience.

Dimensions of seamless learning

A team at the National Institute of Education, Singapore has proposed ten dimensions for Mobile Seamless Learning (MSL):

(MSL1)	Encompassing formal and informal learning;
(MSL2)	Encompassing personalized and social learning;
(MSL3)	Across time;
(MSL4)	Across locations;
(MSL5)	Ubiquitous access to learning resources (online data and information, teacher-created materials, student artefacts, student online interactions, etc.);
(MSL6)	Encompassing physical and digital worlds;
(MSL7)	Combined use of multiple device types (including 'stable' technologies, such as desktop computers, interactive whiteboards);
(MSL8)	Seamless switching between multiple learning tasks (such as data collection, analysis and communication);
(MSL9)	Knowledge synthesis (a combination of prior and new knowledge, multiple levels of thinking skills and multi-disciplinary learning);
(MSL10)	Encompassing multiple pedagogical or learning activity models.

Each of these shows one kind of seamless learning, though people may combine many of these during a single day. The versatile technologies of smartphones and tablet computers can mix all ten dimensions, so they have been a basis for recent seamless learning projects.

The Singapore team ran a three-year project with a primary school, where children aged 9–10 used mobile phones to support seamless learning. Their activities included taking photos and making notes on plants in their neighbourhood, using an animation program on the phones to illustrate the transport system of plants and creating concept maps. A template encouraged the students to write and reflect on 'What do I already know?', 'What do I want to know?' and 'What have I learned?'. A main aim of the study was to extend learning outside the classroom, for example to involve parents in growing hydroponic (without soil) plants, and to encourage the students to record and present their hobbies.

Seamless learning in practice

Nan Chiau Primary School in Singapore is a pioneer school for learning with mobile technology. It has adopted seamless learning in science and Chinese language. The aim is to break down barriers between classrooms and outdoors and between scheduled lessons and informal times. The students explore plants and animals in the school's 'eco-garden', collect evidence on their mobile devices during school trips, and learn vocabulary by taking photographs to illustrate idioms.

A group of universities around Lake Constance which borders Germany, Austria and Switzerland, has formed a four-year initiative to develop seamless lifelong learning in higher education and lifelong learning. The projects to teach science, mathematics, computing and design involve universities and local employers.

Conclusions

Seamless learning has developed from two directions. One is concerned with connecting learning experiences in higher education and lifelong learning. The other, notably in Singapore, has shown how mobile phones and tablets can help children to continue learning during school breaks, after school, at home and on trips. Both are based on a philosophy of holistic education, that people learn best by continually engaging mind, body, spirit, experience and knowledge.

While extending classroom learning seamlessly into the playground, school garden, or home may be liberating, it's also a way for schools to colonize these more informal spaces with curriculum-led projects. Seamless learning doesn't need to start with a curriculum topic. A more radical approach is to let new learning start in any setting and then help it to continue across many settings and communities. Children can pursue hobbies at home then continue them in a class project or an after-school club. University students can join open-access courses to learn alongside students in other countries. Lifelong learners can meet up to share their ideas and skills. The challenge is how to use a combination of technology and pedagogy to make the learning seem fluid and natural despite changes in time, setting, device and community.

Resources

Lake Constance seamless learning project:
http://www.seamless-learning.eu/en/hintergrund/

Historical overview of mobile seamless learning:
Wong, L.-H. (2015). A brief history of mobile seamless learning. In L.-H. Wong, M. Milrad, & M. Specht (Eds.), *Seamless Learning in the Age of Mobile Connectivity*, pp. 3–40. London: Springer.
https://bit.ly/2QZAtpw

Description of seamless learning projects in Singapore schools:
Wong, L.-H., & Looi, C.-K. (2012). Enculturing self-directed seamless learners: Towards a facilitated seamless learning process framework mediated by mobile technology. In

Proceedings of IEEE Seventh International Conference on Wireless, Mobile and Ubiquitous Technology in Education (WMUTE), 2012, pp. 1–8. Takamatsu, Japan: IEEE Computer Society.
https://bit.ly/2qRa3vG

Lifelogging for people with impaired memory:
Lee, M. L., & Dey, A. K. (2008). Wearable experience capture for episodic memory support. In *Proceedings of Wearable Computers, 2008. ISWC 2008. 12th IEEE International Symposium on Wearable Computers*, pp. 107–108. Los Alamitos, CA: IEEE Computer Society.
https://bit.ly/2CwlQGn

Benefits and risks of sharing data from life-logs:
Rawassizadeh, R. (2012). Towards sharing life-log information with society. *Behaviour and Information Technology*, 31(11), 1057–1067.
https://bit.ly/2PQD31a

This chapter draws on material from *Innovating Pedagogy 2013*, published under a Creative Commons Attribution Licence:
Sharples, M., McAndrew, P., Weller, M., Ferguson, R., FitzGerald, E., Hirst, T., & Gaved, M. (2013). *Innovating Pedagogy 2013: Open University Innovation Report 2*. Milton Keynes: The Open University.

Incidental learning

10

Harness unplanned or unintentional learning

Overview

Incidental learning is not planned or intended – it just happens. This is usually in the context of some other activity, such as exploring a city, reading a book, watching TV or doing a job. Young children engage in incidental learning as they develop abilities to speak, play with toys and interact with their family and friends. Through unstructured play, they can learn problem solving, language use, social, physical and self-regulatory skills. Incidental learning continues throughout life, whenever we learn without a specific aim in mind. By its nature, we can't predict when this will happen, but we can open ourselves and others to the possibilities. For example, visiting a foreign country offers the opportunity to pick up words and phrases by reading signs and deciphering menus. We can also manage the consequences, by kindling a spark of interest into a project. In general, incidental learning is enjoyable and encourages curiosity. But it doesn't fit into the structure and timetables of formal classroom education.

Learning in daily life

We learn throughout our lifetimes. Figure 10.1, from the LIFE Center, shows the percentage of waking hours over a lifetime that a person typically spends in formal learning environments (in the centre row) and informal (the rest). Even during school years, only around 18% of the day is spent in a classroom.

Pre-school children learn in a variety of ways. As well as some direct instruction from parents or in daycare, children engage in incidental learning through

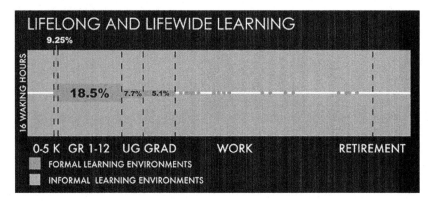

Figure 10.1 Estimated time spent in school and informal learning environments throughout a person's lifetime (LIFE Center: Stevens, R., Bransford, J., & Stevens, A. 2005)

creative play and improvization. For example, a toy house and cars can become a place for pretending to be a parent, negotiating who uses the car or creating a car racing game. Children are also learning language. By the time they start school, children are gaining 10 to 20 new words a week.

In a study of how young children learn arithmetic, children aged 5–6 were tested on their ability to do sums that require approximation ('more or less'). It found that 65% of the young children could answer such problems as: 'If you had 24 stickers and I gave you 27 more, would you have more or less than 35 stickers?'. It seems that many young children can perform approximate arithmetic without being taught, by incidental learning of the skills of estimation. These skills can boost later learning in school. In a different study, researchers gave children aged 3–5 a game on tablet computers to improve their skills at estimation. These children performed better in arithmetic when they started school than children who had played a memory game.

Schools are recognizing that young children can learn through play and discovery. Many schools make time for unstructured exploration. But there is still little awareness that children starting school have already gained skills of estimation, creative problem solving, wordplay and game design that could form the basis of a new kind of early years curriculum.

Incidental learning takes place outside formal education, in the playground and at home. It continues into adulthood, but it generally isn't recognized, celebrated or rewarded. Giasemi Vavoula studied adult incidental learning by asking people to keep a diary of every learning episode over two weeks. Some of the participants found real difficulty in identifying a 'learning episode' since they saw learning as a continuous process. Almost half of the reported learning episodes took place away from home or workplace – outdoors, in a friend's house, or in a place of leisure, such as a park. There was no consistent relation between the topic and the location. Many of the episodes involved equipment, such as a young mother who was "figuring out how to use a type of soft curler in [my] child's hair".

Unlike formal education, incidental learning is not led by a teacher, nor does it follow a structured curriculum or result in formal certification. However, it may trigger self-reflection, and this could encourage people to reconceive what could otherwise be isolated learning fragments as part of more coherent and longer-term learning journeys.

Success in incidental learning

What counts for success in incidental learning depends on what the person wants to achieve. For the young mother, there was an immediate goal to get the curlers to stay in the child's hair and a longer-term aim to make her child look more beautiful. Researchers have identified factors that make incidental learning successful. These include: the goals of the learners, people nearby for discussion and interaction, the tools they have at their disposal, their location and the time they have available. Persistence and confidence contribute to success. Being aware of these factors helps people understand the incidental learning that takes place in their lives and create environments to support it, such as places and resources to study, meet and play. People may seek out situations where learning can occur, such as public seminars or book-reading clubs. The social environment is important since incidental learning often puts learners in a vulnerable position when they need to ask for help.

Assisting incidental learning

Game designers embed opportunities for incidental learning within computer games by setting challenges and offering rewards, as well as by providing landscapes to be navigated, rules to be inferred and the motives and actions of game characters to be interpreted. Some 'serious games' employ similar forms of incidental learning to teach language and cultural skills by immersing players in a foreign environment. This builds on the longstanding approach (from the European 'grand tours' of the 18th century) of taking young adults on trips abroad to pick up the language and culture of a foreign country.

Travellers and migrants often pick up languages much faster than classroom students can. Techniques to mimic immersive incidental learning include encouraging learners to hold everyday conversations in the language they are learning, teaching exclusively in the language and bringing examples of use (for example, from watching a foreign movie with subtitles) back into the classroom for reflection and discussion.

Educators are also exploring how to design learning experiences that build upon incidental learning that takes place elsewhere. Approaches include support for learners in reflecting on learning that takes place throughout their lives and making connections between incidental learning and deliberate learning.

Incidental learning in practice

Incidental teaching is a form of behavioural therapy for children with autism. It involves creating an environment where children initiate 'teachable moments'. The first step is to observe what the child likes to play with and enjoys most. The teacher, parent or therapist, then puts some of these items just out of reach, but visible. Then they wait. Soon, the child will reach up for one of the toys and the adult waits for the child to ask for it. If that doesn't happen, the teacher asks: 'What do you want?'. The idea is for the adult carer to hold a dialogue based on the child's immediate interest, to get the child to engage socially.

Incidental teaching for autism is just one specific form of teachable moment. In a typical school classroom, a good teacher can create many such teachable moments by asking students to describe memorable incidents from their past, such as words learned on a trip abroad, or the colours of a rainbow. Such incidents harness children's experience, curiosity and sense of wonder when teaching a complex topic.

The European MASELTOV project developed a set of applications on mobile phones for immigrants to become integrated into their new cities. These included tools to learn language related to immediate needs, such as healthcare, aids to navigate around the city and a 'help radar' to identify people nearby who could help solve an immediate problem.

New forms of citizen science are engaging people of all ages to carry out individual or collaborative investigations. The iSpot website is designed for anyone to spot and share observations of wildlife. For example, a hiker can upload photos of an unusual bird, insect or flower to iSpot, adding basic information and, if possible, a suggested identification. Others respond by adding, amending or confirming the identification. Once confirmed, the software links this new addition to other identifications of the species with photos by their finders. This simple act of incidental learning can set the contributor on a path of discovery that includes comparisons with other sightings and a developing understanding of how experts classify species.

Conclusions

Although incidental learning can enrich formal learning and occurs throughout a lifetime, it presents challenges for teachers and learners. Incidental learning is inherently messy. It can be difficult for a teacher to know when the learning has occurred, given that it cannot be planned and often is not recorded. There is the challenge of providing learners with well-timed opportunities for reflection, make learning more transparent and helping them reconceive isolated learning fragments as part of more coherent, longer-term learning journeys. Equally, there are challenges for learners who need to value their own learning experiences and journeys, find time to pursue their hobbies and interests, and resist attempts by others – parents, teachers, managers – to over-formalize and validate their personal learning.

We still know very little about how young children acquire abilities related to language, arithmetic, science and social interaction, let alone the beginnings of creativity, art appreciation, psychology and philosophy. As researchers start to uncover these processes of incidental learning, we may see the emergence of new pedagogies that build on children's pre-existing skills and develop these into adulthood.

Resources

The iSpot community to identify wildlife and share nature:
www.ispotnature.org/

Short article on incidental teaching for autistic children:
https://www.special-learning.com/article/incidental_teaching

A brief overview of serious games and incidental learning:
Gamelearn (2017). *Eight Examples that Explain All You Need to Know about Serious Games and Game-Based Learning.*
https://bit.ly/2S3yCRX

Study of how pre-school children can solve addition and subtraction problems through approximate arithmetic:
Gilmore, C. K., McCarthy, S. E., & Spelke, E. S. (2007). Symbolic arithmetic knowledge without instruction. *Nature*, 447(7144), 589–591.
https://bit.ly/2qb1wDb

Short overview of research into incidental learning for the workplace:
Kerka, S. (2000). *Incidental Learning*. Trends and Issues Alert No. 18: Center on Education and Training for Employment.
https://bit.ly/2J88Vf3

MASELTOV project using smartphones to support incidental learning by immigrants:
Jones, A., Gaved, M., Kukulska-Hulme, A., Scanlon, E., Pearson, C., Lameras, P., Dunwell, I., & Jones, J. (2014). Creating coherent incidental learning journeys on smartphones

using feedback and progress indicators. *International Journal of Mobile and Blended Learning,* 6(4), 75–92.
https://bit.ly/2OD2oyI

Diary study by Giasemi Vavoula of incidental learning:
Vavoula, G. (2005). *A Study of Mobile Learning Practices,* Internal Report, Deliverable 4.4 for the MOBIlearn project (IST-2001-37440).
https://bit.ly/2NOVp0A

This chapter draws on material from *Innovating Pedagogy 2015,* published under a Creative Commons Attribution Licence:
Sharples, M., Adams, A., Alozie, N., Ferguson, R., FitzGerald, E., Gaved, M., McAndrew, P., Means, B., Remold, J., Rienties, B., Roschelle, J., Vogt, K., Whitelock, D., & Yarnall, L. (2015). *Innovating Pedagogy 2015: Open University Innovation Report 4.* Milton Keynes: The Open University.

Learning from gaming　11
Exploit the power of digital games for learning

Overview

Games can be played in any setting, including classrooms, and offer many ways to learn. They provoke interest by presenting content in ways that students immediately understand. They set up situations that demand strategy and problem solving. They allow the player to act and see the consequences of actions. They teach that failure is inevitable and that we can learn from mistakes. But they can also be addictive, time-consuming and violent. When computer games are added onto traditional teaching, they give superficial elements of entertainment and reward. These may encourage learners to continue, but they miss the power of games for engagement, reflection and self-regulation. New approaches of 'intrinsic integration' link the motivation of games with specific learning activities and outcomes, so that the gameplay is both engaging and educationally effective. Game designers can achieve this by manipulating elements of challenge, personal control, fantasy and curiosity that match the pedagogy. This can create a productive cycle of engagement and reflection. The shared goals and actions in games also help learners in working together to solve problems and create self-organizing communities.

Games, play and learning

In ancient Greece and Rome, just as now, games were a way to improve the physical skills of coordination, the intellectual powers of planning and strategy and the social values of teamwork. From medieval times, chess provided

Figure 11.1 The effect of computer games on learning

training for strategy, patience and cunning. In the early 20th century, influential educational theorists, such as Vygotsky and Piaget, drew attention to links between children's play and learning. During the past decade, research has explored the connections between digital games and learning.

Board games, such as chess, depend on having a partner with the right level of skills and cunning to keep a player engaged and challenged. What computer games bring is the ability to continually manipulate the challenge of a game to promote engagement and thus learning. It works as shown in Figure 11.1. The computer game can set a task that needs just a little more skill and judgment than before. Or it can increase the level of the game so that the whole environment becomes more challenging. The player is always at the edge of competence and this makes the game engaging. If the engagement also includes educational tasks, then the player learns.

Chocolate-covered broccoli

These relations between games, challenge, engagement and learning have resulted in widespread interest in the 'gamification' of learning. The idea is to take a curriculum subject that is hard to learn, such as arithmetic or physics, and present it in the form of a game, with challenges, levels and rewards, so that the students become engaged and successful learners. It sounds appealing and seems to fit with the theory of learning by gaming but doesn't work in practice.

Such games have been called 'chocolate-covered broccoli' because they offer a layer of fun to cover a boring educational task. The game may offer a stimulus or reward, but the underlying exercise does not change. A related approach is to use the trappings of games – including badges, scores and timed challenges – to make drill-and-practice work appear more appealing. At best, the student may learn routines to gain scores and win badges but never understands the topic in depth.

Intrinsic integration

A more radical approach is 'intrinsic integration' where the designer of the game integrates the learning activity into the gameplay. A familiar example is the game of Hangman where children learn spelling by challenging each other to fill the blanks with letters to form a word. In Hangman, the activity of selecting letters and spelling a word correctly is an essential part of the game.

Virtual worlds, such as Minecraft, offer environments where learners take part in activities that would be too difficult, dangerous or impossible in the physical world, such as building a Chinese city or carrying out an explosive chemical reaction. When used effectively, such settings can promote creativity and the development of '21st-century skills', such as collaboration and problem solving. Students can take on new identities and act out stories. For example, the Education Edition of Minecraft has a lesson to explore part of the city of Shakespeare's Verona and users act out what might have happened there after the deaths of Romeo and Juliet. They use the virtual camera to collect a portfolio of evidence for writing an argumentative essay on crime in the city.

Affinity spaces

Complex digital games require their players to develop new skills and to build detailed understanding of the gaming environment, its characters, capabilities and stories. This learning is key to success within the game, but these skills and knowledge need to be developed in an engaging way, or players will simply switch off and give up. The methods used by video game designers to motivate, train, inform, support and reward gamers, both individually and in teams, might usefully be applied to other areas of online and distance learning. James Paul Gee has identified 36 principles of learning in game environments. These include:

- **Self-knowledge principle**: the virtual world is constructed in such a way that learners learn not only about the topic but also about themselves and their current and potential capacities.
- **Achievement principle**: for learners at all levels of skill, there are intrinsic rewards from the outset, customized to each learner's level, effort and growing mastery, and signalling the learner's on-going achievements.
- **Discovery principle**: overt telling is kept to a well-thought-out minimum, allowing ample opportunity for the learner to experiment and make discoveries.
- **Affinity group principle**: learners constitute an 'affinity group', that is, a group that is bonded primarily through shared endeavours, goals and practices and not primarily by race, gender, nation, ethnicity or culture.

Gee went on to expand the concept of affinity spaces as real or virtual places where learning occurs. In doing so, he combined findings from the science of learning and from gaming. The affinity space is a pedagogically informed way to organize learners and learning environments. It can be applied not only in gaming but also in other online settings and in face-to-face environments. Affinity spaces are organized around a passion. Within them, people use 'smart tools', such as interactive maps to be productive; they do not simply consume. The groups are not graded by age – they bring beginners and experts together. Within these spaces people mentor and are mentored, knowledge is both distributed and dispersed, learning is proactive but aided and everyone is still a learner.

The principles of the affinity space can be seen in action in the work of the Lifelong Kindergarten group at Massachusetts Institute of Technology (MIT). This section of the MIT Media Lab investigates how people learn by designing, creating and inventing things. The group's work with the Lego toy company led to the development of the internationally successful Lego Mindstorms robotics kits that can be used for both play and learning. They also developed the Scratch programming language, with an online community to create and share stories, games and animations.

Learning from gaming in practice

Quest to Learn is a school in New York City for students from 6th to 12th grade (age 11–18) based on principles of game-based learning. The classroom games can be detailed and long-lasting. As an example, students in ninth-grade biology spend a year as workers in a fictional bio-tech company. They clone dinosaurs and create environments for them. Through playing this elaborate game, the students learn about genetics, biology and ecology. In the sixth grade, students play the roles of designers, doctors and detectives to learn about the human body.

Conclusions

Games and gaming environments may develop knowledge and skills within the game, but these have little use in the wider world. Adding the trappings of games – colourful avatars, bright badges and staged challenges – to traditional instruction is not enough. A new approach of intrinsic integration matches the gameplay to the learning so that the flow and challenge of the game reflect the skills needed to learn the topic. Affinity spaces allow gamers to meet and engage in informal learning.

Resources

Lifelong Kindergarten at MIT whose "ultimate goal is a world full of playfully creative people who are constantly inventing new opportunities for themselves and their communities": http://llk.media.mit.edu/

A lesson for Minecraft Education Edition on Shakespeare's Verona, to teach project work, communication and critical thinking:
https://education.minecraft.net/lessons/verona-adventure/

The Quest to Learn School:
http://www.q2l.org/about/

James Paul Gee on the benefits of video games for education:
Gee, J. P. (2008). *What Video Games Have to Teach Us about Learning and Literacy* (2nd edition). New York: Palgrave Macmillan.

Intrinsic integration in educational games:
Habgood, M. P. J., & Ainsworth, S. E. (2011). Motivating children to learn effectively: Exploring the value of intrinsic integration in educational games. *Journal of the Learning Sciences*, 20(2), 169–206.
http://shura.shu.ac.uk/3556/

Impact of flow (heightened challenge and skill), engagement and immersion on learning in game-based learning environments:
Hamari, J., Shernoff, D. J., Rowe, E., Coller, B., Asbell-Clarke, J., & Edwards, T. (2016). Challenging games help students learn: An empirical study on engagement, flow and immersion in game-based learning. *Computers in Human Behavior*, 54, 170–179.
https://bit.ly/2J9FF7A

This chapter draws on material from *Innovating Pedagogy 2013*, published under a Creative Commons Attribution Licence:
Sharples, M., McAndrew, P., Weller, M., Ferguson, R., FitzGerald, E., Hirst, T., & Gaved, M. (2013). *Innovating Pedagogy 2013: Open University Innovation Report 2*. Milton Keynes: The Open University.

Geo-learning   **12**
Learn in and about locations

Overview

Students of geography, environmental sciences and history all seek to understand visible landscapes, as do tourists at heritage sites and visitors to unfamiliar cities. A school nature walk or a visit to a playground garden involves
learning about the surroundings. We can distinguish *learning in* and *learning
about* locations. For learning in a location, students are immersed in a setting
that offers a rich sensory experience, such as a museum that re-creates a street
from the 19th century. For learning about a location, the aim is to understand
features of the terrain, their function or how they were formed. An example is
students on a geology field trip understanding how a glacial valley was formed.
In both cases, being there is essential to the learning. Understanding comes
from being immersed in the setting and getting a sense of scale, perspective
and relationship to parts of the environment.

Being there

A group of geology students stand on a mountain top and look down at a glacial
valley, discussing how the landscape was sculpted by the glacier 20,000 years
ago. Children in a school garden look for signs of growth after winter. Visitors
explore an historic city, taking in the atmosphere of the narrow streets. All
these people are learning about their immediate environment. Geo-learning
isn't new – Thomas Cook organized grand tours to the sights of Europe from
the 1860s – but combinations of pedagogy and technology offer new opportunities to learn from being there.

Some types of knowledge are embedded in the environment and cannot be separated from it. If you want to learn how to sail, then no amount of classroom instruction will substitute for setting the sails by the feel of the wind or navigating across a tidal stream. The pedagogy comes from engaging all the senses to create an integrated impression of the environment. It also involves learning to filter out those stimuli that aren't relevant, to focus on the task at hand. As anyone who has learned to sail a boat or fly a plane will know, the first few lessons can be overwhelming in starting to make sense of the surroundings.

That's why field trips are so important to geology students – they first need to gain a sense of the immediate landscape, then perform activities to interpret and transform it: to understand how it looked in the past, or how it might be changed by a wind turbine. On a smaller scale, school students can learn in and about a school garden: to see plants are affected by sunlight, feel the texture of soil and understand how a garden changes through the seasons.

The geologist Steven Semken has developed a place-based pedagogy which:

- focuses on the natural elements of a location, such as its rock structure, plants and climate;
- acknowledges the diverse meanings that a place has for the teacher, students and community;
- teaches through authentic specimens, maps and measurements;
- promotes sustainable and culturally appropriate activities with local people;
- enriches the sense of place of students and teacher.

School gardens

Around a quarter of elementary schools in the USA have gardens. A roundup of studies into the benefits of school gardening shows a positive relationship between gardening and academic performance in science subjects, including skills in measuring space and understanding plant processes. But curricula should focus on specific subject areas, e.g. mathematics, if they want to influence achievement in those subjects.

Augmented reality outdoors

Augmented reality uses technology to help students learn about their immediate environment. It can be as simple as a transparent sheet marked with an outline of the view and labels to describe the sights (see Figure 12.1). This has been effective on geology field trips. Applications for mobile phones can detect the

Figure 12.1 Transparent sheet showing outlines of mountains and their names

user's location and overlay the camera display with information about where the user is looking. Ordnance Survey, Britain's mapping organization, now provides an augmented reality application for mobile phones.

CAERUS was a project with location-aware mobile devices for visitors to a botanical garden. It was designed to tell stories of the plants, such as where the specimens were collected, and to highlight features of the garden that visitors could see but didn't notice, such as the different shapes of petals. Telling stories behind the visual scene is a powerful form of teaching, as it gets visitors to perceive an environment in a new way and situates information within a visual memory.

The 'Out There, In Here' project supported geo-learning through collaboration. A group of students took part in field-work outdoors and communicated in real time with other students working indoors in a distant laboratory. They could use a range of technologies including interactive tabletops, large screen displays, tablet computers and mobile phones. The outdoor students had the advantage of being in the landscape, while those indoors could quickly search for information and offer guidance.

Urban drama

Geo-learning can take place in cities as well as in the countryside. Some cities now provide audio guides for walking tours. The textopia application takes the urban tour a step further by offering literary texts and poetry that reveal hidden stories and personal experiences about the locations.

An even more ambitious project was 'Riot! 1831'. In 1831, Queen Square in the British city of Bristol was the site of riots against a decision by Parliament not to give more people the vote. The educational project re-created the riot as an audio landscape. As visitors wearing headsets moved around the square, they heard sounds and voices from the battle between rioters and cavalry.

Geo-learning in practice

The head teacher of Charlton Manor Primary School in the UK describes how gardening has become a central part of the school's curriculum. A creative writing task on buried treasure took on new meaning with the garden as a backdrop. In mathematics, children measure and map the flower beds. For science, they produce charts and graphs of sprouting sunflowers.

Each year, geography students from the University of Nottingham go on a field trip to the English Lake District. As part of the trip, they are asked to use and evaluate technologies for understanding the landscape, ranging from transparent acetate sheets to hold up over a view, Google Earth on a tablet computer, to an immersive head-mounted display showing the surrounding scenery during the Ice Age. The students work in groups and one member of the group produces a video diary of the activity. Back in the study centre, the students discuss whether, and how, the technology has helped them to interpret the landscape.

Conclusions

Handheld devices for learning about locations are already widespread at tourist sites and museums. Most offer maps and descriptions of locations. Some tell stories behind the landmarks. But despite much collected data on people's movements and activity, we still know little about how people learn in and about the landscape. People look for meaning in their surroundings according to their pre-existing expertise. A geologist will see evidence of erosion. An urban geographer will recognize cultural signs of fashion and taste. A biologist will look for growth and decay of living things. What they have in common is a way to look beyond the immediate visual pattern of their surroundings to infer the hidden structures and stories. Landscapes and locations do not offer up knowledge in an easily digestible way. The noted geographer Pierce Lewis wrote that "like books, landscapes *can* be read, but unlike books, they were not *meant* to be read". A pedagogy of geo-learning can help students to read their surroundings, with a teacher or technology guiding them in the skills of interpretation.

Resources

Roundup of research on the impact of school gardens on academic success:
https://bit.ly/2AkwNcm

Augmented reality application from Ordnance Survey to overlay labels on camera images from mobile phones for outdoor locations in the UK:
https://bit.ly/2PauIbo

Guidelines for place-based education with mobile devices:
Zimmerman, H. T., & Land, S. M. (2014). Facilitating place-based learning in outdoor informal environments with mobile computers. *TechTrends*, 58(1), 77–83.
https://bit.ly/2runNg8

A review of methods for place-based education in geoscience:
Semken, S., Ward, E. G., Moosavi, S., & Chinn, P. W. (2017). Place-based education in geoscience: Theory, research, practice, and assessment. *Journal of Geoscience Education*, 65(4), 542–562.
https://bit.ly/2ytpXjB

A paper on the 'Riot! 1831' soundscape:
Reid, J., Hull, R., Cater, K., & Clayton, B. (2005). Riot! 1831: The design of a location based audio drama. In *Proceedings of the 3rd UK-UbiNet Workshop*, pp. 1–2. Bath, UK: University of Bath.
https://bit.ly/2J7MPJy

Location-based literature and the textopia mobile application to give recordings of literary texts about nearby places:
Løvlie, A. S. (2009). Textopia: Designing a locative literary reader. *Journal of Location Based Services*, 3(4), 249–276.
https://bit.ly/2I96p71

Users' reactions to the CAERUS guide for learning about a botanic garden:
Naismith, L., Sharples, M., & Ting, J. (2005). Evaluation of CAERUS: A context aware mobile guide. In H. van der Merwe & T. Brown (Eds.), *Mobile Technology: The Future of Learning in Your Hands, mLearn 2005*, 4th World Conference on mLearning, Cape Town, 25–28 October 2005. Cape Town: mLearn 2005.
https://bit.ly/2R49adL

'Out There, In Here' project to connect learning in the field and lab:
Coughlan, T., Collins, T. D., Adams, A., Rogers, Y., Haya, P. A., & Martin, E. (2012). The conceptual framing, design and evaluation of device ecologies for collaborative activities. *International Journal of Human-Computer Studies*, 70(10), 765–779.
https://bit.ly/2PJAuxB

Field trips by University of Nottingham students to use and evaluate technologies to learn about the landscape:

Priestnall, G., Brown, E., Sharples, M., & Polmear, G. (2009). A student-led comparison of techniques for augmenting the field experience. In D. Metcalf, A. Hamilton & C. Graffeo (Eds.), *Proceedings of 8th World Conference on Mobile and Contextual Learning (mLearn 2009)*, 28–30 October, 2009, pp. 195–198. Orlando, Florida: University of Central Florida. https://bit.ly/2J8tnMN

Classic paper on how to read cultural landscapes:
Lewis, P. B. (1979). Axioms for reading the landscape: Some guides to the American scene. In D.W. Meinig (Ed.), *The Interpretation of Ordinary Landscapes: Geographical Essays*, pp. 11–32. New York, NY: Oxford University Press. https://bit.ly/2K8BMiE

This chapter draws on material from *Innovating Pedagogy 2013*, published under a Creative Commons Attribution Licence:
Sharples, M., McAndrew, P., Weller, M., Ferguson, R., FitzGerald, E., Hirst, T., & Gaved, M. (2013). *Innovating Pedagogy 2013: Open University Innovation Report 2*. Milton Keynes: The Open University.

Learning through social media

13

Use social media to offer long-term learning opportunities

Overview

Beyond schools and colleges, people learn less formally. Many use social media, such as Twitter, Facebook and Snapchat, to share ideas and engage in conversations. These sites offer a range of learning opportunities to access expert advice, encounter challenges, defend opinions and amend ideas in the face of criticism. Unfortunately, the same sites can present learners with fake news, offensive comments and hostile responses. Some organizations have set up social media specifically to offer learning opportunities. Learners are helped to share experiences, make connections and link these with teaching resources. Other educational sites are based on projects, such as 'Real Time World War II', 'The Diary of Samuel Pepys' and NASA's 'MarsCuriosity' Twitter account. Running these projects requires not only expertise but the time and ability to take on different roles. Anyone can engage and leave at any time, but a skilled facilitator who takes on the tasks of filtering resources and engaging people can keep a social media project running for many years.

Bringing learning to life

Millions of people access social media sites to keep in touch with their friends and exchange information. In Asia, over a billion people use the WeChat mobile application to send text messages, share photos, hold videoconferences, read news, write blogs, make friends, order taxis, transfer money and buy goods.

Most of these activities could only be described as 'learning' in the loosest sense of the word. However, social media can bring learning to life by summoning up different times, spaces, characters and possibilities. They can support creativity, collaboration, communication and sharing of resources. These media support exploration of the past and outer space in real time, engaging learners in new ways. They can be used to develop extended projects for learning on a grand scale.

Where the pedagogy is successful, social media can give learners reliable and interesting content, as well as opportunities to access expert advice, to encounter challenges, to defend their views and to amend their ideas in the face of criticism. When the pedagogy fails, sites may present learners with misleading information. Educators on social media sites designed to offer learning opportunities therefore have multiple roles that differ from a teacher in more formal settings. Unless the projects have experts to inspire and inform people, the project falls flat. A facilitator is also needed to initiate the project and to take on the tasks of filtering resources, moderating comments and engaging people. Anyone can engage at any time, anyone can leave at any time, but skilled facilitators can keep people engaged and actively contributing.

Self-regulated learning in social media

Self-regulated learning is the process of taking control of and evaluating one's own learning. Social media can support this process at three levels. The first level is for learners to create their own personal learning space by finding and organizing content. They need to know where to look for valuable and reliable resources and how to be a critical reader. The second level is to take part in the online community through commenting, responding and sharing of media. At the third level, students reflect on the material from the first two levels, organizing it around their personal learning goals. When this works well, the social media sites become resources for personal and collaborative learning, matched to the learner's goals. Too often, though, a student gets caught up in an enclosed world of misleading information, self-confirming theories and aggressive communication. Social media communities that educate by expanding minds and engaging critical thinking are rare and precious.

Real Time World War II

A good example of learning and teaching through social media is @ RealTimeWWII, a Twitter account with over 500,000 followers. The goals of the project are to educate followers about the sequence of events in the Second World War and to give a sense of what the war felt like to ordinary people.

The author bases his tweets on eyewitness accounts, photographs and videos, giving the impression that his tweets are coming straight from the time. He includes views from around the world, some commenting on well-known events, some giving the view of a private individual. The war is presented and experienced through the words of people who were involved.

The account includes events that were not widely known at the time, but that we now know were significant. For example, tweets in August 2016 outlined treatment of Roma people at Auschwitz, the thousands of deaths from disease and starvation, the many murders and the experiments on children.

People around the world engage with this project, re-tweeting resources or providing links to their own selection of tweets. Some Twitter accounts translate the thousands of tweets into languages including Chinese, Italian, Turkish, Latin and Finnish. Others contribute to the conversation with reflective posts that link the tweets with current events.

Pepys' diary

Another project that encourages reader participation is www.pepysdiary.com. This uses historical material from a single writer, Samuel Pepys, who lived in London during the 17th century. For nearly ten years, he kept a private diary.

Pepys' journal provides a first-hand account of national events, as well as detailed descriptions of day-to-day life and his sexual adventures. It is a key primary source for English history of that period. It is also long and sometimes difficult to understand. Usually, only highlights are shared, particularly Pepys' accounts of the Great Fire of London.

Pepysdiary.com restores the diary to an account of daily life by publishing its full text, day by day. The shared timescale provides a sense that Pepys and the reader are moving through time at the same pace.

@Samuelpepys also tweets several times a day and has more than 58,000 followers. Although it is clear that Pepys has been dead for 300 years, his tweets provoke a social response. Sometimes these are brief, throwaway comments; others suggest a continued engagement with the character.

The site encourages readers to engage by sharing ideas and collaborating on the project. By the time the entire diary had been posted online, the site had been annotated almost 60,000 times. Now that the diary is being posted for the second time, readers are adding new ideas as well as continuing discussions that began in the comments section ten years ago.

Chaucer and medieval literature

Pepys' diary and @RealTimeWWII both use direct quotes from historical sources to bring the past to life. Chaucer Doth Tweet takes another approach, constructing a character in order to engage people with medieval literature.

Chaucer was a medieval poet who wrote in Middle English. His spelling, references and vocabulary are often difficult for modern readers to understand. Nevertheless, the quality and impact of his writing mean that it is still well known. His poem *The Canterbury Tales* has often been reworked as drama and film.

A version of Chaucer has now been active on social media for more than ten years. 'Geoffrey Chaucer' began his blog with a post in Middle English on internet abbreviations. Once his blog was well established, he started to tweet as @ LeVostreGC. The author behind this character is a lecturer who is fascinated by the possibilities that Chaucer's work opens up for interpretation and for play.

The blog and Twitter stream are not intended as first-hand accounts of medieval life. Instead, they create a world in which the 21st century and the 14th century collide in unexpected ways. Mismatches and anachronisms are skillfully woven together in Middle English.

> Chaucer Doth Tweet
>
> Spydere man spydere man
> Doth al things a spydere kan
> Sondry webbes he kan weaven
> Thieves lyke flyes he kan cacchen
> Lo anon comth spydere man

The learning possibilities come from the author's ability to bring a language to life. In these tweets and posts, Middle English is presented as an inventive and amusing medium to be read for pleasure. Comments and responses allow people to try the style for themselves.

@LeVostreGC prompts readers to explore other works from the period and to consider the different characters and styles of their writers. He answers questions, offers links to more academic sources and provides accessible and helpful

Curiosity Rover ✔ @MarsCuriosity · 16 Dec 2014
Certified organics! I detected **organics** for the 1st time on the surface of Mars #AGU14 go.nasa.gov/1A5NeSQ
💬 388   🔁 7.5K   ♡ 5.1K   ✉

Figure 13.1 Tweet as if from the NASA Mars Curiosity Rover

information. He is also responsible for an annual celebration of dead languages, 'Whan That Aprille Day'. This prompts readers to bake cakes, produce videos, sing songs and generally engage with activity in languages from the past.

NASA

Social media support learning about distant times. They can also help us to learn about different spaces. In the USA, the National Aeronautics and Space Administration (NASA) uses a range of social media to share its work. Each NASA spacecraft has its own Twitter account and personality.

Engaging with these spacecraft produces a variety of learning opportunities. A well-known example is NASA's Mars Curiosity Rover which has nearly 4 million followers on Twitter (See Figure 13.1). Followers receive regular updates on the Rover's activity, such as its detection of organic molecules in a rock sample on Mars.

NASA also engages learners in exploration and discovery through NASA Social. This includes in-person events and provides opportunities for its social media followers to learn and share information about NASA missions, people and programs.

For those who want to learn more, NASA Solve enables people to engage in the USA's aerospace program. The site invites members of the public to contribute their time and expertise to advance research and solve problems. Projects include crowd-sourced challenges, citizen science projects and competitions for students.

Conclusions

Social media make it possible to involve and draw on the experience of people around the world. The projects described here have all developed over time. Each one helps people to learn by creating a social network around events that are remote in time or space.

To run projects like these requires long-term commitment as well as expertise, enthusiasm and the ability to coordinate and facilitate. The coordinator must be able to keep people inspired and engaged, sometimes for many years.

Although these social media projects bring large numbers of learners together internationally, each one has an individual at its heart. These individuals have no set program of study for others to follow. They have an area of expertise and they use it to filter ideas and resources, to facilitate engagement and interaction. They may also act as co-learners, open to new ideas and willing to engage with developments suggested by other participants.

In this role, they manage a learning space that has multiple entrance and exit points. In a space that an individual may find accidentally and with no intention of staying for long, they offer ways of engaging at different levels – attracting people to stay and learn when there is no compulsion to do so. On these sites, engagement is under learners' control – they can engage very briefly, they can learn by watching others or they can take part extensively over a long period of time.

Resources

Tweets in real time from the Second World War:
twitter.com/RealTimeWWII

Pepys' diary in blog form:
www.pepysdiary.com

The associated Twitter account:
twitter.com/samuelpepys

'Geoffrey Chaucer' tweets:
https://twitter.com/levostregc

NASA social media:
www.nasa.gov/socialmedia

Collected posts from the Chaucer blog, along with essays about the blog and medieval scholarship:
Bryant, B. L. (2010). *Geoffrey Chaucer Hath a Blog: Medieval Studies and New Media*. New York: Palgrave Macmillan.

Case studies of using virtual media to enhance learning about the real world:
Sheehy, K., Ferguson, R., & Clough, G. (2014). *Augmented Education: Bringing Real and Virtual Learning Together*. New York: Palgrave Macmillan.

New York Times article on RealTimeWWII twitter feed:
Schuessler, J. (2011). The tweets of war, what's past is postable. *The New York Times*, November 27, 2011.
https://nyti.ms/2S7Hg1W

Social media for learning and Personal Learning Environments for students to construct their own learning spaces:
Dabbagh, N., & Kitsantas, A. (2012). Personal Learning Environments, social media and self-regulated learning: A natural formula for connecting formal and informal learning. *The Internet and Higher Education*, 15(1), 3–8.
http://www.anitacrawley.net/Resources/Articles/DabbaughPLE.pdf

This chapter draws on material from *Innovating Pedagogy 2016*, published under a Creative Commons Attribution Licence:

Sharples, M., de Roock, R., Ferguson, R., Gaved, M., Herodotou, C., Koh, E., Kukulska-Hulme, A., Looi, C.-K., McAndrew, P., Rienties, B., Weller, M., Wong, L. H. (2016). *Innovating Pedagogy 2016: Open University Innovation Report 5*. Milton Keynes: The Open University.

Navigating knowledge   **14**
Assess claims and form sound arguments

Overview

Fake news and information bubbles are not new, but the internet has boosted their impact on public opinion. People need to be able to evaluate and share information responsibly. This involves recognizing different types of knowledge, distinguishing fact from fiction, forming valid arguments and acting wisely. One educational approach is to develop students' awareness that knowledge is complex and changing. Another is to help students appreciate that some pathways to knowing are more reliable than others. These can make the students aware of their assumptions about truth and understanding. They also help learners to develop strategies for evaluating and constructing knowledge.

Challenges for navigating knowledge

The term 'post-truth' refers to a world where appeals to emotion and personal belief are more influential in shaping public opinion than objective evidence. In its most extreme form, post-truth embraces conspiracy theories, plausible but false stories and deliberate fake news items.

The internet has created opportunities for individuals and groups to produce and share information. These developments have many positive effects. For example, blogs and Wikipedia offer huge amounts of current information for free. But they have created new challenges to find, select and assess reliable knowledge as a basis for wise action. We survive in a complex world by floating within a familiar bubble of friends and news. None of us can check and validate all the new information we receive, so we adopt strategies to cope with the flood of information.

The first coping strategy is to rely on sources of news that are **ready to hand**, such as Facebook friends, or familiar news sites. We avoid searching for alternative explanations.

Another strategy is to choose what **seems right at the time**. For example, if we find conflicting positions on the web, then we might choose the one with most 'likes', or that has endorsements by people we know.

A third strategy is **making do**. We only look at the first page of Google search results or don't check a source if it seems authoritative.

Alongside these coping strategies, there is a general psychological trait of **confirmation bias**. This is a tendency to prefer information that supports our beliefs. We also enjoy passing on snippets of news that are strange or outrageous. So, when following and spreading news, we tend to be lazy, biased and mischievous.

Critical reading

Overcoming these traits involves not only being critical of what we read and watch but also questioning our own ability to tell fact from fiction. A study by the Stanford History Education Group of 203 middle school students revealed over 80% believed that an advertisement with the phrase 'sponsored content' was a real news story.

One starting point is to explore how knowledge is complex and ever-changing. For example, students could investigate eating fads – looking at how diet supplements and health foods have changed over the past century, from arsenic pills to wholegrain, and which diets are backed up by modern nutrition.

Another entry point is that differing explanations or arguments are not equally right but need to be supported by evidence. Libraries and fact-checking websites have proposed guidelines for spotting fake news. Figure 14.1 is a poster on how to spot fake news, produced in multiple languages by the International Federation of Library Associations and Institutions. It is based on an article from the FactCheck.org website.

Consider the source. Some fake news sites appear to be newspaper or TV news sites, with similar names to the real news broadcasters, such as ABC News. Others claim to be sources of satire or fantasy. For many years, Snopes.com has been writing about false news and it maintains a list of known fake news websites.

Read beyond the headline. If you are drawn to a provocative headline, check further before spreading the shocking news. Does it seem possible? Have

HOW TO SPOT FAKE NEWS

CONSIDER THE SOURCE
Click away from the story to investigate the site, its mission and its contact info.

READ BEYOND
Headlines can be outrageous in an effort to get clicks. What's the whole story?

CHECK THE AUTHOR
Do a quick search on the author. Are they credible? Are they real?

SUPPORTING SOURCES?
Click on those links. Determine if the info given actually supports the story.

CHECK THE DATE
Reposting old news stories doesn't mean they're relevant to current events.

IS IT A JOKE?
If it is too outlandish, it might be satire. Research the site and author to be sure.

CHECK YOUR BIASES
Consider if your own beliefs could affect your judgement.

ASK THE EXPERTS
Ask a librarian, or consult a fact-checking site.

IFLA
International Federation of Library Associations and Institutions

Figure 14.1 A poster on how to spot fake news, from the International Federation of Library Associations and Institutions

major news sites picked up the story? Read the entire story to see whether there are clues that show it to be satire or fantasy.

Check the author. Some authors of fake news, such as Paul Horner, are well known. Others may claim to be doctors or prize-winning writers. If so, it is worth doing a quick check of their credentials. Also, try typing the author's name into Urban Dictionary to see if it is urban slang.

What's the support? Many fake stories reference official-sounding sources. These may link to genuine news, government or science sites that don't support the claims. Or they may go down a labyrinth of fake news and conspiracy pages. Check whether the sources provide clear evidence to support the claim.

Check the date. Some false stories are distortions of real events that happened in the past. Check whether the story refers to a current event. See if there has been coverage in the past of the same event.

Is it some kind of a joke? Satire comes in many forms. The story could be deliberately provocative and satirical. Or it could describe a genuine event that has been set up as satire – such as the painting by the artist Banksy that automatically shredded itself during an art auction.

Check your biases. We like stories to be true if they support our prejudices. Consider whether your own beliefs and assumptions are affecting your judgment. If you are appalled by a Facebook post about a politician you oppose, then check it out.

Consult the experts. At least one of FactCheck.org, Snopes.com, the *Washington Post* Fact Checker and PolitiFact.com is likely to have checked the claims of a sensational news story, so try using words from the sensational headline to search these sites.

The ultimate goal in learning to navigate knowledge is to appreciate that fake news can be dangerous (for example, in claiming that HIV and AIDS aren't related or that vaccines cause autism) and that we all deserve not to be treated like idiots, but to find truth through evidence and reason.

Navigating knowledge in practice

A teacher in Irvine, California, has devised a scheme to help students aged 10–11 to spot fake news. He starts by asking the students to examine seven elements of a news article: copyright; verification from different sources; credibility; date of publication; author's expertise; match to prior knowledge; and if it seems realistic. Next, he runs a game in the style of 'Simon Says', where he presents articles from the web and the children have to respond by sitting or standing to signal whether the article is true or fake. Then they work in teams to try and prove which one of three articles is the fake. This exercise within a class has extended to an online game where students challenge other teams across the United States to identify the fake news.

A project by the Ministry of Education in Italy is educating students in 8,000 schools to recognize fake news and conspiracy theories online. It involves students creating their own blogs to expose fake news and explain how they investigated the story.

Conclusions

Since the time of ancient Greece, philosophers have sought to establish the truth behind claims. We now know that truth is not 'out there' to be found. It must be constructed by relating language to how we perceive the world. But that does not mean all claims are equally valid or that every appealing story on the web should be liked and forwarded. Here's an analogy. A furniture designer may deliberately design an uncomfortable chair: to be provocative or to challenge assumptions about what is a chair. Similarly, an author might write an article that is provocative or uncomfortable to read. But a designer who sells a chair that's unsafe, that collapses when the buyer sits on it, is simply a danger to the public. That too is the case when a writer presents falsehood as truth, fails to check sources, offers no evidence, or just gives one side of an argument. Navigating knowledge is about testing those dangerous products and finding ways to make them safer.

Resources

Practical guide for evaluating information on social media:
Caulfield, M. A. (2017). *Web Literacy for Student Fact Checkers*. Pressbooks.
https://webliteracy.pressbooks.com/

Newsela takes news from trusted sources and publishes digests at different reading levels:
https://newsela.com/

Guidelines from FactCheck.org on how to spot fake news:
https://www.factcheck.org/2016/11/how-to-spot-fake-news/

Poster on how to spot fake news from the International Federation of Library Associations and Institutions, based on the FactCheck.org article:
https://www.ifla.org/publications/node/11174

Website from University of West Florida on spotting fake news:
https://bit.ly/2J9GcXk

List of fake news sites from Snopes.com:
https://www.snopes.com/news/2016/01/14/fake-news-sites/

Washington Post Fact Checker:
https://www.washingtonpost.com/news/fact-checker/

The *Reading Like a Historian* curriculum by the Stanford History Education Group offers resources and lesson plans for developing critical reading and thinking skills:
https://sheg.stanford.edu/rlh

Poster on some trends in healthy eating from 1880 to the present day (an exercise could be to check the reported eating fads, such as arsenic pills, tapeworm eggs and cabbage soup for accuracy and whether they are still considered healthy):
https://theculturetrip.com/north-america/usa/articles/the-ultimate-history-of-healthy-eating/

Article by Scott Bedley on how he taught fifth-grade students to spot fake news:

Bedley, S. (2017). I taught my 5th-graders how to spot fake news. Now they won't stop fact-checking me. *Vox*, March 29, 2017.

https://bit.ly/2p7nX9v

Project in Italy to teach high school students to spot fake news:

Troop, W. (2017). The Italian politician wants kids to become 'fake news hunters'. *PRI's The World*, October 31, 2017.

https://bit.ly/2EBW2LJ

Urban dictionary:

https://www.urbandictionary.com/

This chapter draws on material from *Innovating Pedagogy 2017*, published under a Creative Commons Attribution Licence:

Ferguson, R., Barzilai, S., Ben-Zvi, D., Chinn, C. A., Herodotou, C., Hod, Y., Kali, Y., Kukulska-Hulme, A., Kupermintz, H., McAndrew, P., Rienties, B., Sagy, O., Scanlon, E., Sharples, M., Weller, M., & Whitelock, D. (2017). *Innovating Pedagogy 2017: Open University Innovation Report 6*. Milton Keynes: The Open University.

Part III

Reflection

Explore first   15
Draw on experience to gain deeper understanding

Overview

Explore first is a method of teaching that gives students complex problems to explore before they receive direct instruction. The aim is for students, working together, to use their prior knowledge to consider possible solutions, then evaluate and explain the best answer. By struggling and sometimes failing to find a solution, the students gain a deeper understanding of the structure of the problem and its elements. After this process, their teacher explains the essential concepts and methods of the solution, helping students to firm up their knowledge by comparing good and bad answers. The pedagogy requires students to embrace challenge and uncertainty. They may feel less confident at first, but this experience can help them become more creative and resilient. To implement explore first, teachers will need a deep understanding of the topic and may need to make fundamental changes to how they teach.

Productive failure

In explore first, students try to solve complex problems in small groups before being taught the relevant principles and correct methods. The pedagogy has also been called 'productive failure', because students' initial efforts at problem solving may cause them to fail or find a poor solution. But the process of exploring different paths can lead to deeper understanding. The teacher then follows up this phase of exploration by explaining the correct solution and its underlying principles, addressing any misunderstandings that the students have shown.

The theory of learning from productive failure has its roots in work by Kurt VanLehn and colleagues. They found that learners sometimes reach a block (or impasse) when trying to solve a problem. If they are working alone, they may try to find a way round the impasse by coming to a wrong solution. Consider a child who is faced with the subtraction sum:

$$\begin{array}{r} 35 \\ -17 \\ \hline \end{array}$$

but has not learned how to subtract a larger number in a column from a smaller one. The child might try to get around the impasse ('I don't know how to take 7 away from 5') by taking the smaller number from the larger one, with the wrong result:

$$\begin{array}{r} 35 \\ -17 \\ \hline 22 \end{array}$$

A teacher who understands that the child is being entirely rational in trying to solve the problem, but just has some missing knowledge, can then help to correct that faulty knowledge.

Learning from productive failure

The learning scientist Manu Kapur suggests that this process of failure and repair can be an effective form of learning. He proposes that students should work in groups to solve difficult problems. Often they will fail, but that failure may cause them to explore the problem in more depth. They may go back to basic principles, or they may be creative and look for alternative routes to the solution.

There are four key learning mechanisms behind productive failure. Learners:

1. access and explore their prior knowledge in relation to the problem or concept;
2. attend to important parts of the problem;
3. discuss and explain these critical features;
4. organize these important conceptual features and include some of them in a solution.

These can be planned into problem-solving lessons in two phases. The first phase encourages students to explore a problem and generate possible solutions (mechanism 1). The second phase teaches the important concepts and helps students to build these into a correct solution (mechanisms 2 to 4).

Say, for example, a teacher is running a class on the statistics of standard deviations. She might give the students a complex data analysis problem: to calculate the most consistent tennis player in an annual tennis tournament over a three-year period. During the first phase, the students work in small groups to produce answers. In the next phase, the teacher gathers, compares and contrasts the student-generated solutions. The teacher then explains how to find the answer, using the student solutions as examples. Finally, the students are asked to solve a similar problem using their new knowledge.

Explore first

Explore first is a more general version of productive failure, where the students first explore a complex topic in small groups, then get direct instruction. It can be done in the classroom, or online, or a mixture of the two. In science, the students might try different ways to measure the speed of sound. In history, they might look up material online to try and determine why the Roman Empire rose and fell.

What's important is that they initially explore the topic in breadth as well as depth, testing a variety of hypotheses and theories. Also important is for the teacher to choose a good topic to explore. It has to be understandable by the students, have many possible solutions, build on students' existing knowledge of the topic, not be so easy that the answer can be found by a quick search online and not be so difficult that the students don't know where to start.

A research study compared two methods for teaching the topic of combinatorics – the mathematics of combinations and permutations. One group of college students watched a video of a university professor giving a lecture on permutations. Then, in groups, they explored the topic with the aid of an interactive table-top display. The second group of students explored the topic first and then watched the lecture.

Those students who explored first showed significantly greater learning gains. The authors suggest that the explore-first students had gained a broad understanding of the topic which helped them to understand the lecture. The ones who began by watching the video focused more narrowly on memorizing, recalling and applying the formulas they had been shown.

Explore first in practice

Since 2008, learning through productive failure has been tested for teaching mathematics in Singapore schools. In a study with ninth-grade students of mathematics, one class was given direct instruction through a series of worked examples and problems to solve. The other class worked in groups of three to solve problems on their own, followed by a session where the teacher discussed the students' solutions and used these as a basis for presenting a correct solution, then a session for students to solve further problems. In a final test, the productive failure students performed better than the direct instruction ones, in their understanding of the concepts and in their ability to transfer their knowledge to solve a different but related problem.

Similar findings have also been found in independent replication studies in the USA, Canada, Germany and Australia. These studies have shown that this technique can effectively be used with learners of various abilities and with different levels of prior knowledge.

Conclusions

This pedagogy requires students to manage an open-ended process of challenge and exploration, so they may feel less confident in the short term. The approach helps them to become more creative and resilient over time.

The teacher has a strong presence in learning through productive failure; first setting the problem, then correcting and building on the students' answers. This is a demanding process. It requires the teacher to understand the problem in depth, to be able to discuss and correct the students' faulty knowledge. To implement productive failure, school structures and classrooms may have to be altered to give students more time and space for group activities.

Despite being a relatively new pedagogy, productive failure is gaining traction. It has been implemented in over 26 Singapore schools. The Ministry of Education in Singapore has incorporated this approach into the Mathematics A-level curriculum for junior college students. As an innovative pedagogy, productive failure flips the traditional notion of direct instruction followed by problem-solving and is backed by rigorous empirical testing of its effectiveness.

Resources

Paper on impasse-driven learning and repair theory:
VanLehn, K. (1987). Towards a theory of impasse-driven learning. *Technical Report PCG-1.* Departments of Psychology and Computer Science, Carnegie-Mellon University. bit.ly/2dlGUCZ

Kapur's original paper on productive failure:
Kapur, M. (2008). Productive failure. *Cognition and Instruction*, 26(3), 379–424. https://bit.ly/1RwcTvM

Website describing the pedagogy of productive failure:
www.manukapur.com/research/productive-failure/

Study comparing 'explore first' with 'instruct first':
Schneider, B., & Blikstein, P. (2016). Flipping the flipped classroom: A study of the effectiveness of video lectures versus constructivist exploration using tangible user interfaces. *IEEE Transactions on Learning Technologies*, 9(1), 5–17.
https://bit.ly/2J9GBci

Paper comparing teaching by productive failure and teaching by direct instruction:
Kapur, M. (2012). Productive failure in learning the concept of variance. *Instructional Science*, 40(4), 651–672.
https://bit.ly/2wTyIVA

This chapter draws on material from *Innovating Pedagogy 2016*, published under a Creative Commons Attribution Licence:
Sharples, M., de Roock, R., Ferguson, R., Gaved, M., Herodotou, C., Koh, E., Kukulska-Hulme, A., Looi, C.-K., McAndrew, P., Rienties, B., Weller, M., & Wong, L. H. (2016). *Innovating Pedagogy 2016: Open University Innovation Report 5*. Milton Keynes: The Open University.

Teachback 16

Learn by explaining
what has just been taught

Overview

As well as learning from teachers, we can learn by explaining to other people what we think we know. This is the basis of teachback. One person (who may be a teacher, an expert or another student) explains their knowledge of a topic to a learner. Then that learner attempts to explain, or teach back, what they have understood. This offers two benefits. It helps learners to understand a topic or problem by reframing it in their own terms. They also need to explain they have learned in a way that is understandable. If the listener cannot make sense of the learner's explanation, then they discuss the topic until they understand each other. Teachback has been used in healthcare. Doctors and nurses can check that they have explained a treatment clearly by asking their patients to explain or demonstrate what they have been told. The method could be adopted more widely, for any topic where it is important to reach a shared understanding. However, if neither person is knowledgeable, the outcome could be shared misunderstanding.

Explaining what you've learned

Teachback is a way to understand a topic, and to show that you have understood it, by means of a structured conversation (see Figure 16.1). One person (usually an expert or teacher) explains something they know about a topic to another person (usually someone new to the topic). Then the novice tries to teach their new understanding back to the expert. If the novice gives a good

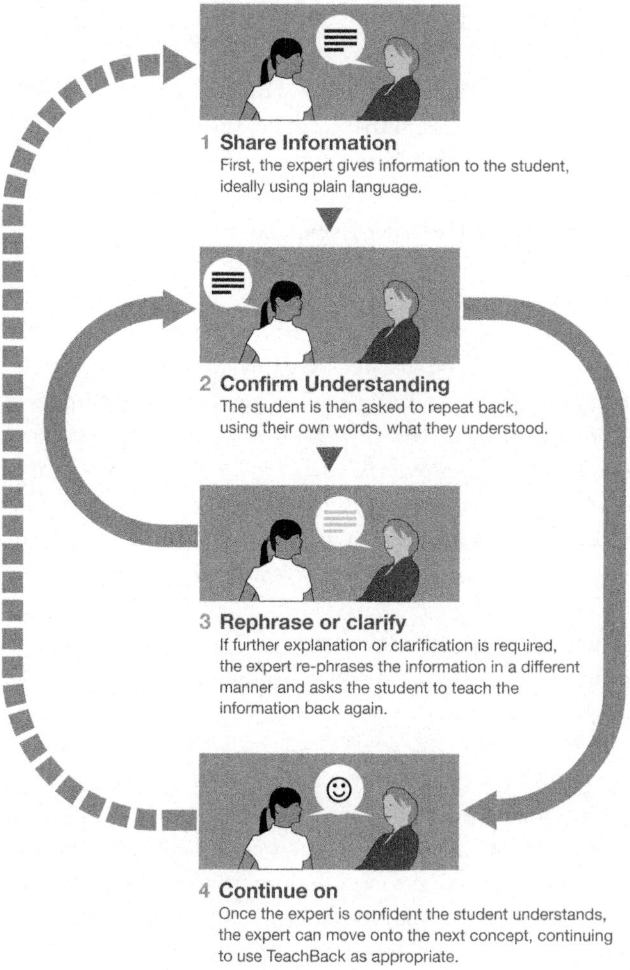

1 Share Information
First, the expert gives information to the student,
ideally using plain language.

▼

2 Confirm Understanding
The student is then asked to repeat back,
using their own words, what they understood.

▼

3 Rephrase or clarify
If further explanation or clarification is required,
the expert re-phrases the information in a different
manner and asks the student to teach the
information back again.

4 Continue on
Once the expert is confident the student understands,
the expert can move onto the next concept, continuing
to use TeachBack as appropriate.

Figure 16.1 The teachback process (adapted from culturallyconnected.ca/skills/
supporting-health-literacy/)

response, the expert goes on to explain some more about the topic. If the novice is struggling to teach back, then the expert tries to clarify the explanation and the novice teaches it back until they reach a shared understanding.

Say, for example, an apprentice is trying to understand the basics of how a car engine works. The experienced car mechanic explains the 'four-stroke' engine cycle of sucking in air and fuel, compressing it, igniting it and pushing it out the exhaust. Then the apprentice tries to explain the four stages back to the mechanic, step-by-step, perhaps with diagrams. If the apprentice makes a mistake, then the mechanic explains again and asks the apprentice to teach back, until they both agree on the explanation.

Learning through conversation

The concept of teachback originated in the 1970s with the educational technologist Gordon Pask, as part of his grand theory of 'learning through conversation'. Pask emphasized that this method need not always involve a trained teacher or expert. It could involve two people with similar knowledge of a topic – each person in turn asking the other to expand on the topic, and then attempting to explain back, until they both gain a better shared understanding.

Three aspects of teachback are particularly important:

- The process of learning should be visible and explicit, with the conversations heard by both participants and anyone else who cares to listen.
- Both partners should gain from the conversation. The one with more expertise has the opportunity to explain that knowledge in a structured way and to find out whether it is being understood. The less-expert person learns by receiving direct instruction and also by going through the process of recalling and teaching back the new knowledge, to find gaps in understanding.
- There should be some way of verifying the new understanding, for example through a teacher-marked test to apply the knowledge, to ensure that what has been taught is accurate.

Teachback can be used for any type of teaching and learning, including sports coaching, science teaching and language learning. It can also be used for people with similar knowledge to explore a complex topic from multiple perspectives.

It does require at least one of the participants to provide accurate knowledge of the topic. If all involved are equally ignorant or misinformed, then either the conversation can't get started or it supports everyone's false knowledge. Even if one person is knowledgeable, it raises the issue of how the others know which knowledge to trust. That usually comes from the knowledgeable person having acknowledged status, as a trained teacher or expert. Alternatively, awareness arises through the conversation as everyone sees how the emerging understanding fits with their prior experience or verifiable facts. That can make learning through conversation an exciting and creative process of coming to know.

Teachback in the classroom

The teachback method could be used for school and university teaching but has not yet been widely adopted. A small study of school science students showed that after teaching back their current knowledge (but not receiving any new teaching) the students produced richer diagrams to explain how objects move under gravity than the ones they had drawn before the teachback.

In a school classroom, a teachback session might involve students working in pairs. They start by explaining to each other what they know about a topic. Next, they receive instruction from a teacher or a video presentation. One student in each pair teaches back to the other what they have learned. The other student questions the explanation, using queries like "What do you mean by that?". If either is not sure, or they disagree, then they ask the teacher. They may also write a brief explanation, or draw a diagram, to explain their new understanding.

Reciprocal teaching is a similar method to teachback. Students work in groups to read a text, then take it in turns to act as teacher. First, they combine their knowledge to understand what the author means, or to predict what will come next in the text. Then, they question their knowledge by asking about puzzling information or unclear sections of the text. Next, one of them is chosen to clarify the text and attempt to answer the questions. Finally, another student will summarize the text by pointing out its most important parts. This is a more complex procedure than teachback and requires a teacher to understand the purpose of each activity and how to assign students to the different roles.

Teachback online

Teachable agents are computer characters that students attempt to teach. In one example, a student starts by creating a picture of the agent on the screen. Then the student goes into the agent's 'brain', shown on the screen as a set of cards representing key concepts of the topic. The student connects these items with arrows to form a concept map. Artificial intelligence software creates a representation of the agent's knowledge, based on what the student has taught it. The agent can answer questions asked by the student, with the concepts lighting up when they are activated. Students then enter their agents in an online competition to discover which one gives the most accurate answers to questions about the topic.

Another variation on teachback comes from Paul Rudman's work on computer-assisted teachback by phone. In this study, one person learns a new topic (herbal remedies) from a book and becomes the teacher. Another person tries to learn about the same topic through a phone conversation with the teacher. The novel part is that the phone conversation is continually monitored by software that recognizes keywords in the spoken conversation. As soon as the software recognizes a word related to herbal remedies (such as the name of a herb, or its medicinal properties), it displays helpful information on the learner's screen but not on the teacher's screen. In this way, the conversation becomes more balanced. The teacher has some basic book knowledge of herbal remedies, and the learner is provided with instant information to help with asking relevant questions or clarifying the teacher's information.

Teachback in practice

Some medical professionals have adopted a form of teachback to make sure that patients with ailments, such as diabetes or heart failure, have understood instructions about how to manage their medication. In a study of people with diabetes, 43 patients with low levels of literacy took part in three weekly 20-minute sessions with a nurse. The nurse used teachback methods to confirm their understanding by asking questions like "When you get home, your partner will ask you what the nurse said. What will you tell them?". When tested six weeks after the final session, those patients who learned through teachback had significantly better of knowledge of diabetes, and of keeping to their diet and medicines, than those in the control group who had spent similar times with the nurse in normal consultations.

Other studies of teachback for patients also found positive results. More research is needed to check whether the results in healthcare are better than other methods, such as giving the patient a well-designed leaflet with pictures and talking about it step-by-step.

Conclusions

Teachback is a simple yet powerful idea that we can learn by explaining what we know to another person, who then explains what they know. The conversation continues until both reach new understanding. The person doing the initial teaching should have a good knowledge of at least part of the topic to avoid spreading misunderstanding. Teachback is used routinely in healthcare to make sure patients understand how to manage their medicines but has not yet been widely taken up in classrooms.

Resources

Introduction to teachback in healthcare from the Scottish Health Council, with a video of the technique being used for a patient interview:
bit.ly/2aY7bFu
Toolkit to help health professionals learn to use teachback:
www.teachbacktraining.org

Original formulation of teachback from Gordon Pask. The book is a fascinating exploration of how to formalize the learning process but is a challenging read:

Pask, G. (1976). *Conversation Theory, Applications in Education and Epistemology.* Amsterdam, The Netherlands: Elsevier.

A photocopy of the book is available online at: bit.ly/2aY5Y1c

Review of 12 published articles on teachback for patients. The methods showed positive effects on a variety of outcome measures, though not always statistically significant:

Dinh, T. T. H., Bonner, A., Clark, R., Ramsbotham, J., & Hines, S. (2016). The effectiveness of the teach-back method on adherence and self-management in health education for people with chronic disease: A systematic review. *JBI Database of Systematic Reviews and Implementation Reports*, 14(1), 210–247.

The use of teachback for science learning:

Gutierrez, R. (2003). Conversation theory and self-learning. In D. Psillos, P. Kariotoglou, V. Tselfes, E. Hatzikraniotis, G. Fassoulopoulos, & M. Kallery (Eds.), *Science Education Research in the Knowledge-Based Society*, pp. 43–49. Heidelberg: Springer Netherlands.

An extract with the section on teachback is available at: bit.ly/2bjO6QA

Study of the use of teachback with diabetes patients:

Negarandeh, R., Mahmoodi, H., Noktehdan, H., Heshmat, R., & Shakibazadeh, E. (2013). Teach back and pictorial image educational strategies on knowledge about diabetes and medication/dietary adherence among low health literate patients with type 2 diabetes. *Primary Care Diabetes*, 7(2), 111–118.

bit.ly/2aWak5y

The method of reciprocal teaching:

Palincsar, A. S., & Brown, A. (1984). Reciprocal teaching of comprehension-fostering and comprehension monitoring activities. *Cognition and Instruction*, 1(2), pp. 117–175.

bit.ly/1mBKkT8

Teachback by phone:

Rudman, P. (2002). Investigating domain information as dynamic support for the learner during spoken conversations. *Unpublished PhD thesis*, University of Birmingham.

Websites on Teachable Agents, from Stanford University and Vanderbilt University:

aaalab.stanford.edu/research/social-foundations-of-learning/teachable-agents/

www.teachableagents.org/

This chapter draws on material from *Innovating Pedagogy 2016*, published under a Creative Commons Attribution Licence:

Sharples, M., de Roock, R., Ferguson, R., Gaved, M., Herodotou, C., Koh, E., Kukulska-Hulme, A., Looi, C.-K., McAndrew, P., Rienties, B., Weller, M., & Wong, L. H. (2016). *Innovating Pedagogy 2016: Open University Innovation Report 5*. Milton Keynes: The Open University.

Learning through argumentation

17

Develop skills of productive argumentation

Overview

Students can deepen their understanding of contested topics in science, history or arts by arguing in ways similar to professional scientists and academics. Argumentation helps students attend to contrasting ideas and discover the value of evidence. It makes reasoning public, for all to learn. It allows students to refine ideas with others, so they learn how scientists work together to establish or refute claims. Teachers can spark meaningful discussion in classrooms by encouraging students to ask open-ended questions, re-state remarks in more precise language, back up their statements with evidence and use models to construct explanations. When students argue in productive ways, they learn how to take turns, listen actively and respond constructively to others. Professional development can help teachers to learn these strategies and overcome challenges, such as how to share their intellectual expertise with students appropriately.

Making claims and providing evidence

The pedagogy of argumentation prepares students for a world where the consequences of science, technology and public policy – such as climate change, genetic engineering, artificial intelligence and sustainable energy – affect every person and are publicly debated.

Students can only understand these issues in depth by engaging in the kinds of inquiry and communication processes that scientists use. These involve reasoning and arguing from available evidence to improve and refute ideas and explanations while communicating understanding through the use of precise language. The methods of productive argumentation are not confined to the traditional sciences but can be applied to mathematics, history, language, arts and the human sciences.

The ancient Greek philosopher Aristotle set out the basic process of a productive argument that still holds today and can be the basis for teaching:

1. Introduce your issue.
2. Adopt a position (are you for or against the issue?).
3. Present your case by explaining the issue.
4. Provide evidence to support your case.
5. Listen to the opposing case.
6. Address the opposing case and try to refute it point by point.
7. Present your conclusion.

This is for arguing through discussion. If the argument comes in a written essay, then the writer will need to do all the work in understanding, presenting and then refuting the opposition case. The form of the argument relies on three elements:

Claims: *What* you are arguing. Other claims can help to support and build the main claim.
Evidence: To support your claims.
Warrant: *How* the evidence supports your claims.

Suppose a class is asked to discuss the issue of whether eating sugar is bad for you. A claim would be 'Sugar harms your health'. Evidence to support that claim includes: 'Sugar rots your teeth' and 'Eating sugar causes people to become overweight'. Each piece of evidence should be backed up by a warrant to say *how* it supports the claim, for example, 'Sugar rots your teeth by feeding bacteria in the mouth that produce acid'. An opposing claim might be 'Sugar gives you energy', which also needs to be backed up by evidence and warrant, and then either acknowledged or refuted.

Arguments without winners and losers

Classical arguments are about trying to outwit your opponent through strong claims and forceful presentations. Another type of argument, proposed by the psychologist Carl Rogers, aims to find a middle ground between differing views. It could work equally well when discussing one-to-one, or as a group debate, or in writing. The steps of a Rogerian argument are:

1. Introduce the issue.
2. Acknowledge the other side's case before you present your side of the argument.
3. Present your case in a form that doesn't dismiss the other side.
4. Find ways to bring the differing sides together by making a careful proposal for a middle ground. Be willing to change your own views.
5. In concluding, make clear how everyone can benefit when they meet in the middle.

This kind of argument can be effective when there is no clear right or wrong, there are good facts to support both sides, and a compromise is a suitable outcome. It doesn't work well for claims like 'Sugar rots your teeth', where the overwhelming evidence is on one side. Example topics for a Rogerian argument could be: 'Should mobile phones be banned in school classrooms?' and 'Should children have more freedom to play outdoors?'.

How teachers can encourage productive argumentation

To benefit from argumentation, students must listen and talk carefully, justify claims and discuss ideas using reason and evidence. This kind of classroom discussion does not come easily to most students and needs to be thoughtfully supported. The teacher takes a role of facilitator to:

- support discussion and listening;
- show students examples of productive arguments;
- propose an issue to discuss, or allow students to propose one;
- encourage students to share ideas and take differing positions, for, against or neutral;
- help students to find reliable evidence;
- explain what a warrant is, and how that evidence can support a claim;
- help students to construct good arguments through discussion or in writing;
- encourage students to consider opposing views and counter-arguments;
- reflect on the argument process and how it could be improved.

A good way to spark serious discussion of scientific ideas is to pose a thought-provoking question that has no simple answer and that requires discussion of theory and evidence. Here are some examples, ranging across topics and levels:

Why aren't birds electrocuted when they land on electric cables? Why don't we feel the weight of a plane when it flies over us? Can we measure intelligence? Is time travel possible? How can we know whether Jesus was a real person?

Technologies to support productive argumentation

Teachers may ask students to investigate a topic in groups, then share and compare their responses. Classroom communication technologies can help this process. Classroom 'clickers' are devices handed out to each student in a class, so they can give responses to a question. For example, a teacher might ask students to suggest different answers to a question and then vote for the best answer, displaying a bar chart of the number of students selecting each response. The teacher then asks the class to discuss the responses, perhaps adding further evidence, then they vote again. Typically, the student responses start to converge towards a more evidence-based understanding of the topic.

Students can also argue productively online. Kialo is an online site for thoughtful discussion and collaborative decision-making. Any user can propose a topic and then others contribute claims for and against backed up by evidence (Figure 17.1). Participants can comment and vote on claims, and Kialo shows the impact of votes as bars above each claim. It also provides a chart of the argument structure.

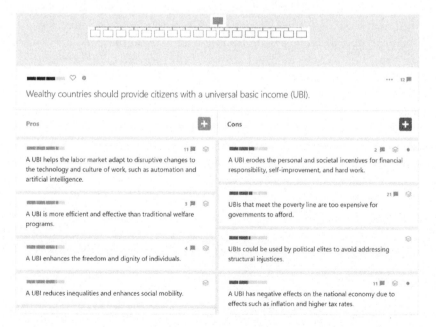

Figure 17.1 Part of a community-created argument in Kialo

Productive argumentation in practice

The Web-based Inquiry Science Environment (WISE) platform offers a variety of science projects on middle and secondary school topics in biology, chemistry, earth science and physics. These projects start with a main question then lead students through a process of online investigation. The WISE Idea Manager helps students to collect evidence and its Explanation Builder allows them to organize the evidence into a structured argument.

Carleton college in Minnesota, USA, runs Argument and Inquiry seminars to prepare students for a liberal arts education. It has provided a set of online resources for classroom discussion where students: set discussion criteria and rules; post discussion material online; identify themselves as preferred teachers or listeners; develop conditions for everyone to contribute.

Conclusions

Managing a session of productive argumentation can be demanding. Most students and teachers are used to questions with known answers, so students can show individual mastery of a science idea or topic. By contrast, argumentation builds knowledge through a process of proposing, critiquing, defending and reconciling ideas by cycles of turn-taking. It can be a laborious process. Students need thoughtful support to learn the specialized forms of argumentation that build deeper understanding. Teachers may require several years to become expert in leading classroom arguments. It can also be hard to develop rich questions or topics for productive argumentation, aligned to the curriculum.

Fortunately, freely available online resources from organizations, such as the Nuffield Foundation, provide examples that have worked well for teachers in the past. Well-designed learning activities that incorporate rich topics for discussion in person or online can be combined with technologies that support communication and show how arguments are built.

Resources

Set of lesson plans from Northwest Association for Biomedical Research on the social nature of scientific research, including scientific argumentation:
https://bit.ly/2Rbb3ph

Teacher resources from Nuffield Foundation for scientific argumentation:
http://www.nuffieldfoundation.org/practical-work-learning/argumentation-quick-start-guide

How to develop a written argument:
https://owl.excelsior.edu/argument-and-critical-thinking/

Introduction to Rogerian arguments from Excelsior Online Writing Lab:
https://owl.excelsior.edu/argument-and-critical-thinking/organizing-your-argument/
organizing-your-argument-rogerian/

20 big questions in science:
Birch, H., Stuart, C., & Looi, M. K. (2013). The 20 big questions in science. *The Guardian*,
    September 1, 2013.
www.theguardian.com/science/2013/sep/01/20-big-questions-in-science

WISE platform for science inquiry and argumentation:
wise.berkeley.edu

Kialo site for community-generated arguments:
www.kialo.com

Carleton College argument and inquiry resources:
https://apps.carleton.edu/curricular/aiseminars/cedi/

Comprehensive survey of research into using 'clicker' technology in large classrooms:
Caldwell, J. E. (2007). Clickers in the large classroom: Current research and best-practice
    tips. *CBE-Life Sciences Education*, 6(1), 9–20.
www.lifescied.org/content/6/1/9.full

Study of classroom conditions that promote, nurture and sustain argumentation practices
among students:
Duschl, R. A., & Osborne, J. (2002). Supporting and promoting argumentation discourse in
    science education. *Studies in Science Education*, 38(1), 39–72.
https://bit.ly/2yRLoKx

To provoke argument among teachers and policy makers, see:
Kirschner, P. A., & van Merriënboer, J. J. G. (2013). Do learners really know best? Urban
    legends in education. *Educational Psychologist*, 48(3), 169–183.
https://bit.ly/1Kz3aPn

This chapter draws on material from *Innovating Pedagogy 2016*, published under a Creative
Commons Attribution Licence:
Sharples, M., de Roock , R., Ferguson, R., Gaved, M., Herodotou, C., Koh, E., Kukulska-
    Hulme, A., Looi, C.-K., McAndrew, P., Rienties, B., Weller, M., & Wong, L. H. (2016).
    Innovating Pedagogy 2016: Open University Innovation Report 5. Milton Keynes: The Open
    University.

Computational thinking **18**
Solve problems using techniques from computing

Overview

Computational thinking takes methods of thinking used in programming computers and applies them to solving everyday problems. The aim is to structure problems so they can be solved. It involves breaking large problems down into smaller ones (decomposition), recognizing how these relate to problems that have been solved in the past (pattern recognition), setting aside unimportant details (abstraction), identifying and developing the steps that will be necessary to reach a solution (algorithms) and refining these steps (debugging). These computational thinking skills can be valuable in many aspects of life. They can help in writing a recipe to share a favourite dish with friends or planning a holiday or expedition. The same methods can guide a scientific team to cope with an outbreak of disease. Computational thinking is not about teaching children to be computer coders but helping them master the art of thinking to tackle complex challenges in all aspects of their lives.

Skills for life

As we learn science, we understand how to perform experiments. As we study music, we develop a sense of timing and rhythm. Each area of the curriculum is associated with a set of skills that can be applied throughout life, offering new ways to understand the world.

In the case of computing, as we learn its principles and methods, we also acquire a set of problem-solving skills. Together, these are known as computational thinking. 'Computational' does not mean teaching children to think like unimaginative machines that can only solve a problem when supplied with a set of instructions to follow. Computational thinking is a way for humans to think when they try to solve problems. It can be set out as a set of clear steps, but adapting these steps to the problem and then performing them is a creative human activity.

Although this way of thinking was developed in the context of computer programming and computer science, it can be applied more widely. It can help people to deal confidently with complexity and with open-ended problems. It is essential when developing computer applications, but it is also valuable in any discipline.

Countries are adding computational thinking to the list of key school subjects. In England, the National Curriculum states that children should be offered high-quality computing education that will equip them with skills in computational thinking and creativity to understand and change the world. Outside education, large companies, such as Google and Microsoft Research, regard computational thinking as an essential set of problem-solving skills and techniques for software engineers.

Elements of computational thinking

Computational thinking uses the same basic elements to deal with a variety of problems.

Decomposition – Break a large problem down into smaller ones.
Pattern recognition – Recognize how these smaller problems relate to ones that have been solved in the past.
Abstraction – Identify and set aside unimportant details.
Algorithm design – Plan the steps to reach a solution.
Debugging – Refine those steps.

A final step that is usually implied without being included in the main list is:

Present a solution in a usable form.

Let's say a team of school students uses computational thinking to explain an eclipse of the moon. They **decompose** the problem into finding out: how the moon moves around the earth; how the earth moves around the sun; what happens when the moon is in the earth's shadow; how to explain this to others. A lunar eclipse has a similar **pattern** to a solar eclipse (which the students have already studied). An **abstraction** of this is when one heavenly body (such as a moon or planet) moves into the shadow of another heavenly body. They set up an **algorithm** in the form of a model of the sun, moon and earth (with a lamp to represent the sun and balls for the earth and moon) to show the steps of the moon moving into the earth's shadow. The team needs to **debug** this to choose a lamp and size of balls to best illustrate the lunar eclipse. Finally, the team **presents a solution** through a demonstration to the class and by making a short video.

How computational thinking differs from problem-based learning

Computational thinking involves understanding a problem in enough detail to break it down into parts then finding steps to solve it. It differs from problem-based learning in that it arises from a need to solve practical problems rather than work through pre-prepared exercises. It breaks an initial problem down into smaller elements, then relates these to ones that have been solved in the past. It also assumes that solutions will be tested and refined until an acceptable one is reached. Thus, it can be more useful for practical problems than problem-based learning, particularly ones that have a step-by-step solution. But computational thinking may not be suited to solve human and social problems that can't easily be decomposed into sub-problems.

Computational thinking skills

Solving problems through computational thinking develops a set of skills that include:

Experiment and iterate – Develop something, try it out and then develop some more.
Test and debug – Find, test and fix to reach an acceptable solution.
Reuse and remix – Build on existing projects or ideas.
Abstract and modularize – Explore connections between the whole and the parts.
Express – Recognize that working in this way is a creative activity.
Connect – Exploit the power of creating with and for others.
Question – Feel empowered to ask questions about the world.

These emphasize that computational thinking is more than a set of steps to be worked through, but also a way of exploring and solving difficult problems.

Computational thinking in practice

As mentioned previously, the National Curriculum in England has been altered to include computational thinking, ensuring that all pupils can analyze problems in computational terms, as well as understand and apply the fundamental principles and concepts of computer science, including abstraction, logic, algorithms and data representation. At Key Stage 1 (age 5–7), pupils learn about algorithms and how to follow precise instructions. They also create and debug simple computer programs. At Key Stage 2 (age 7–11), they solve problems by decomposing them into parts, use logical reasoning to explain how algorithms work, and design, write and debug programs to accomplish goals that include controlling or simulating physical systems. At Key Stage 3 (11–14), they design computational abstractions to model real-world problems. At Key Stage 4 (14–16), they develop creativity and analytic knowledge to solve problems and design digital media.

Green Dot Public Schools in the United States put a strong emphasis on integrating computational thinking into the curriculum across all disciplines. This involves students solving hard problems using ideas from computer science. For example, Excel Public Charter School in the state of Washington sets open-ended problems, such as 'How does the National Basketball Association (NBA) analyze basketball play?', which the students address by finding different ways to collect, decompose, visualize and analyze data. The Green Dot organization has published its computational thinking lessons for others to use for free.

Google has produced a course on Computational Thinking for Educators. It consists of five units and a project for teachers in humanities, mathematics, science and computer science. Each unit includes practical examples, such as planning a road trip across Europe, that can be modified for the classroom.

Conclusions

Computational thinking involves much more than learning to code. It enables learners to engage in abstraction, by defining patterns and generalizing from specific instances. It introduces ways of processing information and representing it in different ways. It requires learners to work systematically to identify and remove errors. Perhaps most importantly, it provides them with a way to break down problems and work to solve them across every area of life. But computational thinking isn't a universal method of problem solving. Many human problems, such as how to live a happier life or how to make friends, may be better addressed by thinking holistically and exploring possibilities rather than breaking the problem down into bits.

Resources

Lessons and projects in computational thinking from Green Dot Schools:
http://ct.excelwa.org/

Google's Computational Thinking for Educators:
https://computationalthinkingcourse.withgoogle.com/unit

National Curriculum in England for computing education, including computational thinking:
https://bit.ly/1f7PIFU

The importance of computational thinking and how it can be incorporated into the curriculum for children aged 5–11:
Berry, M. (2013). *Computing in the National Curriculum: A Guide for Primary Teachers*. Bedford, UK: Computing at School.
https://bit.ly/1J417r

Computational Thinking resources from The International Society for Technology in Education (ISTE) and the Computer Science Teachers Association (CSTA):
https://bit.ly/2FVuK28

Google for Educators offers a curated collection of resources related to computational thinking:
http://bit.ly/2NW751q

What is Computational Thinking? A framework developed by Harvard based on studies in the context of the Scratch programming environment:
scratched.gse.harvard.edu/ct/defining.html

Scratch programming environment for children:
scratch.mit.edu

Framework that includes lesson planning, classroom techniques and assessment methods:
Curzon, P., Dorling, M., Ng, T., Selby, C., & Woollard, J. (2014). *Developing Computational Thinking in the Classroom: A Framework*. Computing at School.
http://bit.ly/2PU35QM

Detailed review of publications on computational thinking:
Grover, S., & Pea, R. (2013). Computational thinking in K–12: A review of the state of the field. *Educational Researcher*, 42(1), 38–43.
http://bit.ly/2NSNXBr

This chapter draws on material from *Innovating Pedagogy 2015*, published under a Creative Commons Attribution Licence:
Sharples, M., Adams, A., Alozie, N., Ferguson, R., FitzGerald, E., Gaved, M., McAndrew, P., Means, B., Remold, J., Rienties, B., Roschelle, J., Vogt, K., Whitelock, D., & Yarnall, L. (2015). *Innovating Pedagogy 2015: Open University Innovation Report 4*. Milton Keynes: The Open University.

Learning from animations

19

Watch and interact with short animations

Overview

When learning from animations, students watch short animated movies showing dynamic processes, such as how the heart beats or how to solve a maths problem. Compared to looking at static images in a textbook, animations can be better at revealing movement and speed. They can also show how an expert tackles a difficult problem through a worked example. To be successful, animations should highlight the relevant parts and zoom into the most important movement. They work best when longer sequences are split into short chunks, with pauses for reflection. The learner should decide when to start the next section and have control over stopping, starting and moving back in the animation. Learners should be encouraged to explain to themselves what they are learning, perhaps by predicting the next step, and watch the animation three or four times to fully understand what the movement and sequence is trying to explain.

Principles of learning from animations

A picture is worth a thousand words, and an animation is worth a thousand pictures – or is it? Twenty years of research into learning from animations have shown when they are helpful and how to design successful educational animations.

The idea behind learning from animations is that some topics are hard to teach through text or static pictures. These include processes showing movement (how molecules diffuse through a liquid), dynamics (how the heart pumps blood), procedures (how to tie a bandage) or steps in solving a problem (how to solve a differential equation). Presenting these as animations can reveal processes that are too slow or small to see, or that are abstractions from the real world, such as an animated weather map showing changes in air pressure.

There are three basic principles of how people learn from animations:

- We actively process information, by selecting, organizing and integrating those parts of an animation that are relevant to what is being taught.
- We respond to different modalities (visual, spoken) in different ways.
- Our ability to process information is limited by short-term (working) memory.

What this means is that animations need to be carefully designed to help students process the relevant information (and ignore distracting parts), to link vision and sound and to make sure that students aren't overloaded and have time to reflect on what they have learned. Watching an animation as if it were a video presentation isn't enough. Learners need to try and solve the problem or perform the task to fully understand it.

How to design a good educational animation

Research has led to a set of animation design principles for successful learning. Some of the early studies showed that animations were no better than textbook pictures, but recent work has focused on the conditions that make animations successful as tools for learning.

The prime aim is for a student to form an accurate mental model of a dynamic process. Thus, to design a good animation involves the following steps:

1. Analyze the dynamics of what is being taught – what's important to understand and what can be ignored.
2. Choose appropriate graphic elements to show the processes and relationships of properties. Some studies have shown that photo-realistic animations can be more effective than cartoon ones.
3. Decide how to present the main events or processes.
4. Devise the sequence of events and how that will be presented – from which angle, in what colours, at what speed.
5. Determine when to add pauses if it's a long animation.
6. Choose what will be included, highlighted and zoomed, so the learner can see the crucial information and how the processes work.
7. Add relevant sounds, but not distracting music.

8. Devise a spoken narration to explain what's happening.
9. Produce the animation on a software platform that allows the student to stop, start and rewind the animation.
10. Test the animation with typical students to check that they gain a deep understanding of the concepts and processes.

A teacher who adopts animations in the classroom needs first to choose good examples to show, based on the design principles just listed. Then, the teacher might show the animation to the class and describe what it is teaching. Next, each student should have an opportunity to watch and interact with the animated sequence, at least three or four times. If the animation shows a process, then the teacher should encourage each student to describe it in words. If it shows the steps in solving a problem, then the students should be given further problems to solve, referring back to the example solution if needed.

Are animations better than pictures?

Compared to static images, animations show movement and speed directly, without a need for arrows to indicate the direction or rate of flow. However, some movements are subtle and not easy to understand. For example, to fully understand the process of diffusion requires knowing how *lots of particles move* through liquids and gases, why the *speed that particles move* means diffusion is faster in a gas than in a liquid, and how the *concentration of particles* at the start affects the rate of diffusion. Putting all these elements together is a complex mental task. Some animations can be overwhelming when they try to show multiple processes happening at once, or they can miss crucial pieces of information. Worst of all, students can mentally switch off and treat the animation just as a video to be watched but not understood.

So, studies have shown that animations are better than pictures when:

- they are well-designed;
- they teach processes or skills;
- students are in control.

Learning from animations in practice

Khan Academy has produced a huge set of free teaching resources based on animated worked examples. Topics include mathematics, science and engineering, computing, arts and humanities, and economics and finance. A typical presentation uses an animated blackboard showing the example problem being solved, with a spoken commentary. It sounds boring, but the combination of colour in the animations, being able to stop and scroll back, and a lively narration can make topics, such as 'Introduction to the Atom' or 'The Krebs Cycle', engaging and understandable.

Explainers are animations to introduce or explain a topic. They are often used by companies to introduce a new product or services, but the same principles can be applied to education. Explainers generally have a strong narrative to tell a clear story, such as how a star is formed. They are short (typically 90 seconds or less), present the key message in the first 30 seconds, generally use a conversational tone and often have a touch of humour.

Animations are not just for explaining difficult topics. The Literacy Shed has hundreds of short videos and animations to prompt children's creative writing. They are organized into themes, such as 'adventure', 'anti-bullying', 'fantasy' and 'history'. Most are photo-realistic animations. For example, 'Mourning Dove' raises themes of love and loss, while 'The Rocketeer' is set during the Second World War and features a young boy who dreams of flying.

Resources

PCCL is a website with animations for mechanics, electricity, optics, chemistry and matter. Examples include how waves move, electrical short circuits and phases of the moon: http://www.physics-chemistry-interactive-flash-animation.com/

Beauty of Science has some photo-realistic animations to show complex molecules: http://www.beautyofscience.com/molecular-animations/

The Literacy Shed has collected short videos and animations to prompt creative writing: www.literacyshed.com

PowToon is a tool for creating simple animations for education or training: www.powtoon.com

Example of a longer animation to explain a complex topic (cryptocurrencies) to a general audience:
http://bit.ly/2Cwtl1a

Introduction to explainer videos and animations in marketing, with some good examples: http://bit.ly/2PaNPCc

BBC animated video that explains how to create educational explainers: https://vimeo.com/53710994

Khan Academy for learning through instructional animations. www.khanacademy.org

Survey and meta-analysis of the educational benefits of instructional animation and static pictures:
Höffler, T. N., & Leutner, D. (2007). Instructional animation versus static pictures: A meta-analysis. *Learning and Instruction*, 17(6), 722–738.
http://bit.ly/2EDQK2i

People learn best about dynamic systems from a combination of video and static pictures:
Arguel, A., & Jamet, E. (2009). Using video and static pictures to improve learning of procedural contents. *Computers in Human Behavior*, 25(2), 354–359.

Learning to learn   **20**
Learn how to become
an effective learner

Overview

We are always learning. Throughout our lifetime we take on board new ideas
and develop new skills. What we find difficult is learning what others want
to teach us, to achieve specific goals. Learning to learn involves becoming an
effective learner and knowing how to manage one's own learning processes.
Central to this is not only working out how to solve a problem or reach a goal,
but also reflecting on that process as a whole, questioning assumptions and
considering how to become more effective. Effective learners seek and compare sources of knowledge and make use of online networks for advice and
support. Web tools and activities, such as reflective journals and concept mapping, have been designed to support learning to learn, but these are rarely well
integrated into a learner's social world.

Learning in a complex world

Learning is a fundamental part of life that shapes us as human beings and gives
purpose to what we do. The irony is that as human beings we rarely want to
learn what others want to teach us. Young children are indulged as they learn
by exploring the world around them. Gradually, they learn to accept instruction from their parents and teachers. But learning by being told isn't sufficient
preparation for life in a rapidly changing world of new products and contested
knowledge. Young people must also learn how to manage the learning process.
Effective learners know how to:

- choose appropriate strategies for different problems;
- seek new knowledge from a variety of sources;
- take a critical stance to assess and compare new knowledge;
- reflect on what they have learned;
- work well with others;
- adapt their skills to unfamiliar situations.

For a teacher, considering the process of learning to learn can help in seeing learning from the student's perspective – how students learn, what motivates them and how to give students the skills they need to manage their own learning.

Educational content remains important, but with a shift from delivery and assessment towards self-management of learning. Students discover how best to acquire knowledge and skills – in the classroom, workplace and at home – through a combination of study, discussion, investigation and practice. A teacher may provide resources, but the learner takes command of deciding how to organize them into a coherent course of study.

Connected with learning to learn is the ability to determine one's own learning needs and to reflect continuously on the learning process. This involves developing skills of open communication and teamwork, being flexible in approach and creative in new situations and becoming confident in the ability to take appropriate and effective action in changing circumstances.

Mindful learning

This is all based on the assumption that learners want to determine their own learning and know how do this. Therefore, there is an emphasis on learning to learn on enabling young learners to make sense of their world and helping them develop creative strategies for organizing their studies. Learning to learn courses can indicate how to diagnose learning needs, set goals, find valuable resources including other people to learn with, choose learning strategies, reflect on progress, develop creative skills and evaluate personal learning outcomes. If learning to learn aligns with what students actually want to learn, and how they learn most effectively, then it's more likely to be empowering and enjoyable.

Another perspective on learning to learn is how to combine personal priorities with learning opportunities. In working life, the need to get through a seemingly impossible To-Do list can make for inefficiencies and too much switching of attention as we try to decide what needs to be done while more work piles in. There are many self-help books that suggest ways to prioritize the important tasks as well as the urgent but more mundane ones. These organizational techniques are also part of some approaches to learning to learn.

A more holistic approach is to step back and ensure a mindful approach to life, by considering the impact our learning has on ourselves and others, paying attention to personal actions. Mindfulness is about becoming more aware of our thoughts and feelings, connecting with the sights, sounds, smells and tastes of the present moment. By seeing the present moment more clearly, we can make positive changes in the way we run our lives. This can be supported by meditation and understanding how much of what appears to be true is in the mind. Whether something is upsetting to study, too difficult, or not worth the effort is an internal judgement. Mindful learning encourages full attention on what is important, balanced by the investment in time to gain that full attention.

Double-loop learning

An aspect of mindfulness is being able to reflect on ourselves as learners and how we have carried out a recent learning activity, in order to adjust the processes of learning. This 'double-loop' approach contrasts with the normal process of 'single-loop' thinking that involves reacting to events, solving a problem in a familiar way and accepting information at face value (Figure 20.1). Double-loop thinking involves considering the problem at hand in relation to a greater system, so as to achieve personal development. The philosopher and educator Donald Schön made a distinction between reflection-in-action, where we become more mindful of our current activity, and reflection-on-action where we learn how to reflect on the activity as a whole, so we control how to perform it and how to improve it in the future. That is the essence of double-loop learning. Both reflection-in-action and reflection-on-action contribute to learning how to learn.

For a teacher, helping students achieve double-loop learning puts the educational content into a larger framework where each student is encouraged

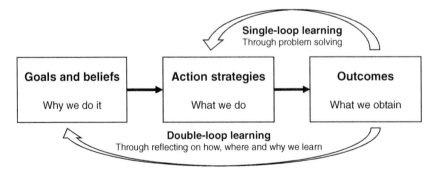

Figure 20.1 Single-loop and double-loop learning (based on Argyris, 1976)

to determine how, where and why they learn. They learn to negotiate a curriculum and learning strategies with themselves, their teacher and their peers. Open learning materials and free online courses fit into this framework by providing resources for study that suit the needs and strategies of each learner. Thus, learning to learn is part of a broader educational movement for empowering learners and helping them to develop competencies to manage their own learning.

Technology for learning to learn

Many software tools have been developed to support learning to learn, including Personal Learning Environments (PLEs), e-portfolios and concept mappers. Personal learning environments provide a set of personal tools for learning. These can include tools to set goals and manage the progress of learning projects, self-assessment surveys, resources including guides to successful learning and ways to access and communicate with other learners. E-portfolios can have a dual role – as records of achievement to show to potential employers and as diaries of learning activities, outcomes and reflections. Concept maps allow learners to create visual maps of the structure of a problem or a set of interlinked ideas. What binds all these tools is that they are designed around the individual learner, to be accessed in and outside formal classes and across institutions.

But there is little evidence that students want or will use technologies specifically designed for learning, particularly if they don't integrate well with other personal, social and professional tools. It may be better for students to adopt widespread web-based tools and services, such as Trello, Pinterest or LinkedIn, to organize learning projects, share ideas and record achievements.

Learning to learn in practice

A paper by Lisa Maria Blaschke lists elements of learning to learn that have been designed and promoted by colleges and universities, including:

Learning contracts that support students to set goals and define their learning paths.

Flexible curriculum where learners create personal learning plans assisted by tutors or mentors. In Finland, upper secondary education is designed around modules, with students having freedom to decide their study schedules, combine academic and vocational study, and complete the syllabus in two, three or four years.

Learner-directed questions where students are guided to ask 'big questions' that help make sense of course content and promote reflection.

Negotiated assessment that involves the student in designing appropriate assessment based on the learning contract and personal goals.

All these may seem utopian, for a world where students are highly motivated and can manage their own learning. Indeed, the main impetus for learning to learn has come from adult distance education, where students are expected to be capable of managing their time and resources. But setting appropriate goals, knowing how to learn effectively, managing learning projects and reflecting on progress are skills that every student needs.

Conclusions

Learning to learn makes sense in a world where many job titles will change within 20 years. But the reflective thinking and techniques that are required for learning to learn are neither easy to acquire nor easy to teach in a classroom. Becoming a self-managed learner is not enough. Part of the problem in learning is too many options and unclear aims. The essential steps include realizing that learning to learn is worth the investment in time and looking for learning frameworks that bring together opportunities for learning around a mindful and reflective approach to life.

Resources

Free course from The Open University on learning to learn:
http://bit.ly/2CAqOlc

SUNY Empire State College policy for student learning contracts:
http://bit.ly/2R8jnWN

Overview of education in Finland:
http://bit.ly/2S8OeUu

Introduction to heutagogy (self-determined learning):
Blaschke, L. M. (2012). Heutagogy and lifelong learning: A review of heutagogical practice and self-determined learning. *The International Review of Research in Open and Distance Learning*, 13(1), 56–71.
http://bit.ly/2OEq1qF

Idea of double-loop learning, based on a model of how feedback loops should help organizations work:

Argyris, C. (1976). Single-loop and double-loop models in research on decision-making. *Administrative Science*, 21(3), 363–375.
bit.ly/2JQBZKN

Overview of concept mapping and its underlying theory:
Novak, J. D., & Cañas, A. J. (2008). The theory underlying concept maps and how to construct and use them. *Technical Report IHMC CmapTools 2006-01 Rev 01-2008*. Florida: Florida Institute for Human and Machine Cognition.
cmap.ihmc.us/docs/theory-of-concept-maps

Pebblepad e-portfolio and personal learning environment:
www.pebblepad.co.uk

Mahara e-portfolio platform:
mahara.org

LinkedIn:
www.linkedin.com

Trello:
trello.com

Pinterest:
www.pinterest.com

This chapter draws on material from *Innovating Pedagogy 2014*, published under a Creative Commons Attribution Licence:
Sharples, M., Adams, A., Ferguson, R., Gaved, M., McAndrew, P., Rienties, B., Weller, M., & Whitelock, D. (2014). *Innovating Pedagogy 2014: Open University Innovation Report 3*. Milton Keynes: The Open University.

Assessment for learning 21
Support the learning process through diagnostic feedback

Overview

Assessment can support the process of learning, not just measure its outcomes. In diagnostic testing with rapid feedback, students and teachers are given the immediate results of a computer-based assessment in a form that helps to address student misconceptions and provide supplementary teaching. The teacher can be shown a dashboard that displays the progress of each student and proposes a range of actions from simple, automated prompts to online student–tutor conversation. Students can be offered 'open learner models' that show their progress in relation to peers and what steps to take in improving performance. There is strong evidence that well-designed diagnostic assessment does improve learning.

Constructive feedback

Assessment for learning (or 'formative assessment') goes beyond measuring the outcomes of learning and taking snapshots of students' performance, towards integrating assessment fully into the learning process. The most immediate benefits come from giving students advice on how to meet their learning goals and improve performance. For this, assessment is embedded into the teaching materials and students are given immediate constructive feedback. It can be done in various ways: by having quizzes within a textbook, by the teacher questioning students, through peer feedback or by computer-based assessment. Each has its benefits and drawbacks.

Embedded quizzes need no computer technology and the students can work through the material at their own pace. But the book needs to be carefully designed, with a question on one page and the answer on the next, and the students need self-discipline not to flick forward and peek at an answer. The teacher can get a rough idea of each student's progress by seeing which page they have reached but gets no immediate report on how they answered each question.

The traditional method of assessment for learning is for the teacher to **ask students questions**. As every teacher knows, this is more difficult than it sounds. Knowing when to stop and ask, what questions to pose, who to select and how to respond to wrong answers are all skills that a teacher learns through practice. The benefit is that the teacher can respond immediately to misconceptions and the whole class learns from the discussion. But only one student is quizzed at a time, so differences in understanding can be missed.

In **peer feedback**, students work in pairs or groups to check to other students' answers, discuss differences in understanding, spot missing details and offer praise. The objective is not for students to mark each other's work but to give constructive feedback. When it works, students learn by looking closely at other students' assignments and working together on how to improve them. However, students need to be taught how to give constructive feedback and how to manage the discussion.

Computer-based assessment ranges from setting multiple-choice questions and giving fixed responses to wrong answers, through to Cognitive Tutors® that guide students through the steps of solving a problem. The main benefits are that students work at their own pace, they must attempt the assignment before seeing the feedback and the teacher can see a dashboard showing the progress and responses for each student. Against that, the range of feedback that a computer can give is limited, the experience can be isolating and setting up the technology can be expensive and time-consuming.

For all these, the approach is that students already attempt to monitor their own performance, so feedback should build on this process of self-regulation. Conditions for successful feedback are:

1. Set up a classroom culture that encourages interaction and feedback.
2. Help students set learning goals and track the progress of each student towards those goals.
3. Use appropriate methods to assess student understanding (e.g. peer assessment for essay assignments, computer-based feedback for steps in solving a problem).
4. Give individual feedback to each student.
5. Give general feedback to the whole class on frequent issues and misunderstandings.

Computer-based feedback

Computer-based feedback works for multiple-choice questions where there are fixed responses and wrong answers can be corrected. More sophisticated systems guide the student through steps in solving a problem, such as solving a quadratic equation. Beyond that, we are in the realms of intelligent tutoring systems – programs that attempt to respond in ways similar to knowledgeable human tutors.

For example, the computer method of 'latent semantic analysis' can offer limited feedback on student essays. It processes a set of texts (such as previous student assignments at different grade levels) to find similarities in meaning between words and phrases. Then, it uses these to simulate human judgements of the coherence and style of a new piece of student writing. The main problem with this approach is that the computer does not understand the essay in depth, so it cannot spot a highly original piece of good work.

Other techniques, adapted from computer games, provide visible indications of a student's performance over time. The software generates an 'open learner model' of performance that is shown to the student as a bar chart or a graph of progress across topics. More complex versions show how the student is progressing through a web of connected topics.

Such methods must be used with caution. They cannot provide the precision or the insight of a human response and there is a danger that giving continual feedback will channel a student into continually adjusting performance to match the response, rather than planning and then engaging in a fluent piece of work. Rather than the student just viewing the feedback or learner model, a more useful approach may be to have the student and the system (and in some cases a human tutor) cooperate to produce an agreed representation of the student's skill, knowledge and performance. In this way, the student takes a more reflective approach to self-regulation and managing feedback.

A simple but effective example of this negotiated approach is 'confidence-based marking' (also called 'certainty-based marking'). Let's say a student in a calculus class is asked 'What is the derivative of x^3?' with a set of answers to choose from, such as: $2x^2$, $3x^2$, $4x^2$, $2x^3$, $3x^3$ or $4x^3$. The student not only has to choose an answer, but also indicate a level of confidence by selecting 'low', 'medium' or 'high'. The feedback to the student can then be based on a combination of confidence and correctness, such as:

> You had low confidence, but you got the answer right! Let's see if you can now find the derivative of x^4.

Or

> You had high confidence and you got the answer right. Here's a harder problem to solve: What is the derivative of $3x^2$?

Confidence-based responses help the student to think more carefully about an answer, but designing good feedback can be difficult.

Involving humans in computer-based assessment for learning

Human tutors or teaching assistants can be brought into the process of computer-based assessment for learning in two ways. The first is to provide tutors with 'dashboards' showing a continuous indication of how each student is performing. One type of dashboard is a grid with each row indicating a student and each column showing a question that has been set. The cells show green or red for correct or incorrect answers, and amber if confidence is also assessed. From this display, the tutor can see at a glance how each student is performing, and so can focus effort in assisting students that show misunderstandings or lack confidence in their responses. A version of the dashboard, perhaps with the rows anonymized, can also be shown to the students as part of the open learner model, so they can see how they are performing in relation to their peers and when to seek help.

The second way of involving tutors is to help them improve the quality of their responses to open questions. For example, tutors typically give extended comments on the written work of poor-performing students, but terse responses to high-quality work. Yet high-achieving students also value encouragement and advice. If they cannot see other students' marks, they may not know how well they have performed.

These methods represent a shift from assessing the outcomes of learning towards guiding the learning process. They also break with the previous use of computers for adaptive tutoring, where the computer tries to infer students' knowledge from their performance and then adapts the teaching with additional hints or supplementary teaching. For some topics, for example in maths or language learning, adaptive tutoring can be successful, but to do it well requires intensive analysis and modelling of the topic and possible student misunderstandings. Assessment for learning is more flexible, in that it can be easily applied to new topic areas and it involves students, computer systems and tutors in a cooperation to enhance understanding and performance.

Assessment for learning in practice

For the Re-engineering Assessment Practices in Higher Education (REAP) project, three universities in Scotland designed assessment and feedback for learning across 19 first-year classes. In a psychology class, students wrote collaborative essays and gave feedback to their partners. These students later performed better in exam essays than students from previous years. Students on a pharmacy course were presented with examples of medical prescriptions. They were asked to click on areas of the form with incorrect or missing information and they received immediate feedback. The project produced evidence of effective assessment and principles for transforming education in universities.

A school study in Israel compared the benefits of receiving feedback and grades on motivation and performance. Students who were given grades did not improve their performance between two lessons. Students who only received comments improved, on average, by 30%. Surprisingly, students who were given both grades and comments did not improve. It seems that the students with grades and comments focused on their marks and largely ignored the comments.

Conclusions

One of the pioneers of formative assessment, Dylan Wiliam, later said that he regretted using the word 'assessment' because it made people think about exams and tests. A better label would be 'responsive teaching'. A challenge for the future is to find effective ways to combine the different methods without overwhelming student or teacher. Assessment for learning is a process of mutual adaptation: students reflect on, share and regulate their learning; teachers monitor and assist the learning progress; and computer systems manage the process, providing timely feedback and overviews.

Resources

Presentation by David Wees on 56 methods of formative assessment:
http://bit.ly/2EzgtZq

Report from the OECD/CERI on formative assessment:
http://bit.ly/2R6cOUu

Assessment for learning in vocational education, with a case study:
Jones, C. A. (2005). *Assessment for Learning*. London: Learning and Skills Development Agency.
http://bit.ly/2yrQYDQ

JISC report on technology-enhanced assessment and feedback for higher education:
JISC (2010). *Effective Assessment in a Digital Age: A Guide to Technology-Enhanced Assessment and Feedback*. Higher Education Funding Council for England.
http://bit.ly/2S76H3B

Overview of certainty-based marking:
http://www.ucl.ac.uk/lapt/lpcfhelp.htm

Re-engineering Assessment Practices in Higher Education (REAP) project:
https://www.reap.ac.uk/reap/index.html

Thought-provoking article on why formative assessment hasn't worked (yet) in schools:
Booth, N. (2017). What is formative assessment, why hasn't it worked in schools, and how can we make it better in the classroom? *Impact: Journal of the Chartered College of Teaching*, September 2017.
http://bit.ly/2CYC0t5

OpenMentor approach to support tutors in providing more effective feedback to students:
http://bit.ly/2D1pDwm

Literature review of technology-enabled assessment:
Oldfield, A., Broadfoot, P., Sutherland, R., & Timmis, S. (2012). *Assessment in a Digital Age: A Research Review*. Bristol: University of Bristol.
http://bit.ly/2EDosou

Classic paper by the pioneers of assessment for learning, and a follow-up project:
Black, P., & Wiliam, D. (1998). Assessment and classroom learning. *Assessment in Education: Principles, Policy & Practice*, 5(1), 7–74.
http://bit.ly/2OGBiH0

Black, P., Harrison, C., Lee, C., Marshall, B., & Wiliam, D. (2004). Working inside the black box: Assessment for learning in the classroom. *Phi Delta Kappan*, 86(1), 8–21.
http://bit.ly/2CAudAu

Study on the benefits of receiving feedback and grades:
Butler, R. (1988). Enhancing and undermining intrinsic motivation: The effects of task-involving and ego-evolving evaluation on interest and performance. *British Journal of Educational Psychology*, 58(1), 1–14.
http://bit.ly/2yT4S1p

This chapter draws on material from *Innovating Pedagogy 2012*, published under a Creative Commons Attribution Licence:
Sharples, M., McAndrew, P., Weller, M., Ferguson, R., FitzGerald, E., Hirst, T., Mor, Y., Gaved, M., & Whitelock, D. (2012). *Innovating Pedagogy 2012: Open University Innovation Report 1*. Milton Keynes: The Open University.

Formative analytics   **22**
*Develop analytics that helps
learners to reflect and improve*

Overview

Learning analytics aims to measure and predict the learning processes of students by tracking their behaviour and inferring their thinking processes. For example, it tracks time spent learning online or performance on an assessment. Summative learning analytics provides teachers or administrators with a digest of performance and insight into who needs support. By contrast, formative analytics supports learners to reflect on what they have learned, what can be improved, which goals can be achieved and how they should move forward. By providing analytics *for* learning rather than analytics learning, formative analytics has the potential to empower each learner through timely, personalized and automated feedback, including visualizations of potential learning paths.

Analytics to support teachers

Learning analytics presents and analyzes the data produced during learning and teaching. This is intended to help teachers or administrators understand the process of learning. As institutions and teachers collect more data about each learner's profile and behaviour, they are starting to use learning analytics to predict which students need additional support.

Learning analytics tools have been embedded in commercial learning management systems, such as Blackboard and Desire2Learn. These collect behavioural data that includes time spent in an online learning unit and performance on an assessment. From these data, these tools measure and predict the performance of learners. By identifying who is struggling, learning analytics applications provide teachers with insight into which students may need additional support.

Formative analytics for students

There is also a new approach in learning analytics called 'formative analytics'. In line with feedback for learning, formative analytics supports learners to reflect on what is being learned, what can be improved, which goals can be achieved and how to move forward. It differs from assessment for learning in that the feedback is not just based on a quiz or essay, but on analysing a variety of learning actions including which materials the student has seen, time spent on each activity, answers to assessments, whether the student has asked for help and how the student contributes to online discussions.

Some commercial applications already include forms of personalized automated feedback, providing suggestions about what to study next based on analysis of performance. For example, with the ALEKS tutoring system students are continuously assessed to determine their knowledge of key concepts and inter-relations. Based on their learning behaviour, students get feedback on what they know and how they can further improve their understanding. They also have the option to choose a new topic that fits with their abilities to learn and interests.

How formative analytics works

There are many ways to track progress and provide feedback to students on whether they are struggling and how to improve. The basic method is to interpret whether activities, such as answering a quiz or viewing supplementary material are effective or not, based on the activities of a previous cohort of learners and their exam scores. This approach produces advice, such as 'Most students who passed this module viewed this document'.

Another approach is to compare the behaviour of each learner with the performance of the current set of students, offering responses, such as 'Most students have viewed this document', 'The average score for this test is...' or 'There's an active online discussion on this topic'.

More advanced methods of monitoring student behaviour are also possible, such as eye tracking using the camera on a laptop to detect whether a student's attention is wandering. Each of these methods has the potential to give richer feedback but could also be seen as intrusive. Alongside ethical concerns about tracking student behaviour are the risks of distracting students from managing their own study by giving them too much guidance. Formative analytics must achieve a delicate balance between support and disruption.

Formative analytics in practice

OU Analyse from The Open University applies a range of learning analytics techniques to existing distance learning courses. It traces what successful students are doing in a range of learning activities, including contributing to specific discussion forums, watching a key video or engaging with a quiz. The system analyzes this information about successful strategies and then gives advice to students who need additional support or who want to push themselves to achieve excellence.

Figure 22.1 shows a dashboard that would provide student Suzie with an indication of how well she is doing relative to her peers who have similar

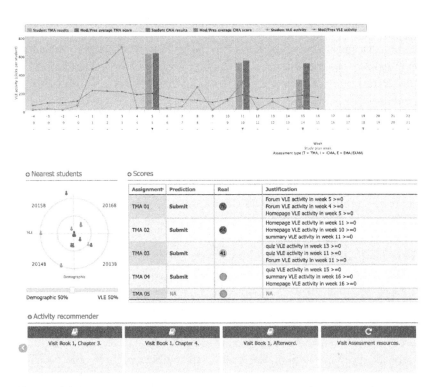

Figure 22.1 The OU Analyse dashboard, showing performance of a distance-learning student

learning paths and personal profiles. Suzie can see whether she is predicted to submit the fourth tutor-marked assignment (TMA) in week 18, based on the actions she has taken since the third assignment. Suzie may decide not to do the fourth assignment if she has already gained sufficient credit or judges it not to be important. But if she does want to do well on the assignment, the system recommends specific learning activities based on analysis of similar students.

Conclusions

As institutions collect more data about learning behaviour, they will be able to show learners how to progress both cognitively and emotionally. Some learners will be discouraged if formative analytics feedback indicates that they are potentially at risk or they need to complete many more activities to pass an assignment. Some may want to see the details of data that determine why certain activities are recommended. Others may just want to know what they should do to achieve, say, a 5% increase in their grade and how much time this is likely to take. A dialogue is needed between students, teachers, learning designers and learning analytics experts to decide how formative analytics results and feedback can be most effectively shared with different learners. One obvious approach would be to provide a range of information and automated advice, from simple activity recommenders through to more advanced underlying metrics.

Resources

The ALEKS system, marketed by McGraw-Hill Education, assesses each student in relation to a topic and gives advice on what to study next:
www.aleks.com

Report on the value of analytics to higher education, including formative analytics:
Higher Education Commission. (2016). *From Bricks to Clicks: The Potential of Data and Analytics in Higher Education*. London: Higher Education Commission.
http://bit.ly/2D1q7ma

Overview of OU Analyse:
https://analyse.kmi.open.ac.uk/

Tracking eye gaze to understand the relation between students' attention and their performance:
Sharma, K., Jermann, P., & Dillenbourg, P. (2014). How students learn using MOOCs: An eye-tracking insight. In *Proceedings of EMOOCs 2014*, pp. 80–87. Lausanne, Switzerland: European MOOCs Stakeholders Summit.
http://bit.ly/2J95R2h

Study of the effectiveness of two learning analytics tools (the Concept Trail and Progress Statistics) to give information about students' cognitive activities:

van Leeuwen, A., Janssen, J., Erkens, G., & Brekelmans, M. (2015). Teacher regulation of cognitive activities during student collaboration: Effects of learning analytics. *Computers & Education*, 90, 80–94.
http://bit.ly/2EzTUny

This chapter draws on material from *Innovating Pedagogy 2016*, published under a Creative Commons Attribution Licence:

Sharples, M., de Roock , R., Ferguson, R., Gaved, M., Herodotou, C., Koh, E., Kukulska-Hulme, A., Looi, C.-K., McAndrew, P., Rienties, B., Weller, M., & Wong, L. H. (2016). *Innovating Pedagogy 2016: Open University Innovation Report 5*. Milton Keynes: The Open University.

Part IV

Extension

Threshold concepts   **23**
Teach troublesome concepts and tricky topics

Overview

A threshold concept is something that, when learned, opens up a new way of thinking about a problem, a subject or the world. An example is the physics concept of 'heat transfer' that can inform everyday activities, such as cooking or home energy use. These concepts help to define subjects, and they shift learners' perceptions of a topic area. Teachers may use threshold concepts as starting points for the design of effective lessons. A challenging aspect of threshold concepts is that they often seem strange and unintuitive. Students who appear to have understood these troublesome concepts may be unable to put them into practice, instead falling back on common-sense, but inaccurate, beliefs. Momentum for using threshold concepts to help teaching is growing across disciplines. One approach is to develop standard sets of threshold concepts for different subject areas; another is to embed them in teaching and learning processes and practices.

Understanding threshold concepts

The idea of threshold concepts can itself be difficult to understand. How to identify them and distinguish them from other learning topics has provoked debate among academics. There is general agreement that a threshold concept is fundamental to understanding a topic, opening up a new way of thinking about it. Once the student 'gets' the concept, the whole area of knowledge makes more sense. A threshold concept has one or more of these characteristics:

- **troublesome** – it appears difficult and unintuitive;
- **transformative** – it shifts a learner's perceptions of a subject;
- **irreversible** – once learned, it is hard to unlearn;
- **integrative** – it exposes the inter-relatedness of some things;
- **bounded** – it borders with other threshold concepts to define a disciplinary area.

Troublesome knowledge

It is unclear how many of these five characteristics are needed to define a concept as a threshold concept. A simple approach is to say that threshold concepts are core topics in education without which students cannot progress in the subject. The characteristic of 'troublesome knowledge' is central. Especially within science and technology, a good starting point for teachers is to explore which curriculum topics seem strange and counter-intuitive.

In computing, for example, the concept of 'recursion' causes problems for learners because it relates to one computing structure being embedded inside another, like a set of dynamic Russian dolls. So using Russian dolls as an analogy might be a way to start teaching the concept. As always with analogies in teaching, there is a need to balance a compelling image against its power to explain.

Although engineering and the sciences have been the main focus of projects to identify and map threshold concepts, they have been identified in other disciplines. Examples of threshold concepts include: 'opportunity cost' in economics, 'gravity' in physics and engineering, 'depreciation' in accounting and 'deconstruction' for text analysis in English literature.

Threshold concepts can also be part of workplace learning. For example, trainee doctors and nurses need to understand and apply the concept of 'emotional intelligence' when working with patients.

Meyer and Land give the example of 'opportunity cost' as a threshold concept in economics. In brief, opportunity cost describes the benefits that an individual or business misses out on when choosing another alternative. Central to economics is how people and organizations make choices, such as how they choose to spend their time or invest their money. Opportunity cost expresses the basic relationship between scarcity and choice – every choice (including not choosing) means rejecting alternatives. A student who understands this has come to look beyond immediate consequences of choosing one alternative or another, towards a more abstract way of thinking, and has a powerful means to explore aspects of economics, such as investment decisions and risk.

Threshold concepts to guide teaching and learning

Classroom education is designed to transform learners so they gain a deep knowledge of the concepts needed to understand and apply a curriculum topic and can fit these concepts together appropriately and accurately. Threshold concepts can provide a starting point for this transformation. Effective design of a curriculum around these key concepts provides a structure for teaching, promotes dialogue among students, helps in introducing complex topics and prompts inquiry into the nature of student and teacher understanding. They allow teachers to reflect on important points in learning from the students' perspective, indicating areas of misunderstanding and barriers to deeper learning of a subject.

Threshold concepts can also guide assessment practices. By breaking a concept into related elements, each anchored to a threshold concept, a teacher can guide and assess knowledge of each part, then fit them together into a composite whole.

Just as with a jigsaw puzzle, there is also value in showing the 'big picture' of a threshold concept – why it is important and how it can be applied in practice – before putting together the component parts. The true value of threshold concepts is that they provide an approach to teaching across different disciplines that is based on fostering deep understanding of difficult concepts.

Threshold concepts in practice

The Juxtalearn European project worked with teachers in science, technology, engineering and mathematics (STEM) to overcome the barriers of teaching threshold concepts. They broke the process down into eight steps.

1. The teacher identifies 'tricky topics' (threshold concepts) in teaching based on previous experience with students. Each of these can be divided into smaller 'stumbling blocks' that students find difficult to understand.
2. The teacher creates one or more teaching activities to address each stumbling block.
3. The teacher, helped by the research team, also develops a diagnostic quiz to test the students' understanding of the tricky topic.
4–6. Students work in teams to plan, produce and share short videos that explain the tricky topic.
7. The students discuss their different video presentations and try to reach a shared understanding.
8. Students take the diagnostic quiz again to re-assess their understanding.

The process of students working together to create videos that explain the topic by visual analogies is central to the Juxtalearn process. The Juxtalearn team tested this with STEM teachers who were able to manage the process of testing students' understanding of threshold concepts and helping students create the videos. In a project in Portugal, three teachers worked with students aged 13–15 to identify tricky topics in mathematics, such as simplifying an algebra equation. The students found it difficult to plan a video to explain a topic but enjoyed the creative process and some reported it helped to clarify misunderstandings.

Newman University College in the UK carried out a review of its undergraduate course on 'Working with Children, Young People and Families'. The review found that students were not grasping some central concepts in sociology. The course team re-designed the course around three 'big ideas': the critical practitioner; professional identities and values; and the links between theory, policy and practice. The aim was to emphasize and explore the key threshold concepts that had previously been hidden by the mass of course content.

Conclusions

It may be hard to define what threshold concepts are, but it's clear that they are central to understanding many curriculum topics. For a learner, grasping a threshold concept opens a gateway to understanding. It provides a way to think about a difficult subject at a more abstract level and to organize new knowledge. For a teacher, threshold concepts offer ways to organize a curriculum and plan lessons – by introducing the concept, giving examples of its use, helping students to understand it in their own terms and then progress to re-conceiving the topic around the new concept. Entering the gateway of each threshold concept can be difficult for both student and teacher because it involves reorganizing existing knowledge and taking on a new way of thinking about the topic.

Resources

A short introduction to threshold concepts and a bibliography:
http://bit.ly/2q4tmRr

Short introductory article:
Cousin, G. (2006). An introduction to threshold concepts. *Planet*, 17.
http://bit.ly/2OF3cTV

Key paper by inventors of the term 'threshold concepts':
Meyer, E., & Land, R. (2003). Threshold concepts and troublesome knowledge: Linkages to ways of thinking and practising within the disciplines. *Occasional Report, 4, May 2003*,

Enhancing Teaching-Learning Environments in Undergraduate Courses. University of Edinburgh.
http://bit.ly/2yT6ZCn

Edited book on threshold concepts, with a free online copy of the preface, foreword and first two chapters:
Meyer, J. H. F., Land, R., & Baillie C. (Eds.) (2010). *Threshold Concepts and Transformational Learning.* Rotterdam: Sense Publishers.
http://bit.ly/2ytt3UV

Article on a project in Portugal to teach tricky topics in mathematics through the Juxtalearn process:
Cruz, S. M. A., Lencastre, J. A., & Coutinho, C. P. (2018). The VideoM@T project: Engaging students on learning tricky topics in mathematics through creative skills. In *Proceedings of the 10th International Conference on Computer Supported Education* (CSEDU 2018), 1, pp. 342–349. Funchal, Madeira: SCITEPRESS.
http://bit.ly/2yv1J8w

Article on redesign of the 'Working with Children, Young People and Families' course at Newman University College:
Monk, C., Cleaver, E., Hyland, C., Brotherton, G. (2012). Nurturing the independent-thinking practitioner: Using threshold concepts to transform undergraduate learning. *Journal of Pedagogic Development,* 2(3), 10–15.
http://bit.ly/2R5YCux

This chapter draws on material from *Innovating Pedagogy 2014*, published under a Creative Commons Attribution Licence:
Sharples, M., Adams, A., Ferguson, R., Gaved, M., McAndrew, P., Rienties, B., Weller, M., & Whitelock, D. (2014). *Innovating Pedagogy 2014: Open University Innovation Report 3.* Milton Keynes: The Open University.

Learning through storytelling

24

Create narratives of memories and events

Overview

A story provides a narrative structure that helps in remembering and recalling events. The narrator of a story, the storyteller, creates a series of events from a specific point of view to create a meaningful whole. Writing up an experiment, reporting on an inquiry, analyzing a period of history – these are all examples of narrative supporting learning. Indeed, much of our education involves combining things we know to create an understanding of what has happened and, thus, what can be expected to happen in the future. These accounts can be used to link memories of events, binding them together to form larger, more coherent chunks. Narrative approaches to learning emphasize the creation of stories. Learners follow the flow of events and see a sequence of resources and evidence. Storytelling can engage learners and make remote events relevant.

Narrative and human memory

Storytelling is fundamental to human learning. Stories provide narratives that help us to make sense of the past by showing how events are connected over time. Sagas, parables and fables are all ways of making important events memorable by weaving them into a coherent story. They not only recount past events but can also be called upon to predict and plan future actions, by showing how abstract principles can be acted out in practice. Stories can be told in many ways: spoken, written, filmed, mimed, acted and presented through interactive media, such as computer games. What stories have in common is a report of connected events that carries the audience forwards and makes them care about what happens next.

The rise of a scientific approach to learning and teaching has sidelined these narratives in favour of a curriculum that emphasizes mastery of facts and figures. But, as the wealth of online information continues to grow and as society becomes more complex, there is an increasing need for coherent storylines that can help learners to find their way through resources and events.

Here we look in more detail at three approaches to learning through storytelling: storytelling in the classroom, narrative pedagogy and narrative-centred environments.

Storytelling in the classroom

There are many ways for a teacher to tell stories in the classroom – by reading from a storybook, retelling a story from history, telling a family story or recounting a personal narrative. After any of these, the students can retell the story through writing, pictures or by acting it out.

Li'l Stories is a framework for teachers to help young children create and share their own stories. First, the children work in groups to create a storyboard – a series of pictorial frames, like a cartoon strip, that introduces the characters and settings and shows the sequence of actions. It can be a retelling of a story that the teacher has presented, a personal narrative from one of the children, a story from history or a fantasy. Creating the storyboard helps the students to structure a shared narrative and organize their thinking. Then the children act out their stories as plays, puppet shows or films.

Narrative pedagogy

Narrative pedagogy was developed for nursing education, though it could be adopted in other professions, such as social work or business. The approach involves students and teachers working together to discuss and interpret their recent experiences. As well as sharing workplace stories with each other, they may be encouraged to create reflective journals in which they consider their actions, analyze patient situations and evaluate outcomes.

This practice of recounting experiences encourages nursing students and their teachers to consider what is possible and what is problematic in their professional practice. It gives learners opportunities to hear and discuss different viewpoints. Within these different narratives, knowledge is contested and elements of uncertainty are explored. Nothing in the subject area is taken as certain: everything is open and problematic.

Narrative pedagogy supports a context-sensitive approach to learning, where the students examine different perspectives on situations, such as how they coped with a difficult patient, and opportunities to empathize with others. As stories are shared, the nurses are prompted to examine their values and their attitudes. They are also made aware of the importance of continually questioning and thinking things through, rather than reaching for a set answer.

Narrative-centred learning environments

Narrative pedagogy for nurses takes place in the real world. A narrative-centred learning environment, by contrast, provides a fictional 'story world' in which guided exploratory learning can take place. These environments could be created in the classroom or may be based within virtual worlds (such as Minecraft) or game settings. In each case, they place learners within unfolding stories that may require them to take roles, ask questions, make predictions and solve problems.

These environments put the students in control, not only of their route through the landscape but also of their progress towards solving problems and overcoming challenges. The fantasy elements of the scenario contribute to vivid imaginative sequences.

Learning through storytelling in practice

Project Storytelling is a narrative-centred environment in the Minecraft virtual world. A visitor to the Project S Island lands in a village square surrounded by shops and homes, dominated by the 'tree of souls'. Exploring inside the tree reveals temples to earth, water, air and fire. Around the main village are other settlements where students can build homes and businesses. Nearby islands have caves, volcanos and pirate traders. The whole environment is designed to provoke imagination and creative expression.

For adult learners, the University of Strathclyde in Scotland has produced a free introductory Massive Open Online Course (MOOC) on Forensic Science as a story around a murder case. Learners on the course are introduced to a murder set on the shores of Loch Lomond in Scotland. Each week, a video presents more detail of the murder. The learners act as forensic scientists, analyzing data to find who committed the murder. They work together online, to compare witness statements, examine the crime scene, decide who should be fingerprinted and consider blood pattern analysis, footwear marks and the use of firearms. In the final week of the MOOC, there were over 1,300 contributions to the discussion about who had committed the crime, with a final moment of tension as the murderer was revealed on the last night of the course. A current challenge for MOOC creators is to engage learners over time, so storytelling approach offers one way forward.

Conclusions

Listening to and telling stories is a powerful way of learning. Stories can transport learners to another time or place. They create compelling narratives that make abstract principles more real and memorable. They can explore the 'what if' of alternative worlds and different histories. They allow students to use alliterative language. They provide rich content for reflection and sharing. And they allow teachers and students to connect through a shared experience.

But storytelling has to be used with care. Some teachers and students may find it difficult to tell stories of their own lives, especially if these have been harrowing. A school classroom is not the place for group therapy. Telling stories of historical events risks distorting the past – presenting a complex event, such as a war, as a series of inevitable actions. Stories about scientists, such as Newton and the apple or Archimedes in his bath, can present science as if it were invented by great men. With the great power of storytelling comes great responsibility.

Resources

Minecraft Education Edition, Project Storytelling:
https://education.minecraft.net/worlds/project-storytelling/

FutureLearn Introduction to Forensic Science course based on weekly videos to investigate a murder:
https://www.futurelearn.com/courses/introduction-to-forensic-science

L'il stories:
https://kck.st/2AlW1qZ

Website for educational uses of digital storytelling, with example stories:
http://digitalstorytelling.coe.uh.edu

StoryMap is a free tool to see and tell stories linked to map locations:
http://storymap.knightlab.com

Practice-led research project to make the transition from story listeners to storytellers:
Reason, M., & Heinemeyer, C. (2016). Storytelling, storyretelling, storyknowing: Towards a participatory practice of storytelling. *Research in Drama Education: The Journal of Applied Theatre and Performance*, 21(4), 558–573.
http://bit.ly/2S7Jnmc

Narrative pedagogy for nursing education:
Ironside, P. M. (2003). New pedagogies for teaching thinking: The lived experiences of students and teachers enacting narrative pedagogy. *Journal of Nursing Education*, 42, 509–516.
http://bit.ly/2PgkfuW

Benefits of narrative-centred learning environments and the Crystal Island guided exploratory environment:
Mott, B., McQuiggan, S., Lee, S., Lee, S. Y., & Lester, J. (2006). Narrative-centered environments for guided discovery learning. In *Proceedings of the AAMAS Workshop on Agent-Based Systems for Human Learning*, pp. 22–28. Hakodate, Japan: Association for Computing Machinery.
http://bit.ly/2q49kq0

Storytelling in the classroom:
Heinemeyer, C. (2018). The dying art of storytelling in the classroom. *The Conversation*, April 11, 2018.
http://bit.ly/2S7Zlgk

This chapter draws on material from *Innovating Pedagogy 2014*, published under a Creative Commons Attribution Licence:
Sharples, M., Adams, A., Ferguson, R., Gaved, M., McAndrew, P., Rienties, B., Weller, M., & Whitelock, D. (2014). *Innovating Pedagogy 2014: Open University Innovation Report 3*. Milton Keynes: The Open University.

Learning through wonder

25

Evoke a sense of wonder

Overview

When one encounters a wondrous event, such as a brilliant rainbow or a majestic mountain waterfall, it creates an experience that provokes curiosity. By questioning and investigating encounters in the everyday world, a child's desire to understand leads to learning. A nature walk can reveal patterns, such as Fibonacci spirals, fractals, vortices, waves, bubbles, tessellations and cracks that are at once beautiful and open to mathematical modelling. Visual illusions and magic tricks with familiar objects can provoke questions of causality, conservation, action at a distance and free will. Such wondrous encounters motivate learners to see a phenomenon from many different perspectives. Teachers can include wonder in learning activities through magic shows, object lessons, nature tables, cabinets of curiosities and outdoor quests, as well as through literature that evokes 'a sense of wonder'.

Seeking wonder

Wonder invites learning. The everyday phrase 'I wonder how that works' can be the start of a quest to understand. Philosophers, such as Aristotle and Plato, saw wonder as a spur for learning, when we confront our familiar conceptions and explore strange new ideas. Since antiquity, teachers have created curious mechanical toys, displayed wondrous objects for their pupils and organized tours to see the wonders of the world. 'Wonder Rooms' with their 'Cabinets of Curiosities' were forerunners of museums in Renaissance Europe of the 16th

Century. In more modern times, teachers take students on nature walks to find wondrous objects, such as spider webs, and set up experiments to show the wonders of science.

Thus, wonder can be deliberately sought and designed to support learning. The poet Wordsworth saw wonder in everyday sightings, such as a field of daffodils or a sky of clouds, seen through the eyes of an imaginative child. Lingering on the familiar can provoke a 'joy of being' that inspires creativity.

Wonder has many forms. It can be awe-inspiring in a flame or a plasma globe; or curious in the shape of an ostrich feather or the motion of a gyroscope. A classroom nature table can be a focus for exploration and classification; it can form connections between nature, science and mathematics. Wonder is based on kindness and positive experience that leads to observation and an urge to find out more.

Anticipation, encounter, investigation, discovery, propagation

A pedagogy of wonder has some similarities to guided discovery learning, where a teacher helps students solve a problem or understand a principle through a process of hands-on exploration. But it differs in how the quest begins: by showing an object or event that sparks curiosity; presenting the familiar in a new way; setting up a puzzle; or conjuring with science and nature. Much in this chapter is based on explorations by Matthew McFall into designing wonder in school settings. He builds on previous work to describe wonder as a series of phases:

Anticipation – a sense that something is going to happen and a desire to know more;

Encounter – the moment of experiencing the wondrous;

Investigation – pursuit of the wondrous, to understand it better or continue the experience;

Discovery – coming to understand, or realize how much more there is to know;

Propagation – continued working with this wonder, to share and celebrate.

Each phase can be designed for learners. A sense of anticipation can be seeded with riddles, questions, mysterious conversations or posters. There could be an event that takes students to a strange place, either by physically moving to another room or outside, or by evoking the strangeness through storytelling.

The encounter with wonder should be inspiring, not frightening. It can be deliberately constructed, as with a table showing peculiar objects: a fossil, a sea urchin skeleton, a seed pod, a sparkling stone, a kaleidoscope, a tooth, a marble, the workings of a clock or anything else that inspires curiosity. It can be a journey to a new place, such as a walk to find spider webs or seeds. It can be a puzzle or magic trick. It can be an 'object lesson': time to consider the remarkable qualities of an object.

Each design for wonder and learning should be constructive. It should allow learners to share their ideas of wonder and to find or create their own wondrous objects. The encounter should prompt questioning and a search for meaning that spreads beyond the encounter. How does it work? Why does it have that shape? What makes it so beautiful? What happens next? Each of these questions can start a journey to understand more about the encounter.

The phase of discovery can continue throughout a lifetime through a profession or hobby, such as geology, botany or engineering. Memorable exposures to the wondrous are key. A school offers many opportunities to display and share – such as curated classroom cabinets and 'wonder walls'.

Principles for wonder lessons

McFall offers some general principles for lessons based on wonder:

1. How we are introduced to things makes a difference. Consider how the encounter with wonder is designed, to build anticipation and spark investigations.
2. The rules governing interaction influence the outcomes. If each child can touch the curious object, play with the puzzle and try to re-create the strange event, then the learning will be more engaged than watching a display by the teacher.
3. We are drawn to things that are concealed or are the means of concealment, e.g. containers. A gold envelope lends authority and prestige.
4. Objects afford different interactions; some of these may allow exploration and insight. Seek connections.
5. Consider all the senses when planning an interaction.
6. Try to satisfy. A promise should be met, though not necessarily in the way that a participant expects. Be mindful of frustration. Sometimes questions are more potent than explanations.
7. Be kind.

Practices of learning through wonder

Some educational philosophies, schools and technologies emphasize the wondrous nature of learning.

The educational philosopher Rudolf Steiner saw children's early years as a period to stimulate their imagination through wonder at the beauty of nature, the elegance of numbers, the design of artworks and the telling of a suspenseful story. He built his Waldorf School as a place to foster a spirit of wonder that combines thinking, feeling and doing.

Matthew McFall set up his first 'Wonder Room' in a school in Nottingham, UK, containing objects to provoke wonder, curiosity and investigation. These ranged from an African voodoo lily that once a year gives off the smell of rotting meat to attract flies, to a pre-war mechanical typewriter. His PhD thesis reports high engagement from pupils, staff and community.

McFall has also developed a sequence of eight sessions that form a pedagogy of wonder. He presents the sessions as modules or 'boxes', each with a colour scheme, to be opened into a learning activity.

1. **Black box** is the launch event that stimulates anticipation and piques curiosity. Depending on the teacher and the setting, it might be a table draped with a black cloth that is pulled back to reveal a curious object; or it could be a magic or science show; or a physical box that is opened to reveal a clue or a puzzle. The students share their ideas of wonder and learn more about their roles as 'wonder workers'.
2. **Red box** is a brief 'object lesson'. The students look for objects of wonder outside the classroom and bring them in for a show-and-tell. The exhibits might range from the seemingly mundane (a leaf, a stone, a paper clip, a coin) to the exotic (a porcupine quill, a statuette). The students consider and discuss what makes them wondrous.
3. **Orange box** is a scavenger hunt within the school grounds. The students, with support from staff, go in teams to look for the weird and the wonderful. They are encouraged to question the things they see around them and collect specimens, such as pebbles, acorns and dandelions.
4. **Yellow box** is a nature table gallery. The students examine items they have found and discuss how they can be described and displayed for others to see. They might use a magnifying glass to look at the objects more closely, organize the items into groups and add labels to identify them.
5. **Green box** is a cabinet of curiosities event. The students create interactive exhibits to show and explain. These could be items they collected on the scavenger hunt, displays inspired by wonderous events they have witnessed (such as a lightning storm), objects brought from home (a fossil collection), or stunt (juggling), feat (conjuring trick), challenge (mathematical magic) or survey. For example, a student could take apart an old mobile phone, with all the components displayed; or could plant seeds at different times to show stages of growth. A curiosity need not be a physical object. It could be a question, such as 'How does lightning work?' or 'Why do shells form spirals?'.

6. **Blue box** is a quest to explore and understand. It may involve a visit to an historical site, a zoological museum or a woodland. Students and staff collect and consider their wonders in this new setting.
7. **Indigo box** is an opportunity for students to create displays of their exhibits and conceptions of wonder to a larger audience. They could design a small classroom museum or a 'wonder show' for parents to visit. The emphasis is on bringing previous boxes together. They can seek feedback, learn from the experiences and create something even more ambitious.
8. **White box** is a celebration of wonder with other students or parents. It could be similar to a school science fair, but around the theme of curiosity and wonder, focused on the results of the students' quests. It is a 'grand finale' but with an understanding that wonder and wondering never ceases.

Wonderopolis® is a computer platform created by the US National Center for Families Learning. It offers a 'Wonder of the Day', in the form of an intriguing or curious question supported by text and images. Students can submit their own wonder questions to a 'Wonder Bank'. They can also vote for favourite questions to be promoted as a 'Wonder of the Day'. The platform provides resources for learners to explore wonders in more detail and discuss these online.

Conclusions

Wonder has a rich heritage. It differs from awe, amazement and astonishment in opening pathways to learning. A pedagogy of wonder can design opportunities for anticipation, encounter, investigation, discovery and propagation. At one extreme, this may consist of a teacher dragging reluctant students on nature walks to find the wonder in a pebble or a leaf. At the other extreme, it becomes a diffuse empathy in wondering about how others are feeling. Done well, learning through wonder can fit into a curriculum of science or arts, yet provoke new ways of seeing and understanding where familiar objects become prompts for inquiry and imagination.

Resources

Wonderopolis® is an educational software platform to provoke learning through curiosity and wonder:
https://wonderopolis.org/

John Spencer has developed 'Wonder Day' and 'Wonder Week' projects for schools, based on design thinking and inquiry learning:
http://www.spencerauthor.com/wonder-week/

The book *Wonder* by R. J. Palacio (also made into a film) has been the basis for school projects on wonder and kindness:
https://wonderthebook.com/for-teachers
http://bit.ly/2yUoOkr

Article on wonder in Steiner education:
Puckeridge, T. (2014). Imagination, wonder and reverence: The primary years in Steiner/ Waldorf education. *Nurture Magazine*, Winter 2014, pp. 20–22.
http://bit.ly/2OCVSIk

Article in *The Guardian* newspaper about the 'Wonder Room' created by Matthew McFall in a school in Nottingham, UK:
Arnott, C. (2011). A wonder room – every school should have one. *The Guardian*, May 31, 2018.
http://bit.ly/2Cv4BFo

A book on the centrality of wonder in education:
Egan, K., Cant, A. I., & Judson, G. (Eds.) (2013). *Wonder-Full Education: The Centrality of Wonder in Teaching and Learning Across the Curriculum*. New York: Routledge.

PhD thesis and a pocket 'Cabinet of Curiosities' from Matthew McFall:
McFall, M. (2014). Using heritages and practices of wonder to design a primary-school-based intervention. *Unpublished PhD thesis*, University of Nottingham.
McFall, M. (2013). *The Little Book of Awe and Wonder: A Cabinet of Curiosities*. Carmarthen: Independent Thinking Press.

Learning in remote science labs **26**
Guide experiments with authentic scientific equipment

Overview

Students who engage with authentic scientific tools are learning how to act like scientists. Remote laboratory experiments and telescopes were first provided for experienced scientists and university students. Now, some are open to trainee teachers and school students. A typical remote lab has working scientific equipment, robotic arms to operate it and cameras that give views of the experiments. Remote lab systems can provide user-friendly web interfaces, curriculum materials and professional development for teachers. With appropriate support, operating remote labs offers hands-on investigation and the opportunity for direct observation that complements textbook learning. Access to remote labs can also bring such experiences into the school classroom. For example, students can use a distant, high-quality telescope to make observations of the night sky during daytime school science classes.

Lab experiments at a distance

In a remote laboratory, students control real scientific equipment and collect real data over the internet. The procedure can be guided by a computer so classroom teachers can spend less time setting up equipment and more on supporting student learning. Students can collect large data sets, share results from the same equipment with other schools and engage in replications and extensions.

Through a remote lab, students can now work with scientific apparatus and materials that would otherwise be too expensive, dangerous, difficult or time-consuming. For example, the Radioactivity iLab enables students to measure radiation from a sample of strontium-90. In this iLab, students in the United States move a Geiger counter in Australia up and down to measure the radioactivity at different distances and watch what happened over a live video.

Remote labs are available for many topics including astronomy, biology, chemistry, computer networking, earth science, engineering, hydraulics, microelectronics, physics and robotics. Further, common platforms are emerging, such as iLab Central, Go-Lab and the OpenScience Laboratory. The benefits and growing availability of remote labs mean it is now a good time to focus on the pedagogical innovations needed to realize the full potential of both local and remote labs.

Learning through lab work

As technology makes the mechanics of lab work faster and easier, how can learning be enhanced? Six questions are at the heart of learning by doing science:

1. **What is the learning purpose?** In traditional teaching labs, the purpose was sometimes only to handle scientific equipment safely and precisely. This work is taken out of students' hands in a remote lab. Consequently, in remote labs educators focus on conceptual understanding and inquiry goals related to the curriculum. There is less time setting up (and cleaning) a lab and more time for designing the experiment and processing results. But, hands-on experience may be better for some purposes, such as exploring the properties of materials. A remote lab may give the impression that lab work is distant and always works. Messy experiments with local materials are also valuable for understanding how science is done.

2. **What guidance do students need before and after the lab session?** Instructions guide students during the lab session, labels can show parts of the equipment and sensors can measure and display results. Students also need support before and after operating the equipment, to plan meaningful experiments and analyze the findings. They may need help in relating the data back to their original questions and deciding what to do next. By attending to the complete cycle of planning, acting and reflecting, educators can better help students to develop as self-regulating learners.

3. **How can students get timely feedback to guide their learning?** In traditional physical labs, teachers typically walk around to identify difficulties

students are having and intervene appropriately. In a remote lab, students also need to be tested and assisted during their engagement with the lab, but the teacher may not be present during the session. Digital resources, such as a video showing a typical experiment, can support students in checking their own understanding and progress.

4. **How can collaboration support learning goals?** Educational labs in schools and universities are places where students interact socially to support each other's learning. In remote labs, communication can be set up via online chat. Students also need to learn skills of collaboration, such as adopting specific roles, setting up a shared workspace and taking turns to operate the equipment. These can all be managed for remote labs, but the social interactions need to be carefully organized, especially if the students are working from different locations.

5. **Can the places for sense making and data collection be flipped?** For lab classes, students are normally expected to collect data during school time, then organize and interpret their findings as homework. Bur that requires students to do challenging intellectual work alone at home. With remote labs, students can run experiments from home then share findings back in class. Teachers can help students make decisions about what to investigate and how to interpret the data. Overall, innovative pedagogies can balance the time and support for doing the lab work with time and support for learning from it – making sure that the difficult work of sense-making is not left to students to struggle with alone.

6. **How can teachers prepare?** Remote labs offer new opportunities for teacher learning. Trainee teachers can practise with a remote lab from home or university, then teach students using the same lab during a practical session in a school. Remote labs also offer teachers sample data sets that students have collected, to help with planning their lessons. Teachers in different locations can use the same remote lab and discuss their pedagogical approaches to teaching the lab class.

Remote labs in practice

The Faulkes Telescope Project is a network of telescopes around the world that can be controlled remotely from a classroom or home. It provides free access to the telescopes for teachers. A teacher registers for an account, books an observing time, selects a star or galaxy to observe and receives an image captured by the telescope during that time. A more experienced user can choose the coordinates in the sky and add filters to create beautiful colour images.

Go-Lab is a portal to remote and virtual labs for use by schools. Its remote labs include a Geiger counter to measure radioactivity, a chemical lab to synthesize the compound methyl orange and a wind tunnel with model vehicles.

Conclusions

Doing practical experiments with real scientific equipment is no longer restricted to science labs in schools or universities during normal working hours. By carrying out experiments remotely over the internet students can operate machinery that is expensive, dangerous or time-consuming. Automating the operation lets students and teachers focus on learning goals and the pedagogy of science learning, rather than just practical handling of apparatus. While remote labs are good for some difficult experiments, they should complement not replace the experience of setting up equipment and carrying out simple investigations in the classroom.

Resources

Go-Lab portal to remote labs for schools:
www.golabz.eu/labs

Remote Experimentation Laboratory (RExLab) provided by the Federal University of Santa Catarina, Brazil:
relle.ufsc.br

OpenScience Laboratory, bringing practical science to students:
learn5.open.ac.uk

Review of remote labs in education:
Cooper, M., & Ferreira, J. M. M. (2009). Remote laboratories extending access to science and engineering curricula. *IEEE Transactions on Learning Technologies*, 2(4), 342–353.
http://bit.ly/2q6F1z7

Study of remote lab use by undergraduate students, indicating a need for realism, such as live video of the lab:
Sauter, M., Uttal, D. H., Rapp, D. N., Downing, M., & Jona, K. (2013). Getting real: The authenticity of remote labs and simulations for science learning. *Distance Education*, 34(1), 37–47.
http://bit.ly/2ODKxbh

Study of introduction of remote lab use in a Brazilian school, indicating importance of access on mobile devices and teacher development:
Simão, J. P. S., de Lima, J. P. C., Rochadel, W., da Silva, J. B. (2014). Remote labs in developing countries: An experience in Brazilian public education. In *Proceedings of IEEE 2014 Global Humanitarian Technology Conference*, 1–13 October 2014, pp. 99–105. San Jose, CA: IEEE Computer Society.
http://bit.ly/2S7OXoD

Review of guidance for supporting student use of online and remote labs:

Zacharia, Z. C., Manolis, C., Xenofontos, N., de Jong, T., Pedaste, M., van Riesen, S. A. N., Kamp, E. T., Mäeots, M., Siiman, L., & Tsourlidaki, E. (2015). Identifying potential types of guidance for supporting student inquiry when using virtual and remote labs in science: A literature review. *Educational Technology Research and Development*, 63(2), 257–302.
https://bit.ly/2Nud7rh

Evaluation of use of remote labs with schools, indicating a need to focus on active manipulation of control devices and to teach key skills, such as experimental design and control of variables:

Lowe, D., Newcomb, P., & Stumpers, B. (2013). Evaluation of the use of remote laboratories for secondary school science education. *Research in Science Education*, 43(3), 1197–1219.
http://bit.ly/2yTYtDe

This chapter draws on material from *Innovating Pedagogy 2015*, published under a Creative Commons Attribution Licence:

Sharples, M., Adams, A., Alozie, N., Ferguson, R., FitzGerald, E., Gaved, M., McAndrew, P., Means, B., Remold, J., Rienties, B., Roschelle, J., Vogt, K., Whitelock, D., & Yarnall, L. (2015). *Innovating Pedagogy 2015: Open University Innovation Report 4*. Milton Keynes: The Open University.

Context-based learning 27
How context shapes and is shaped by the process of learning

Overview

Context enables us to learn from experience. By interpreting new information in the context of where and when it occurs and relating it to what we already know, we come to understand its relevance and meaning. In a classroom or lecture theatre, the context is typically confined to a fixed space and limited time. Beyond the classroom, learning can come from an enriched context, such as visiting a heritage site or museum, or just being immersed in a good book. We have opportunities to create context, by interacting with our surroundings, holding conversations, making notes and modifying nearby objects. We can also come to understand context by exploring the world around us, supported by guides and measuring instruments. It follows that to design effective sites for learning, at schools, museums and online, requires a deep understanding of how context shapes and is shaped by the process of learning.

Making sense of experience

Context is how we make sense of experience, by distinguishing between what is relevant and irrelevant. For example, when reading a book, the meaning of each word and phrase is conveyed not only by its own characteristics but also by its location in relation to other words or illustrations.

Until recently, education has been designed to minimize the effects of context on learning, so that children can gain universal knowledge and take tests that are appropriate whatever the location, time of day or surroundings. Yet many professions, in areas such as medicine, art or engineering, require general professional knowledge to be applied in specific contexts. They also need practical knowledge to be built up from working in many differing situations. Understanding how context relates to learning is essential for innovating pedagogy.

Learning in context and learning by creating context

Consider a group of students standing before a painting in an art gallery. They are in a specific context, comprising the painting, gallery, the student group and other people. They are also creating context by engaging in shared action and conversation, moving closer to see the painting, discussing the artist and comparing this painting with others they have seen. Thus, context is both something we are immersed in and something we create. The same is true when reading a book: we are at a specific word on a page and also creating contextual meaning from our knowledge of language and literature.

This dual nature of context, as something that surrounds us and something we create through our activity, raises problems for teachers at all levels. A teacher of young children needs to offer them opportunities to create context through exploratory play while safeguarding them so they do not stray into dangerous situations either outdoors and online. At university level, a central issue in subjects such as geology, archaeology and environmental sciences, is whether to use a field trip to immerse students in an authentic context, with all its risks and uncertainties, or to provide them with an experience similar to that of a field scientist by manufacturing or simulating typical data.

Augmented reality, virtual reality and environmental modelling can provide students with the experience of viewing and sampling context-based data. For example, the Virtual Microscope allows students to view and compare pre-prepared samples of rock collected from many locations (including by Apollo astronauts on the Moon). For each sample, the students can see on a map where it was collected and view its position on a geological timeline. They can rotate a 3-dimensional image of the chunk of rock, then view a slice of it under the Virtual Microscope – zooming and measuring it under different lighting conditions. Such technology-enhanced approaches allow students to visit or explore many contexts, but the advantages must be weighed up against the value of doing science in real settings.

Context in education

Young children's learning is tied to contexts of time, place, people and objects, so they live 'in the now'. As they mature, children are increasingly able to create context by applying generalized knowledge to a situation. For children and adults, this process can be supported by tools for accessing knowledge in context and for abstracting general knowledge across multiple contexts.

It is often not easy to take what is learned in one setting and apply it in another. Words and ideas vary according to their context. A word like 'set' in English has very different meanings in a kitchen, a tennis court and a mathematics classroom. Similarly, ideas and activities may need to be re-interpreted from one context to another and data items collected at particular locations may need to be checked or modified before they can be used more generally. So, context-based learning is a powerful means to understand places and events and to connect general knowledge with everyday life, but it requires skill in interpreting localized words, concepts and data.

Context-based learning in practice

New context-sensitive technologies offer opportunities to develop enriched contexts for learning. Handheld location-aware guides and augmented-reality applications can offer audio, text and images to describe the current location or object, such as a painting or museum item. The aim is to give the visitor general information that relates to the specific place or exhibit.

The Aris application offers a set of tools to create and deliver location-based games, such as scavenger hunts and re-enactments of historical events. One Aris game re-creates a student protest in the 1960s on the University of Wisconsin Madison campus. A visitor to the university can take the role of a reporter, moving around the campus, witnessing past events through images and video at the campus locations where the events took place and conducting simulated interviews with participants.

Users of Aris can also create contexts by taking photos and making notes that are added to a map, for others to view when they reach the appropriate locations. This and similar context-based systems can be used, for example, in citizen journalism, as people record everyday events, or in language learning for people to add labels in a foreign language to locations and objects that pop up on other people's devices when they visit each location.

When learning across contexts, communities of amateur scientists already share and compare local data on, for example, weather, wildlife, rocks and fossils. Schools can participate in these community activities through sites, such as Journey North, which engages students and citizen scientists around the world in studying wildlife migration and seasonal change, including tracking migration of hummingbirds, recording sightings of butterflies and noting when tulips bloom in spring. Generalized knowledge about migration and climate change develops by exploring patterns of data across time and location.

Conclusions

Contextual learning ties together other pedagogies including geo-learning, seamless learning, event-based learning, crowd learning and citizen inquiry. The common theme is learning that comes from being situated in and understanding a context and from reporting and comparing events across multiple contexts. As an approach to education, contextual learning involves helping students to learn from the world around them and to see how knowledge relates to location and activity.

Resources

Aris web-based system for creating and playing context-based mobile games:
arisgames.org/

Virtual Microscope with rock samples from locations on the Earth and Moon:
https://www.virtualmicroscope.org

Journey North website that engages students and citizen scientists in tracking wildlife migration and seasonal change:
www.learner.org/jnorth/

Rose Luckin's Ecology of Resources design framework for learning, context and technology:
http://bit.ly/2Sa3f8a

Discussion of the 'Salters' courses for context-based science education, focusing on development of the Salters Advanced Chemistry course:
Bennett, J., & Lubben, F. (2006). Context-based chemistry: The Salters approach. *International Journal of Science Education*, 28(9), 999–1015.
http://bit.ly/2NVQpY8

Context-based adult learning:
Hansman, C. A. (2001). Context-based adult learning. *New Directions for Adult and Continuing Education*, 2001(89), 43–52.
http://bit.ly/2CuBodH

This chapter draws on material from *Innovating Pedagogy 2015*, published under a Creative Commons Attribution Licence:
Sharples, M., Adams, A., Alozie, N., Ferguson, R., FitzGerald, E., Gaved, M., McAndrew, P., Means, B., Remold, J., Rienties, B., Roschelle, J., Vogt, K., Whitelock, D., & Yarnall, L. (2015). *Innovating Pedagogy 2015: Open University Innovation Report 4*. Milton Keynes: The Open University.

Event-based learning　**28**
Time-bounded learning events

Overview

Event-based learning runs over a few hours or days and creates a memorable sense of occasion. Examples are Maker Faires that gather together enthusiasts who are keen on do-it-yourself science, engineering or crafts projects. Local events spark national gatherings and these build into international festivals. Many learning events, like the UK's annual Springwatch week or the world-wide Scratch Day for computer programming, are initiated at the national or international level, but all depend upon local enthusiasm and initiative. The time-bounded nature of an event encourages people to learn together, its local setting supports face-to-face encounters between amateurs and experts and the scale of an event can provide access to resources that would otherwise prove inaccessible. Having such an event as a focus gives learners something concrete to work towards and to reflect upon afterwards, together with a sense of personal engagement and excitement.

Events that shape our lives

Events that shape our personal and national histories – births, weddings, funerals, religious holidays and festivals – are what we most remember later in life and record through photographs. In schools, key dates provide convenient hooks on which to hang lessons about culture, history and art. When students learn about the origins of their country or take part in an annual festival, they know they are doing so at the same time as thousands of others and they benefit from the resources that are readily available at these times. There is also a sense of anticipation as they prepare to build on or challenge what they have learned during similar occasions in the past.

Technology provides opportunities to extend these benefits. Social networking systems, such as Instagram and Twitter, enable participation and collaboration, allowing people to share happenings with friends and colleagues around the world. The possibilities opened up by the combination of event-based learning and social networking are being explored in a variety of subject areas, including science, computer science, history and literature.

Community events: Scratch Days, Maker Faires and Raspberry Jams

Scratch is a free computer programming language, designed for children who are learning to program. The Scratch website brings together a user community that shares and builds on the stories, games and animations created by others around the world.

In 2008, the first annual Scratch conference was held with hundreds of the educators, researchers and developers involved in the project. But it was not aimed at the young people who make up the bulk of the Scratch community and it was only accessible to people with the time and money to travel to the East Coast of the USA. This prompted the creation of an annual Scratch Day when Scratch users could gather together in their local communities. Since then, young users have met up annually to collaborate on programming projects, share ideas and experience and have fun together. Each year, more than 1,000 Scratch Day events are run in over 50 countries. The days are used to prompt further activity and interaction, with Scratch computer programs shared across the world in online galleries.

Other events used to catalyze activity and interaction include the Raspberry Jam and Raspberry Jamboree events focused on the inexpensive Raspberry Pi microcomputer; and the Maker Faires around the world that have a focus on do-it-yourself crafts and projects. All these are associated with enthusiastic and growing communities; the time-limited events inspire, support and showcase learning.

Knowledge-building events: BioBlitzes and Hack Days

Event-based learning does not require engagement with an existing worldwide community. A BioBlitz collects groups of people to carry out a biological survey of an area within a short period of time – usually a day or less. These events often have a festival atmosphere and bring scientists and naturalists together with members of the public. They provide opportunities for amateurs and enthusiasts to learn more about biology, ecology and the importance of nature in their area, while increasing scientific understanding of specific ecosystems.

Publicizing and sharing the results of a BioBlitz online extends its reach beyond the local area. In addition, online tools can be shared with participants that may extend the learning experience over time. This enables BioBlitz participants to continue their investigations once the experts have gone home.

A Hack Day is an event for computer programmers to meet and work together on an intensive project. Make Your School is a project in Germany to run school Hack Days where students work in teams to design and implement interactive devices for improving their school. The concept has spread to other topics, so Hack Days could be organized for trainee nurses, police officers or social workers to design creative solutions to shared problems.

Media-led learning events

Television and theatrical events are increasingly being used as a focus for both entertainment and learning. The annual *Springwatch* and *Autumnwatch* BBC television programs combine live and recorded footage of seasonal wildlife activity with opportunities to engage by accessing additional resources, attending events or taking part in citizen science research. For example, viewers may map bumblebee distribution, provide data to help target hedgehog conservation actions, take part in phenology (the study of seasonal phenomena) and participate in research on the breeding behaviour of gannets. The use of technology means that observations made worldwide can be viewed online via webcams, submitted using smartphone apps and shared using social media.

Stargazing Live, another annual event on BBC television, focuses public interest on astronomy and planetary science. Again, there are opportunities to extend the experience by accessing online resources, attending face-to-face events or participating in citizen science. In 2012, online classification work by viewers led to the discovery of a new planet revolving round a distant star; their work the following year identified dozens of previously unknown galaxies. Zooniverse, which runs these online projects, registered over a million classifications per hour when the program was running, resulting in the classification of more than 6.5 million images (with each image classified multiple times to increase reliability).

There are also media-led learning events in the arts and humanities. The Royal Shakespeare Company, in collaboration with Google's Creative Lab, played out its digital retelling of *A Midsummer Night's Dream* in real time over midsummer weekend in 2013 on a variety of social media. The project appeared on 25 million Twitter feeds and opened discussion of Shakespeare and his contemporary relevance to a worldwide audience. Earlier in the same month, the Channel 4 television company ran a one-day event on 6 June, linking television programs about the Second World War D-Day landings to a retelling of the event through social media. In both cases, the events were strongly time-bounded, encouraging discussion and reflection across a wide group for a short period of time.

Conclusions

Technology-enhanced event-based learning offers opportunities for participation, collaboration and distributed expertise. These events not only have the potential to engage millions of people in memorable learning experiences but can also make significant additions to the body of knowledge available to us as a society.

Resources

Scratch Day annual event run worldwide in association with the Scratch programming language:
http://day.scratch.mit.edu

Raspberry Jam, a global network of groups and events associated with the Raspberry Pi computer:
http://raspberryjam.org.uk/raspberry-pi-jams/

Bristol Natural History Consortium organizes BioBlitz events across the UK:
http://www.bnhc.org.uk/bioblitz/

Make Your School Hack Day project:
http://www.makeyourschool.de/ueber-hys/

Autumnwatch BBC website with links to resources and activities:
https://bbc.in/2yQYCqZ

Zooniverse and *Stargazing Live*:
McMaster, A. (2017). Stargazing Live 2017 recap. *Zooniverse*, May 10, 2017.
https://blog.zooniverse.org/tag/stargazing-live/

Midsummer Night's Dreaming – a digital theatre event by the Royal Shakespeare Company:
The Guardian (2013). Shakespeare's Midsummer Night's Dreaming: What did you think?.
    The Guardian, June 24, 2013.
http://bit.ly/2NZa09E

D-Day as it happens – television and social media coverage of some of the events of 6 June 1944:

Mount, H. (2013). D-Day: How technology can bring history to life. *The Telegraph*, June 5, 2013.

http://bit.ly/2Pb2T2I

This chapter draws on material from *Innovating Pedagogy 2014*, published under a Creative Commons Attribution Licence:

Sharples, M., Adams, A., Ferguson, R., Gaved, M., McAndrew, P., Rienties, B., Weller, M., & Whitelock, D. (2014). *Innovating Pedagogy 2014: Open University Innovation Report 3*. Milton Keynes: The Open University.

Learning for the future   **29**
*Prepare students for work
and life in an uncertain future*

Overview

Students need to be educated not just for today but for the future. They should acquire skills and dispositions that will enable them to cope with an uncertain life and a complex work environment. Learning for the future builds human capacity to learn. This includes the ability to change perspectives in the light of new information and understanding. It helps students to acquire critical thinking skills, gain social competencies related to learning and working together and develop resourcefulness in learning. Future-ready learners have agency and autonomy in planning what and how to learn. They have the skills to be responsible citizens, contributors and innovators in an uncertain future. They also have mature cultural and interpersonal understanding.

Future-ready students

The call to be future-ready is intended to prompt schools and educational systems to prepare their students for success in future learning, work and life. The Skills Strategy produced by the international Organisation for Economic Co-operation and Development (OECD) has shifted the emphasis from human capital, measured in years of formal education, towards the skills people gain and enhance over their lifetimes. This shift is reflected in educational policy statements and initiatives to equip learners with the skills and dispositions to cope with an uncertain world, a complex life and a changing work environment.

To give an idea of these skills and dispositions, the Careers 2030 website lists jobs that might be advertised in the year 2030. These include Wearable Technology Therapist, Systems Tangilizer and Aesthetician. An intriguing example from the list is Robot Counsellor – not someone who offers therapy to robots, but a person who helps families and elderly people to integrate robot technology into their lives. A job such as this combines skills of empathy and communication with knowledge of new robot technology.

So, future-ready learners should not only have the cognitive skills of critical thinking, creativity and innovation, and a good knowledge of how to work with new technologies, they also need to build inter-personal skills of collaboration, empathy and cultural awareness. And just gaining the individual skills is not enough – students also need to see how they fit into a changing society, to benefit from new opportunities and overcome challenges.

Future-ready schools

School curricula and teaching materials cover traditional topics and teach basic skills. By contrast, learning for the future needs to prepare students for new technologies in a changing society. That's a huge demand for an already over-stretched education system.

One way to start is by helping students understand, and even look forward to, a changing society. Future-oriented websites and resources, such as Careers 2030, can provide inspiration. Which career would you like to have in 2030? The website describes each future job in detail, so a student might pick one and research it. What skills would be needed to become a Company Culture Ambassador, a SmartCube Technician or a Teacher in 2030? Exploring future careers could be a springboard for students to learn and practice the underlying qualities of resourcefulness, empathy, communication, cultural sensitivity, engagement with technology and ethical action.

Figure 29.1 shows a tool to think about the future, for teachers and students. First, it asks us to reflect on our certainty about the future, for ourselves and in general – is the future open and uncertain, or closed and predictable, or somewhere in between? Second, it asks what is our locus of control – do we feel in control of our future, or will it be determined by someone else? This produces quadrants that indicate a person's orientation to the future: Building Site, Route Map, Into the Future and Carried Away. The purpose of the thinking tool is not to provide answers to the questions, but to confront our assumptions about possible futures and whether we can influence them. What are we basing our assumptions on? Can these be challenged, and if so how? What evidence is there that our future may be more closed, or open, than we might think? What new choices and challenges would come from taking a different orientation to

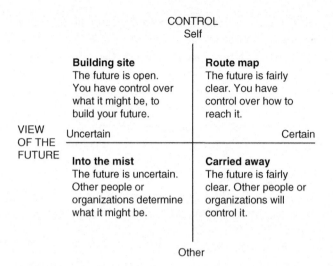

Figure 29.1 A tool for thinking about the future (adapted from Facer et al., 2011, *Building Agency in the Face of Uncertainty*)

the future? The tool and the questions it raises could be a resource for classroom discussion.

Technology can support learning for the future. The US National Education Technology plan for 2017 uses the title 'Future Ready Learning: Reimagining the Role of Technology in Education'. It advocates giving agency to learners that enables them to make meaningful choices about their learning and to play a part in their own self-development as their situation changes over time. For example, online mentoring and jobs forums (such as Indeed and Quora) can provide career advice. Free online course sites (such as Coursera, edX and FutureLearn) give introductions to new careers.

More research is needed in how to nurture and assess learning for the future. Teachers need ways to teach knowledge, skills and dispositions as a whole. Policy makers need to decide how to make space for these within a crowded school year.

Future-ready learning in practice

The focus in most countries on content and exams means that education systems may need wholesale change to accommodate learning for the future. Finland is often considered to be a model of a successful education system, with learning outcomes near the top of global comparisons for literacy, mathematical literacy and science literacy, and differences between schools that are the smallest in the world. This is achieved with average government investment in school education, small amounts of homework and daily lesson hours, and a school system that is not subject to inspections.

Finland bases its school system on principles of equity, flexibility for life-long learning, local freedom and responsibility, high-quality teacher education, formative evaluation and support for children with learning difficulties. The country has a core curriculum for basic education that prepares children for the future. It still has a long list of subjects, but these are taught in relation to the competences of: thinking and learning to learn; cultural competence, interaction and self-expression; taking care of oneself and managing daily life; multiliteracy; ICT competence; working life competence and entrepreneurship; participation, involvement and building a sustainable future.

The goal is to strengthen each student's image of themselves as positive and realistic, discovering the joy of learning, with a strong emphasis on a collaborative school culture and communal methods of studying. The curriculum is intended to make connections between the topics students learn at school and the knowledge they need for their own lives and futures.

Conclusions

There are many possible visions for the future of work, technology, education, society. We can't prepare young people for every eventuality. Nor can we rely on an education system that is grounded in the past. A first step is to help students to become more aware of future opportunities and to have agency in making choices about their careers. But major change will only come when schools and colleges prepare students for many possible futures. That includes helping students to gain 21st-century skills, such as critical thinking, alongside qualities such as cultural awareness and ethical action. We have much to learn from policy initiatives in countries such as Finland, Canada and Singapore that are building education systems around resourceful teachers, adaptable curricula, future-oriented skills, global awareness and close links between education and employment.

Resources

The College and Career Readiness and Success Organizer is an overview of elements that affect a student's ability to succeed in college and careers:
www.ccrscenter.org/ccrs-landscape/ccrs-organizer

Framework for understanding 21st-century learning from the P21 Partnership for 21st Century Learning:
www.p21.org/our-work/p21-framework

Finnish core curriculum for basic education:
http://bit.ly/2D0ONuU

Indeed career advice:
https://www.indeed.com/forum/gen/Career-Advice.html

Quora site for careers choices:
https://www.quora.com/topic/Career-Choices

Some sites offering free online courses that provide a taster for future careers:
https://www.coursera.org/
https://www.edx.org/
https://www.futurelearn.com/

Report on educating for the future, with a Worldwide Educating for the Future Index:
Economist Intelligence Unit (2017). *Worldwide Educating for the Future Index: A Benchmark for the Skills of Tomorrow.* The Economist Intelligence Education Unit Limited.
https://bit.ly/2L1SHaB

A guide to the educational system in Finland:
Niemi, H., Multisilta, J., Lipponen, L., & Vivitsou, M. (Eds.) (2014). *Finnish Innovations and Technologies in Schools: A Guide towards New Ecosystems of Learning.* Rotterdam: Sense Publishers.
http://bit.ly/2R7K2TE

Report on future-ready education from the US Department of Education:
Office of Educational Technology (2016). *Future Ready Education: Reimagining the Role of Technology in Education.* US Department of Education.
tech.ed.gov/files/2015/12/NETP16.pdf

A paper on leadership in future-ready schools:
Sheninger, E. (2015). *Leading Future-Ready Schools.* Rexford, USA: International Center for Leadership in Education.
www.leadered.com/FutureReadySchools.pdf

Tool for thinking about educational futures:
Facer, K., Craft, A., Jewitt, C., Mauger, S., Sandford, R., & Sharples, M. (2011). *Building Agency in the Face of Uncertainty: A Thinking Tool for Educators and Education Leaders.* Economic and Social Research Council.
http://bit.ly/2EBcADC

This chapter draws on material from *Innovating Pedagogy 2016*, published under a Creative Commons Attribution Licence:
Sharples, M., de Roock, R., Ferguson, R., Gaved, M., Herodotou, C., Koh, E., Kukulska-Hulme, A., Looi, C.-K., McAndrew, P., Rienties, B., Weller, M., & Wong, L. H. (2016). *Innovating Pedagogy 2016: Open University Innovation Report 5.* Milton Keynes: The Open University.

Part V

Embodiment

Embodied learning   **30**
Make mind and body work together to support learning

Overview

Embodied learning involves experiencing and controlling one's body interacting with a real or simulated world. The aim is that physical feedback and bodily actions support learning. Technology to aid this includes wearable sensors that gather personal physical and biological data, visual systems that track movement and mobile devices that respond to actions, such as tilting and motion. Embodied learning can be applied to explore aspects of physical sciences, such as friction, acceleration and force, and to understand one's own body and health. Physical activity lets learners feel as they learn. Being more aware of how one's body interacts with the world can also support the development of a mindful approach to learning and well-being.

Experience in the world

Embodied learning comes from self-awareness of one's own body – its movements, biomedical measurements, limits and interactions with the world. Controlling one's body is essential for some forms of learning, such as playing a new sport, becoming a dancer or learning to drive a car. It also relates more generally to how we experience ourselves and act on the world through our bodies.

As we move through environments and interact with people and objects, our bodies and limbs fit into the surroundings. We continually adjust to the terrain, temperature, objects and people we touch. The environment provides opportunities for action (called 'affordances') that our bodies detect and act upon by walking, running, hearing, seeing, touching, smelling, tasting. Learning occurs when this continuous process of action and reaction comes to our attention. It can happen when the body does not fit neatly into the environment (for example, when a child touches a hot plate), or we are learning how to perform a physical activity, such as dancing, or we are shaping the environment to our needs (for example, by drawing, painting, sculpting or building).

By exploring the world around them, young children come to understand their space, their bodies, their time and other people. When they start school, children gain disembodied knowledge from books and teachers. Traditional education separates abstract and embodied learning. The time has come to recognize that learners have bodies and to develop pedagogy for the whole person.

Acts of learning

It follows that physical acts – such as using a pen, pencil or brush to write and draw – affect how we learn. When writing or drawing by hand rather than typing on a keyboard, we are able to cross out, add notes and draw diagrams alongside the text. The process of creating a text, mathematical solution or drawing can be made visible to other learners or teachers. Students may use their workings and crossings out to gain insight into thinking processes, see gaps in knowledge and suggest ways to improve the technique, perhaps by adding notes or drawings. These acts of mind and body working in harmony to express the process of thinking can be powerful aids to teaching and learning. Children show their working of subtraction problems by crossing out and adding figures; poets leave traces of their creative processes on the written manuscript.

Computer devices with pen or touch input can capture these pen strokes and replay them to provide an animation of problem solving. Teachers can create 'worked example' videos to demonstrate the process of solving a mathematical problem or to explain a concept by drawing and adding to a diagram. Free courses from Khan Academy employ a combination of voice and whiteboard to good effect in explaining topics from mathematics and science. New technologies that are sensitive to pressure of touch allow more subtle ways of communicating the process of drawing and painting. However, there are digital limitations in the flow of ink and the colour of pigment. For example, paints create colour by reflecting ambient light, while computer screens transmit and filter light.

Gestures allow people to communicate by indicating or moving real or virtual objects, working together to produce shapes and patterns and creating music and dance. Gestures may also have a fundamental role in children's development of mathematics and science, as they rotate shapes, organize things into categories, pour liquids and move objects into alignment or set them in motion. The speech children use with adults in performing these actions, such as 'push' and 'pour', forms the basis for scientific language.

Fitness trackers

Mobile and wearable devices now contain a range of different sensors that can provide information not only about our external environment (including ambient temperature, light levels and location) but also about an individual's physical and biological data (such as the number of steps walked during a time period, heart rate and even blood oxygen levels). These data, sometimes referred to as 'the quantified self', can be applied to help us learn about ourselves, to improve fitness and diagnose bodily illnesses and weaknesses.

However, this comes with an important warning. Wearing fitness trackers may motivate young people in the short term, but in time can turn them off exercise. A study in the UK gave 84 students aged 13 to 14 fitness trackers for eight weeks. Initially, the students gained interest in fitness, but by the end of the study students consistently reported being bored with the fitness tracker. Many particularly disliked the daily step count of 10,000 steps and felt pressured into performing for the device.

Embodied learning in practice

The educational technologist Seymour Papert developed a notion of 'body syntonic' learning. The idea is that children learn about geometry and mechanics by directing their own bodies to create shapes and movements. For example, a child can walk out a square by stepping 10 paces forward, turning right 90 degrees and repeating this 4 times. Then, what commands would create a rectangle or a triangle? Once the children have understood how to create shapes with their own bodies, they move on to controlling a small robot 'turtle' by giving it similar commands to draw shapes, such as 'Repeat 4 times [Forward 100 Right 90]'.

In a study of body syntonic science learning, university students wore sensors on their hands that detected position and orientation. The student could 'write' distance–time and velocity–time graphs directly onto a computer screen by moving a hand. Figure 30.1 shows an example of two graphs that a student made by moving her hand backwards and forwards. In the distance–time graph, the faster the student moved her hand, the steeper the line. The velocity–time graph shows the steepness of the slope.

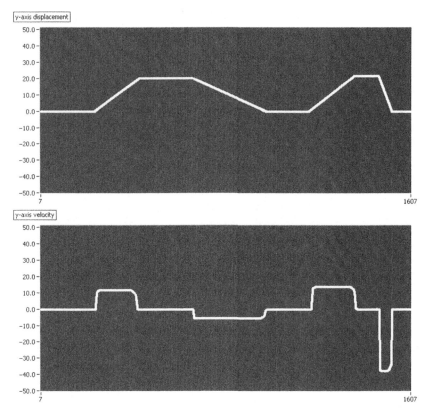

Figure 30.1 Distance–time and velocity–time graphs produced by a student moving a hand wearing a motion tracker (from Anastopoulou et al., 2004[1])

First, each student tried different hand movements to see how these generated graphs of distance and time, then they were given tasks such as looking at a book illustration of a distance–time graph, predicting what hand movement would be needed to generate that graph, then trying it by moving the hand. The study showed that students who wrote the graphs by moving their own hands scored better on tests of graph knowledge than those who watched a teacher perform the actions.

SMALLab is a room-sized environment for students to learn about mathematics and science by moving their bodies. For example, they can learn about gravity, friction and mass by walking and turning, with feedback from motion trackers.

Conclusions

Embodied learning is essential for gaining some skills, such as sports or driving. It also offers new ways to understand space, time and motion through physical movement and gesture. Learning occurs not only in the mind, but through a coordination of mind and body. However, unless it is implemented thoughtfully, embodied learning will present challenges to students who struggle with physical exertion or complex body movements. New developments in wearable and implanted technologies, including internal microchips and digital tattoos, are likely to provide even greater amounts of personal data about physical movements and physiology. But these possible extensions to minds and bodies will not always be a comfort or benefit. We need carefully to consider the potential negative impacts on learning, such as demotivation and intrusion, before we engage with these developments more extensively.

Note

1   Anastopoulou, S. (2004). Investigating multimodal interactions for the design of learning environments: A case study in science learning. *Unpublished PhD thesis*, University of Birmingham, UK.

Resources

Khan Academy videos showing teaching by worked example:
www.khanacademy.org

SMALLab Learning advancing embodied learning in schools and museums:
www.smallablearning.com

Study of school students wearing fitness trackers:
Kerner, C., & Goodyear, V. A. (2017). The motivational impact of wearable healthy lifestyle technologies: A self-determination perspective on Fitbits with adolescents. *American Journal of Health Education*, 48(5), 287–297.
http://bit.ly/2EOsmev

Paper on learning about distance and velocity graphs through hand gestures:
Anastopoulou, S., Sharples, M., & Baber, C. (2011). An evaluation of multimodal interactions while learning science concepts. *British Journal of Educational Technology*, 42(2), 266–290.
http://bit.ly/2CwSwzl

Article on embodied cognition, that understanding comes from embodiment:
McNerney, S. (2011). A brief guide to embodied cognition: Why you are not your brain. *Scientific American Blog Network*, November 4, 2011.
http://bit.ly/2R3lkn6

Evidence from gestures by teachers and learners that mathematical knowledge is embodied:
Alibali, M. W., & Nathan, M. J. (2012). Embodiment in mathematics teaching and learning: Evidence from learners' and teachers' gestures. *Journal of the Learning Sciences*, 21(2), 247–286.
http://bit.ly/2Ao36HH

Survey of interactive surfaces and physical environments for learning:

Evans, M. A., Rick, J., Horn, M., Shen, C., Mercier, E., McNaughton, J., ... & Slotta, J. D. (2012). Interactive surfaces and spaces: A learning sciences agenda. In *Proceedings of 10th International Conference of the Learning Sciences: The Future of Learning*, ICLS 2012, Volume 2: Symposia, pp. 78–85. Sydney, Australia: International Society of the Learning Sciences.
https://b.gatech.edu/2R4vvHY

This chapter draws on material from *Innovating Pedagogy 2015*, published under a Creative Commons Attribution Licence:

Sharples, M., Adams, A., Alozie, N., Ferguson, R., FitzGerald, E., Gaved, M., McAndrew, P., Means, B., Remold, J., Rienties, B., Roschelle, J., Vogt, K., Whitelock, D., & Yarnall, L. (2015). *Innovating Pedagogy 2015: Open University Innovation Report 4.* Milton Keynes: The Open University.

Immersive learning   31
Intensify learning by experiencing new situations

Overview

Immersive experiences transport us to another place, giving a feeling of being in the midst of the action and having some control over what happens next. Reading an interactive computer-based novel is one such experience. Readers can choose how the action in the story will continue or what the characters will do. They may even be able to enter the story as one of the characters and get involved in the action. With virtual reality technology, immersive learning allows people to experience a situation as if they were there, using their situated knowledge and resources to solve a problem or practise a skill. The learning is intensified by bringing in movement, spatial awareness and touch. Taking part in immersive learning is likely to be stimulating and memorable.

Designs for immersive learning

Traditionally, immersion requires people to act out scenarios or take part in activities, with actors and props to simulate reality. A school play or a good book can take learners to different worlds and draw them into experiencing other perspectives and cultures.

Nowadays, playing a video game or watching sports on a virtual reality headset are designed to be immersive, interactive experiences. Students can use technologies such as smartphones, 3D computer screens, large displays, headsets or helmets with screens inside and gloves fitted with sensors. These enable students to experience immersive learning in a classroom, in a museum, in a work setting, at home or outdoors.

Basic technology, such as phone text messages, can be used to send people to real or virtual locations, creating a feeling of partial immersion, but immersive learning often involves Augmented Reality (AR) or Virtual Reality (VR). With AR, learners can look at the world through special glasses or a handheld device, such as a smartphone, and see labels, images, 3D shapes, characters or animations added to the view. This can be part of a game, a puzzle, a trail or any kind of exploration of the environment. With the Pokémon Go game on smartphones, players create avatars (representations of themselves) that interact with artificially generated creatures and buildings that appear in their surroundings.

In VR, learners can themselves become avatars interacting with other virtual beings. They can travel through time and space. They can play 'What if?', by exploring possibilities that cannot be set up in real life. They can engage in activities that would be difficult, dangerous or impossible in everyday life.

Pedagogy of immersive learning

An advantage of immersive learning is that students can repeatedly practise a complex skill in a safe environment. This is particularly valuable where the skill could be dangerous for the learner (such as learning to fly a plane) or others (such as medicine or surgery). A skill like drilling a tooth can be attempted many times under controlled conditions until it is mastered.

Immersion gives a more realistic environment than a classroom to gain social skills like conversing in a foreign language. It sets up a feeling of 'being there' where the learner has to interact in a rich environment with simulated people, surroundings and objects.

It can allow learners in different locations to meet in a shared space and solve a common problem, such as dealing with an emergency.

Flow state

At its most involving, immersive learning can be a flow of continual engagement regardless of the passing time and changing surroundings. The psychologist Mihaly Csikszentmihalyi proposed nine indicators of a flow state, that are equally applicable to the seamless flow of learning:

- There are clear goals every step of the way.
- There is immediate feedback to one's actions.

- There is a balance between challenges and skills.
- Action and awareness are merged.
- Distractions are excluded from consciousness.
- There is no worry of failure.
- Self-consciousness disappears.
- The sense of time becomes distorted.
- The activity becomes 'autotelic' (it is done for personal satisfaction).

In a state of flow, the learner is engaged in an overarching context where they lose awareness of time and surroundings and is caught up in the action.

Computer games are designed for flow, with continual stimulation to the senses, rapid action and response, increasing challenge and immediate feedback. Immersive flow is undoubtedly engaging and sometimes joyful. It allows the learner to try a skill repeatedly at increasing levels of difficulty. But learning also needs reflection, to process the new information and relate it to existing knowledge.

Teachers and designers of immersive educational technology need to understand how learners enter a flow state, how it can be maintained and how it can contribute to effective learning. One way is to restrict each session of immersive activity to 15 or 20 minutes, followed by a time to reflect, take notes on the experience, think about what worked and what could be improved and set a goal for the next session.

Immersive learning in practice

Immersive learning can be effective in medicine and healthcare training. Medical students can practise surgical skills or talk to virtual patients. For example, dental students can now use simulated drills. Each student holds a simulated dental drill and looks down on a screen as if looking into a patient's mouth. The drill vibrates and gives force feedback that feels like drilling into a tooth.

In geology, a project used immersive VR for geology students on field trips. The students stood on the hillside next to a valley that had once been carved by a glacier. Each student in turn put on a VR headset that allowed them to see the same valley, from the same viewpoint, but as it was 20,000 years ago. When they took off the headset, the students sketched the valley with the glacier and looked for marks that the glacier had left on the landscape. The aim was to get an experience of being at the glacier and to understand how the landscape has changed over time.

Greenleys Junior School in Milton Keynes, UK, has an immersive room where students are surrounded by interactive images on the floor, walls and ceiling. It also has an integrated sound system and smoke machine. The room can be set up to explore planets, take a field trip to another city or take part in interactive games and quizzes.

Immersion doesn't need expensive technology. At Shenley Brook End School, also in Milton Keynes, students have immersive learning projects across year groups to cope with real life scenarios. These include: Shipwrecked, to build a community on a deserted island; Murder Mystery, to become police detectives; Olympics, to act as a country that hosts the Olympic Games; and Moving Out, where students live in a simulated apartment with friends, paying bills, meeting with officials and furnishing their rooms on a tight budget.

Conclusions

Immersive learning can allow students to interact with a complex object such as a molecule, visit a setting such as a French café, learn a skill like dentistry or take part in a simulated emergency. An important advantage is the chance to practise real-world skills in a safe environment, repeatedly, avoiding potential harm to real people and damage to equipment or property. The multimedia and multisensory elements can reinforce learning and make it more appealing and memorable.

On the other hand, immersive learning makes use of technologies that require some technical competency or literacy. The equipment and software can be expensive, although cheaper VR headsets use smartphones as displays. Virtual reality cuts off learners from the real world. A classroom with 30 children stumbling around wearing VR headsets would be a nightmare for any teacher. But immersion comes in many forms: a book, a game of chess, a language role-play in the classroom, an online educational game, an augmented reality visit, a simulation of an emergency for first responder training, a virtual reality patient for teaching surgery. What's important is that the pedagogy is designed around a rhythm of engagement and reflection, with each immersive experience extending the skill, offering active engagement and providing material for reflection and discussion.

Resources

Blog post that provides an introduction to virtual reality and learning:
Jagannathan, S. (2017). *Virtual Reality: The Future of Immersive Learning for Development.* World Bank, July 3, 2017.
http://bit.ly/2yv15Ib

Overview of Immersive Learning for teachers:
Burns, M. (2012). Immersive Learning for teacher professional development. *eLearn*, 2012(4), 1.
http://bit.ly/2Pi1Spq

Introduction to Mihaly Csikszentmihalyi and flow:
http://bit.ly/2AmnIzV

Immersive room at Greenleys Junior School:
https://www.greenleysjunior.org/curriculum/immersive-room/

Immersive learning at Shenley Brook End School:
http://www.sbeschool.org.uk/Immersive-Learning

Learning dentistry with haptic feedback:
https://www.sheffield.ac.uk/dentalschool/our_school/haptics

Immersive virtual reality with geology students on field trips to see how the landscape looked during the last Ice Age.
Priestnall, G., Brown, E., Sharples, M., Polmear, G. (2009). A student-led comparison of techniques for augmenting the field experience. In D. Metcalf, A. Hamilton & C. Graffeo (Eds.), *Proceedings of 8th World Conference on Mobile and Contextual Learning (mLearn 2009)*, pp. 195–198. Orlando, Florida: University of Central Florida.
http://bit.ly/2S8vjZV

Augmented reality and language learning:
Godwin-Jones, R. (2016). Augmented reality and language learning: From annotated vocabulary to place-based mobile games. *Language Learning & Technology*, 20(3), 9–19.
http://bit.ly/2R0BfCO

Immersive learning and dental education:
Dută, M., Amariei, C. I., Bogdan, C. M., Popovici, D. M., Ionescu, N., & Nuca, C. I. (2011). An overview of virtual and augmented reality in dental education. *Journal of Oral Health and Dental Management*, 10, 42–49.
http://bit.ly/2hfq2l1

Classic paper on immersion and learning:
Dede, C. (2009). Immersive interfaces for engagement and learning. *Science*, 323(5910), 66–69.
https://b.gatech.edu/2Eztdzd

This chapter draws on material from *Innovating Pedagogy 2017*, published under a Creative Commons Attribution Licence:
Ferguson, R., Barzilai, S., Ben-Zvi, D., Chinn, C. A., Herodotou, C., Hod, Y., Kali, Y., Kukulska-Hulme, A., Kupermintz, H., McAndrew, P., Rienties, B., Sagy, O., Scanlon, E., Sharples, M., Weller, M., & Whitelock, D. (2017). *Innovating Pedagogy 2017: Open University Innovation Report 6*. Milton Keynes: The Open University.

Maker culture

32

Learn by making

Overview

Maker culture involves people in making and sharing artefacts, from jewellery to robots. It emphasizes experimentation, innovation and testing of theory through practical tasks. The pedagogy combines learning by play and taking risks and with rapid iterative development and testing. The maker community provides feedback and support. Learning comes from informal mentoring and progression through a community of practice. Critics argue it is simply a rebranding of traditional hobby pursuits. Proponents say that new technologies for 3D printing and sharing designs over the internet have created global communities that emphasize learning through social making.

Making things is fun

The essence of maker culture is making things is fun – that it's more enjoyable to make one's own clothes than to buy them from a shop; that a computer is not just a box you switch on but a playground to be explored; that a 3D printer is a tool for creative expression. It is suggested that being a maker is a disposition – a way of seeing objects as malleable and understanding oneself as being able to change things by tinkering with them. But that separates Makers (with a capital M) from the rest. Every child has an ability to tinker with things by pulling, squashing, bending, taking them apart and putting them back together.

Social construction and communities of practice

All knowledge is socially constructed. We learn about the world and ourselves through a combination of experiment and conversation. This holds for academic knowledge in arts or science as well as practical knowledge of skills and crafts. What maker culture does is emphasize the combined social construction of objects and knowledge.

Makers produce objects that satisfy needs and desires in their everyday lives – this includes playful or aesthetic needs. Each new object becomes a focus for conversations with peers. Production is an iterative process that involves designing, creating, getting immediate feedback and altering or extending the artefact. Others in the community offer criticism and advice.

Makers gather together in informal gatherings of friends, workshop spaces, organized events, such as Maker Faires, and online communities. The Maker Faire movement holds over 200 events around the world, engaging 1.5 million people in making and sharing. It has an ethos of exhibiting not competing, connecting with other like-minded people and learning through doing.

These and similar events recognize that learning can occur through the gradual introduction of a learner into a community of practice. The educational theorist Étienne Wenger describes a community of practice as a group of people who share a concern or passion for something new and learn how to do it better as they interact regularly. New members may watch and carry out simple tasks, then progress to more complicated challenges, supported through informal mentoring by more expert members.

Learners can ask questions about problems and improve their skills by getting help from others. Most powerful, they begin to teach others as they increase their expertise. Becoming a more central and valued member of the community is a powerful incentive for learning. Maker culture resonates with current interests in lifelong learning and in cross-generational learning, with skills transmitted not only from old to young but also from young to old.

Some families and schools encourage such learning through constructing, valuing the understanding of processes as much the creation of the final object. Maker culture extends beyond the home and school into communities of practice – people with a shared love of sewing clothes, designing jewellery, taking apart radios, building robots or casting intricate trinkets on 3D printers.

The community creates a social framework for learning, based on a willingness to share ideas and experiment with things. By joining a community, members discover a shared way of thinking and acting. They not only swap ideas but also see each other's creations. This is strengthened when they take part in events, such as meetups and fairs, where they can touch the objects and talk with their creators. Lastly, members of a community of practice develop a set of practical skills and produce communal resources such as plans and recipes, getting pleasure from seeing these used by others.

Tools for learning through making

Maker culture has been driven in part by new affordable tools such as 3D printers. These offer production methods, hardware and software previously only accessible to commercial or academic organizations. Freely available web tools, such as Google SketchUp, for producing and sharing designs, cheap single-board computers and sensors have encouraged widespread experimentation with computing projects that interact with the real world: air pollution monitors, footballing robots and clothing with embedded sensors. Online sharing of designs and plans have encouraged the creation of custom-made components, models and artefacts such as jewellery and clothing.

Maker culture embraces a wide range of activities from the high-tech (electronics, programming, computer-aided design) to craft skills, such as sewing, woodworking and soldering. It encourages novel applications of technologies and explores intersections between traditionally separate domains – for example, computer-controlled knitting machines or 3D printed jewellery. New technologies, such as the Raspberry Pi computer on a single printed circuit board and the Arduino open-source electronics prototyping device, offer tools for practical experimentation.

Maker culture has attracted the interest of educators concerned about students' disengagement from STEM subjects (science, technology, engineering and mathematics) in school. Students can find new pathways into engineering that make the subject lively and relevant. The essence of engineering is the creative application of principles to designing and testing practical objects. So, engineering doesn't need to be restricted to engines and bridges. An engineering approach can be applied to any tangible object.

Online communities of interest

Online communities, such as Pinterest, provide the means to share practical knowledge through visual inspirations, designs and recipes. Meeting sites, such as Meetup and Eventbrite, let people join and later organize events. The maker culture celebrates informal, networked, peer-led and shared learning motivated by fun and self-fulfilment.

Proponents argue that the networked aspect is a key distinction between this and earlier construction-centred affinity groups, such as a local woodwork or sewing club. It gives a far larger sphere of communication. It doesn't matter if you are the only person in town interested in building air-pollution monitors on your Raspberry Pi computer: somebody elsewhere in the world will be interested in sharing their plans and designs with you.

Maker culture offers examples of self-organized social learning that can be taken up in school projects and after-school clubs, but also in informal learning environments, such as museums, libraries and community-based settings.

Maker culture in practice

Vigyan Ashram in Pune, India, has run a Fab Lab since 2002. Its aim is to use modern technology to learn how to solve rural problems. Projects have included designing and building an egg incubator and a sanitary incinerator, using tools such as plasma metal cutters and 3D printers. The Lab runs Fab Camps in digital fabrication with projects for beginners. It now provides a full-time course over six months in digital fabrication at its Fab Academy.

Albermarle County Public Schools comprise 26 schools in Virginia, USA. Each school has a commitment to learning through making, which it implements in its own way. One school has a dedicated makerspace; another has mobile carts with equipment; another runs a design engineering camp in a local community room.

At Ocean City Primary School in New Jersey, USA, a class of 8-year-old students were set a broad project to create something that would help the school community and solve a problem. After much discussion, one student suggested building a makerspace. With the help of their teacher, they wrote a proposal to the school board, gained funding and found a room. Their original plans for craft materials and 3D printers were too expensive, with the materials needing to be replaced each year. So, they proposed a Lego makerspace. All the furniture in their room is made from Lego-like blocks (from a company called EverBlocks) and its storage units are filled with 65,000 Lego bricks for building robots, race cars, landmarks and even a water piano.

Conclusions

Maker culture has been criticized as being a parody of factory labour, with privileged youth playing at constructing objects from expensive pre-fabricated parts. Some maker events are just that. But maker culture is also about creating a community of apprenticeship, producing and exhibiting objects, sharing plans and designs and learning through a cycle of design, build and test. The essence of maker culture is to see everyday objects as playgrounds to be explored and other people as co-creators.

Resources

Arduino, an open source electronics prototyping platform for artists, designers and hobbyists:
www.arduino.cc

Raspberry Pi – a single board computer for computer projects:
www.raspberrypi.org

Air Pi: an environmental sensor kit based on the Raspberry Pi computer, devised by UK school children:
airpi.es

The Restart Project: a recycling group encouraging people to have fun and learn skills fixing their broken electronic equipment rather than throwing them away:
therestartproject.org

Vigyan Ashram Fab Lab in Pune, India:
http://vigyanashram.com/InnerPages/FabLab.aspx

Maker Faire movement and Maker Share community to share projects, run by Make: magazine:
https://makerfaire.com/
https://makershare.com/

Albermarle County Public Schools maker education:
make.k12albemarle.org

Makerspace at Ocean City Primary School:
Kohr, R. (2017). A makerspace built by elementary students. *Edutopia*, November 27, 2017.
https://edut.to/2AniP9M

Open-source knitting machine:
Salomone, A. (2014). OpenKnit: An open source knitting machine. *Make:*, February 20, 2014.
http://bit.ly/2S5ScwZ

Maker culture as a heightened sensitivity and capacity to shape one's world:
http://bit.ly/2yTkFNJ

Introduction to Communities of Practice from learningtheories.com:
http://bit.ly/2S57dPL

Critique of maker culture:
Chachra, D. (2015). Why I am not a maker. *The Atlantic*, Jan 23, 2015.
http://bit.ly/2R2PgQn

This chapter draws on material from *Innovating Pedagogy 2013*, published under a Creative Commons Attribution Licence:
Sharples, M., McAndrew, P., Weller, M., Ferguson, R., FitzGerald, E., Hirst, T., & Gaved, M. (2013). *Innovating Pedagogy 2013: Open University Innovation Report 2*. Milton Keynes: The Open University.

Bricolage   **33**
Tinker creatively with resources

Overview

Bricolage is a practical process of learning through tinkering. It involves continual transformation of physical and cultural items, with earlier products or materials that are ready to hand becoming resources for new constructions. It is a fundamental process of children's learning through play, as they create castles out of boxes. It also forms a basis for creative innovation, allowing inventors to combine and adapt tools and theories to generate new insights, while also engaging with relevant communities to ensure that the innovation works in practice and in context.

Tinkering

The term 'bricolage' is French for 'tinkering', or working creatively with whatever tools and resources are available. Originally used in relation to practical activities, such as carpentry, it has since been applied in many fields, from music created by everyday objects like spoons, to cultural identities, such as punk, that are constructed from elements of other cultures.

Improvisation with tools and materials

There are two uses of the term 'bricolage' with relevance to pedagogy. The first refers to the ways in which people learn by improvising around materials. Children learn how to relate to others and to tell stories by playing games with toys and props, such as chairs and sheets. Students of art and drama learn the skills of improvisation with found materials and their own bodies. To combine these in productive ways to produce a deliberate effect is the creativity of bricolage – it is what distinguishes playing with sand from building sandcastles, hitting objects from creating stomp music, scribbling from doodling. Through bricolage, both the learner and the materials are transformed, so that two chairs and a sheet become a house in which children can play at being parents.

It follows that children can be encouraged to learn through imaginative play by providing them with a rich environment of objects that they can combine and modify. What is fascinating is that young children are able to engage in long periods of learning through bricolage, building castles or creating pretend homes, making up stories as they play, without the need for an adult teacher. Rather than seeing this pretend play as training for adult life, to be replaced by school education as they mature, perhaps we should be exploring how young children's bricolage can contribute towards a new theory and practice of creative adult education. Bricolage develops sensitivity to the forms, properties and uses of materials that are important for professions ranging from cooking to chemistry, architecture to engineering.

Practices of educational innovation

The second use of 'bricolage' in education relates to engaging in innovation by creative exploration of the practices and technologies needed to achieve an educational goal. In the classroom, a teacher creates a lesson out of the current educational materials, classroom practices and skills of the pupils. At a larger scale, researchers and entrepreneurs develop innovations in education from resources that are available locally.

Jon Dron offers ten principles and patterns for effective bricolage:

1. Do not design – just build.
2. Start with pieces that are fully formed and useful.
3. Surround yourself with both quantity and diversity in tools, materials, methods and perspectives.
4. Dabble hard – gain skills, but be suspicious of expertise.
5. Look for exaptations (unintentional side-effects) and surf the adjacent possible (possible near futures).
6. Avoid schedules and goals, but make time and space for tinkering and include time for daydreaming.
7. Do not fear dismantling and starting afresh.

8. Beware of teams, but cultivate networks: seek people, not processes.
9. Talk with your creations and listen to what they have to say.
10. Reflect and tell stories about your reflections, especially to others.

Trying things out

Innovation in education has similarities to innovation in many other areas – such product design, pharmaceuticals, mathematics and entrepreneurship. It is a process of well-informed 'trying things out to see how they work'. Tim Berners Lee, developer of the World Wide Web, described how he developed the web from many sources, including the educational theories of Seymour Papert and the HyperCard software that was available on Apple computers at the time.

The World Wide Web began as a way for scientists to learn by sharing information. Berners Lee first wrote a simple computer program called Enquire that kept track of people and programs across different computer systems. The practical process of developing the Enquire code led him to a larger vision of a system to support the decentralized growth of ideas across the world. He describes this process as "the swirling together of influences, ideas, and realizations from many sides, until, by the wondrous offices of the human mind, a new concept jelled". It was a process of bricolage, not the linear solving of one well-defined problem after another.

Big, expansive innovations, such as the World Wide Web, mobile learning or Massive Open Online Courses (MOOCs), not only arose from a process of bricolage, they are themselves sites of bricolage as people use them to explore new methods of teaching and learning.

Bricolage in educational technology

Figure 33.1 shows a process of bricolage for new educational technology. One or more people have a vision for educational change. This is based on a combination of their practical experience, knowledge of educational practices, existing educational technology and technology developments in the wider society. All these provide material for a sustained bricolage that can last many years as the new methods are researched, tested at small scale in classrooms or workplaces and expanded. Sometimes promising developments are abandoned, only to be resurrected for a new generation of technology, educational theory and practice. The best innovations become sites for playful exploration, by inventors and entrepreneurs as well as teachers and learners.

For example, work on mobile learning started in the early 1970s with a vision, from Alan Kay and colleagues at Xerox Palo Alto research centre, of

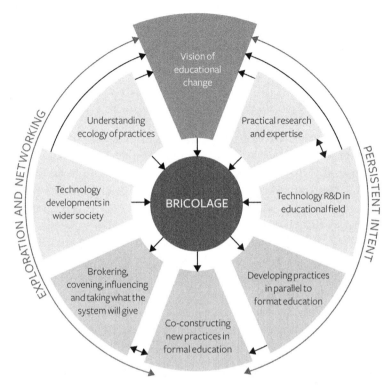

Figure 33.1 The role of bricolage in the innovation process for technology-enhanced learning (from Scanlon et al., 2014, *Beyond Prototypes*)

a Dynabook as a thin portable computer for 'children of all ages'. This idea of a mobile computer for learning reappeared in the early 2000s with educational software on early tablet and handheld computers. Mobile learning then became mainstream in 2010 with the Apple iPad. It's no coincidence that the iPad looks remarkably similar to the 1970s Dynabook concept. It took 40 years of bricolage by individuals and companies with different technologies to realize the early vision of a handheld computer for learning.

Modern technologies for learning – mobile devices, virtual reality, artificial intelligent tutoring – may be marketed as new and exciting, but they all are the result of many years of tinkering and testing in labs and classrooms.

Testing constraints and learning from failure

At a more abstract level, bricolage is a continual testing of constraints and the structures within which imaginative play occurs. Too much constraint means that creativity is stifled; too little constraint and the activity becomes disorganized and formless. The other side of bricolage is evidence. In order to make progress, as a person or as an organization, we need to base new practices on evidence of success and on learning from productive failure. Each insight emerges from a process of testing what does and does not work in practice, and so becomes a resource for further creative exploration.

Bricolage in practice

Bricolage Academy is a tuition-free open-enrolment public school in New Orleans, USA. Its aim is to develop children as creative problem solvers through innovation focused on design, engineering and creativity. For example, on their 'shop nights', parents, teachers and students come together to build devices such as marble runs out of materials like cardboard that are ready to hand.

The Yoza Project is an example of bricolage in educational technology. It started with a novel written for mobile devices. Readers were invited to interact with it as it unfolded. Teens could discuss the plot, vote in polls and submit sequels. This grew into a project to support young people in South Africa to read works of fiction by distributing them to mobile phones. The project team considers the main innovations to include not only the use of phones for delivery of the novels but also the availability of really engaging local stories, with readers able to comment as they read and to see other people's comments. The Yoza Project has now been incorporated into a larger enterprise called FunDza, to get young people reading.

Conclusions

Bricolage is a fairly simple term to understand – it refers to playing in a creative way with things that are ready to hand. It has power to describe how children play creatively with everyday objects such as cardboard or stones, making fantasy worlds and telling stories. It can also describe a more abstract process of innovation through playing with a combination of ideas and tools until new concepts start to form. Rather than seeing these as separate forms of creative play by children and by adults, we might look for ways to teach children how to improvise like adults as well as exploring how the bricolage of young children can contribute towards a theory and practice of adult innovation.

Resources

Bricolage Academy in New Orleans:
http://bricolagenola.org/

Yoza cellphone stories:
m4lit.wordpress.com
www.yoza.mobi

Dynabook project:
http://history-computer.com/ModernComputer/Personal/Dynabook.html

Brief history of the World Wide Web:
Lumsden, A. (2012). *A Brief History of the World Wide Web*. Envato Tuts+.

Introduction of the term bricolage in relation to creative play:
Lévi-Strauss, C. (1962). *La pensée sauvage*. Paris: Librairie Plon. Translated into English as
    The Savage Mind Chicago: Chicago University Press, 1966.

Educational theory and practice of learning through creative play:
Papert, S. (1980). *Mindstorms: Children, Computers, and Powerful Ideas*. New York: Basic Books.
http://bit.ly/2Alyd6t

Ten principles for effective tinkering:
Dron, J. (2014). Ten principles for effective tinkering. In *Proceedings of World Conference on
    E-Learning in Corporate, Government, Healthcare, and Higher Education 2014*, pp. 505–513.
    Chesapeake, VA: Association for the Advancement of Computing in Education (AACE).
http://bit.ly/2NXs5Vy

Role of bricolage in innovation for technology-enhanced learning:
Scanlon, E., Sharples, M., Fenton-O'Creevy, M., Fleck, J., et al. (2014). *Beyond Prototypes:
    Enabling Innovation in Technology-Enhanced Learning*. London: Technology Enhanced
    Learning Research Programme.
http://bit.ly/2q41Q6r

This chapter draws on material from *Innovating Pedagogy 2014*, published under a Creative
Commons Attribution Licence:
Sharples, M., Adams, A., Ferguson, R., Gaved, M., McAndrew, P., Rienties, B., Weller, M., &
    Whitelock, D. (2014). *Innovating Pedagogy 2014: Open University Innovation Report 3*. Milton
    Keynes: The Open University.

Design thinking   **34**
Apply design methods to solve problems

Overview

Design thinking is about solving problems using the methods and thinking processes of designers. These include creative processes such as experimenting, creating and prototyping models, soliciting feedback and redesigning. Design thinking places learners in contexts that make them think like designers, creating innovative solutions to address people's needs. Learners need to solve technical problems, but they also need to understand how users will feel when employing the solutions. Design thinking is a social as well as a mental process. It requires thinking and working across different perspectives and often involves conflict and negotiation. For example, students designing an educational computer game need to think from the perspective of a good teacher as well as from the perspective of a game player. As a pedagogy, design thinking may involve civic literacy, cultural awareness, critical and creative thinking as well as technical skills. When implementing this approach in the classroom, the teacher and students need to take risks and try new methods.

How designers think

The term 'design thinking' was popularized by two books in the 1980s. In *How Designers Think*, the designer and psychologist Bryan Lawson summarizes design thinking as adventurous generation of ideas combined with focused solving of problems. In *Design Thinking*, Peter Rowe describes processes of design in architecture and urban planning, supported by observations of designers at work.

Rowe describes design thinking as a series of 'skirmishes' or 'engaged episodes' with the problem at hand, exploring the relationships between form, structure and technical issues. During each skirmish, a typical designer engages in unconstrained speculation, followed by sober reflection to understand the situation. The skirmish takes on a life of its own, with the designer becoming absorbed in its possibilities and constraints. After that, the designer switches to a process of solving problems, working out the issues needed to bring the design into reality.

Thus, design thinking is more than just creativity or 'thinking outside the box'. It involves a series of episodes that combine creativity with critical thinking, followed by analysis and construction. Designers work with the constraints of their materials – concrete and glass for an architect, or colours and computer code for a web designer – employing these constraints as resources to make decisions about what will be elegant and what will work in practice. Designers also backtrack when they reach a mental block, returning to an earlier stage or exploring a different route.

Principles of design thinking

The books by Lawson and Rowe, together with more recent observation and interview studies of designers at work, have provided a set of principles for design thinking.

1. Design thinkers embrace diverse perspectives. They explore or develop competing alternatives while making choices. They do not jump to immediate solutions. Having more than one solution or idea allows them to understand the problem and evaluate possibilities.
2. Design thinkers combine interdisciplinary knowledge and skills to generate solutions, which may be based on their practical experience.
3. Design thinkers are focused on products. They understand the properties and constraints of materials, working within these constraints while testing the boundaries.
4. Design thinkers possess strong visual literacy. They sketch and develop their ideas visually. This not only makes the ideas more comprehensible and compelling but also helps them see pitfalls, misunderstandings and opportunities that verbal discussion may not reveal.
5. Design thinkers do more than resolve technical problems. They explore how their designs will respond to human needs and interests.
6. Design thinkers look beyond the immediate project and its requirements. They understand the process of design and may invent new design tools or improved ways of working for future design effort.

7. Design thinkers are adept team workers who can effectively work in group settings towards a common goal. They develop and apply inter-personal skills to communicate across disciplines and solve problems collaboratively.
8. Design thinkers are oriented to action. They intend to make changes to the world, in small or big ways.

A long-running course on design thinking at The Open University indicates some properties of designed artefacts that influence the way designers work.

All designed things have a structure, usually made up of many parts. Assembling these parts is a rhythmic activity – the visual equivalent of playing music.

Symmetry brings a sense of order to the design. Asymmetry offers oppor-tunities for more complex and provocative assembly. There are guidelines for achieving attractive proportions in design. These can be traced back to ancient Greece and the Golden Ratio.

Composition involves emphasis through colour, size, position. It also bal-ances positive and negative space.

All these principles are made to be broken. The essence of creative design is understanding where there are rules and constraints, then exploring what hap-pens when these are pushed and flouted.

Design thinking in education

As a pedagogy, the essence of design thinking is to put learners into con-texts that make them think and work like expert designers. Design think-ing can be applied to any subject area that creates innovative products to address people's needs, including engineering, architecture, medicine, computer programming, website production and creative writing. The principles and practices of design thinking are being adopted for industrial and media design courses in college and vocational education. In teacher education, design thinking has been employed to help school teachers with lesson planning.

Typically, students work in pairs or groups on a project of personal mean-ing or community importance. For example, school students might design a school desk suited to collaborative working, then display their products to other students in an exhibition. One issue in design projects for schools is how to provide the sense of satisfaction produced by a completed design project. Just designing a school desk, but not seeing it built and tested may leave the impres-sion that design is only a paper exercise. It is better to propose designs that can be constructed and put into use.

Design thinking in practice

A pioneer of design thinking is the Institute of Design at Stanford, also known as the d.school. Its courses and curriculum are based on a process of design thinking during which students cycle rapidly through a series of processes: observe, brainstorm, synthesize, prototype and implement. The d.school acts as an innovation hub for Stanford University, taking students from the arts, medicine, education, law and the social sciences for classes and projects. For example, an online crash course in design thinking from d.school provides all the materials needed for a 90-minute exercise in re-designing the experience of gift giving. The d.school also runs a K12 Lab for professional development of teachers.

The Design Thinking in Schools website lists schools and programs throughout the world that teach design thinking. Entries include the African Leadership Academy that helps students to design and run business and social enterprises; Ekya Schools in Bangalore, India, that run 6–8-week school projects to solve social problems; and Nazarbayev Intellectual Schools in the Republic of Kazakhstan that run design thinking camps for school students across the republic.

Conclusions

As with many new pedagogies, a major challenge to the implementation of design thinking is finding ways to align it with the curriculum and exam system. The goal is not for students to master a topic but to gain enduring competencies and dispositions, to think about their everyday world as a set of interlocking designs and its obstacles as design problems. Design work is demanding, intellectually and practically, for students and teachers. Students require modelling and support from teachers. Teachers need repeated practice to become effective facilitators. All must embrace the uncertainties and open-ended nature of design problems, taking a positive attitude to acceptable risk and failure.

Resources

Online crash course in design thinking offered by Stanford University Institute of Design: dschool.stanford.edu/dgift/

Toolkit for educators in designing learning experiences, classrooms, schools and communities:
IDEO (2012). *Design Thinking for Educators Toolkit*.
https://designthinkingforeducators.com/toolkit/

Free online short course on design thinking from The Open University, UK:
http://bit.ly/2ySLEZW

Resources for design thinking in schools:
www.designthinkinginschools.com/resources

List of schools engaged in design thinking:
www.designthinkinginschools.com/directory

How designers address 'wicked problems' that have no simple definition nor single solution:
Buchanan, R. (1992). Wicked problems in design thinking. *Design Issues*, 8(2), 5–21.
www.jstor.org/stable/1511637

Detailed study of an interdisciplinary design curriculum in a school, unpacking key characteristics of design thinking:
Carroll, M., Goldman, S., Britos, L., Koh, J., Royalty, A., & Hornstein, M. (2010). Destination, imagination and the fires within: Design thinking in a middle school classroom. *International Journal of Art & Design Education*, 29(1), 37–53.
https://stanford.io/2D128U0

Three core elements of design thinking explained:
Dorst, K. (2011). The core of 'design thinking' and its application. *Design Studies*, 32(6), 521–532.
http://bit.ly/2EAgGM4

Introduction to design thinking:
Cross, N. (2011). *Design thinking: Understanding How Designers Think and Work*. Oxford, UK: Berg.

Fourth edition of a classic book on design thinking, originally published in 1980:
Lawson, B. (2005). *How Designers Think: The Design Process Demystified* (4th edition). London: The Architectural Press.

Uncovering the thought processes of designers in action:
Rowe, P. (1987). *Design Thinking*. Cambridge, MA: MIT Press.

Design thinking applied to the process of creative writing:
Sharples, M. (1999). *How We Write: Writing as Creative Design*. London: Routledge.

This chapter draws on material from *Innovating Pedagogy 2016*, published under a Creative Commons Attribution Licence:
Sharples, M., de Roock, R., Ferguson, R., Gaved, M., Herodotou, C., Koh, E., Kukulska-Hulme, A., Looi, C.-K., McAndrew, P., Rienties, B., Weller, M., & Wong, L. H. (2016). *Innovating Pedagogy 2016: Open University Innovation Report 5*. Milton Keynes: The Open University.

Part VI

Scale

Massive open social learning

35

Free online courses based on social learning

Overview

Massive open social learning brings benefits of collaborative learning and social networking to people taking Massive Open Online Courses (MOOCs). It exploits the 'network effect' where the value of a networked experience increases as more people join in. The aim is to engage thousands of people in productive discussions and the creation of shared projects. Together, they share experiences and build on their previous knowledge. A challenge to this approach is that these learners typically only meet online and for short periods of time. Approaches include linking conversations with learning content, creating short-duration discussion groups made up of learners who are currently online and enabling learners to review each other's assignments. Other techniques, drawn from social media and gaming, include building links by following other learners, rating discussion comments and competing with others to answer quizzes and take on learning challenges.

Massive open online courses

In Massive Open Online Courses (MOOCs), tens of thousands of people access free courses online. Some early MOOC experiments were based on a pedagogy of connectivist learning, where many people and their ideas are connected in a loose online network to learn together. While this approach harnesses the power of many voices and technologies, it is difficult to manage at large scale and requires learners to know how to navigate the web resources and engage with their peers.

More recent MOOCs have taken an instructivist approach. A university creates the course materials and delivers these by video and text. Learners watch the videos, read the text and take quizzes to test their knowledge. While this allows the learner to control where and when to learn, pausing and reflecting on the material, it can be a lonely experience. There are forums for learners to discuss the course and some people may get together in scheduled meetings, but more can be done to engage people as active learners, sharing their ideas and discussing their different perspectives as they learn online.

The social learning effect

The big question is, 'Which pedagogies can improve with scale?'. Some effective methods of teaching, such as sports coaching or personal tutoring, cannot scale up to thousands of learners without huge costs (researchers in artificial intelligence have been attempting for many years to develop computer-based personal tutors). By contrast, methods of direct instruction scale well. A good educational television program can inform a hundred people, a thousand or a million – but television programs are not effective in engaging people in active and reflective learning.

A general theory of scale can be applied to education. The 'network effect' proposes that the value of a networked product or service increases with the number of people using it. For example, a telephone system becomes more valuable when it connects millions, or billions, of phone users worldwide. The World Wide Web benefits millions of interconnected people and their computers. But people are not just points in a network – we have knowledge and perspectives to share. So, the 'social learning effect' can be stated as 'the value of a networked learning system increases as it enables more people to learn easily and successfully from each other'. The more people who take part in social learning, the greater the diversity of their contributions.

Massive open social learning in practice

An example of a large-scale social learning system is Stack Exchange, with over 5 million users. In Stack Exchange, people pose problems, then other members of the community offer answers. Yet more people expand these answers and rate the contributions, so the most interesting questions and the best answers rise to the top – they become more visible to all users. As more people take part, the range of questions is greater, the answers are more varied and the recommendations more powerful.

Another approach to massive open social learning is to support many lines of conversation. The FutureLearn MOOC platform has over 8 million users. Beside each piece of content on FutureLearn is a free-flowing discussion (Figure 35.1). The discussion is prompted by a question from the educator in the video or accompanying text. Any learner can see the discussion about a topic and add a quick contribution or reply. The more people who engage with the course, the faster the discussion flows and the more the content is enhanced with different perspectives.

If online learning environments can harness the power of social interaction, then the more people who take part, the better the learning. Learners enrich the instructional content by sharing their perspectives on a topic or problem. To do this successfully requires the learners to engage with the content and be willing to offer their viewpoints. How can we make sure that people take part openly and constructively? Here are some ways to run effective learning at massive scale:

- It's important that everyone engages willingly and not through coercion. If learners are assessed on the quantity or quality of their contributions that may lead them to post many insincere comments, to please the teacher.

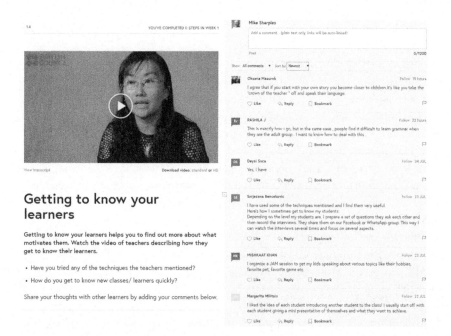

Figure 35.1 A free-flowing discussion alongside a learning element in the 'Teaching for Success: Learning and Learners' FutureLearn course from the British Council

- The educator or platform needs to set good practice by reminding participants to be respectful and to respond constructively to the views of others.
- It's a good idea to begin with a straightforward question that learners can answer from personal experience. For example, a FutureLearn course on 'The Science of Nutrition' starts by asking learners: 'What time did you go to lunch yesterday?'. From that, the course moves on to eating rituals and diets.
- If there is a continual flow of discussion, then negative and unhelpful comments tend to get lost in the flow. Conversely, informative and helpful comments get likes and responses. Learners who search for 'most liked' comments see these and reply further.
- Educators and mentors reply to the most interesting comments, particularly those giving a diversity of views. Then learners who follow the educators can see and respond to those comments. Educators can also feature or pin good comments to the top of the list.
- Question-answering sites, such as Stack Exchange and Quora, prioritize the most liked answers, so learners see these first.

The experience from large-scale social learning environments like Stack Exchange and FutureLearn is that the more the discussion focuses on a specific topic and question, the more the contributions stay relevant and respectful.

Overload and disorientation

Just as telephone networks can become congested and faulty and we may receive nuisance calls, so massive open social learning has its problems. The most obvious of these is overload. A single video on FutureLearn can attract over 15,000 comments. If these are just seen as a flow of conversation, then there is no issue, but if learners feel overwhelmed or believe they may have missed an important comment, then massive scale can cause anxiety. For this reason, discussions in FutureLearn are initially hidden and only shown at the click of a button.

One way to manage this overload is by applying methods of social networking. These include allowing learners to 'like' comments and find 'most liked' comments, and letting educators pin interesting replies at the top of the list.

Another difficulty, experienced by many who have participated in connectivist MOOCs, is the feeling of being 'lost in hyperspace', of having too many options and possibilities, not knowing where they are in a learning activity, who to engage with and where to go next. Challenges for designers of such open social environments include lessening the initial shock of joining for the first time and providing clear guidelines and pathways to progress.

Conclusions

Many consumer technologies have started small, then expanded, then engaged people in networked social interactions. Television, telephones, computers and electronic games are examples of this development pathway. In a similar way, innovative pedagogies generally start small and then increase in scale and sociability. MOOCs, seamless learning, game-based learning, personal inquiry and geo-learning are all now developing as large-scale social activities. This means they face the issues of how to reap the benefits of the 'network effect' while avoiding congestion, overload and disorientation.

Resources

Question-answering and social help sites include:
stackexchange.com
www.answers.com
www.quora.com
www.ehow.com

FutureLearn social learning platform:
www.futurelearn.com

Learners on connectivist MOOCs (cMOOCs) build understanding by connecting with others:
http://bit.ly/2PRk3Q9

The 'network effect', popularized by Robert Metcalfe, states that some network goods or services increase in value as more people are connected:
Metcalfe, R. M. (2007). It's all in your head. *Forbes Online*, April 20, 2007.
http://bit.ly/2OFljsU

Personal network effect (the value of social learning):
Downes, S. (2007). The personal network effect. Blog posting, November 20, 2007.
http://bit.ly/2EDr6L3

Massive-scale social learning in MOOCs:
Ferguson, R., & Sharples, M. (2014). Innovative pedagogy at massive scale: Teaching and learning in MOOCs. In C. Rensing, S. de Freitas, T. Ley & P. J. Muñoz-Merino (Eds.), *Open Learning and Teaching in Educational Communities, Proceedings of 9th European Conference on Technology Enhanced Learning*, Graz, Austria, September 16–19, pp. 98–111. Heidelberg: Springer.
http://bit.ly/2PNvt78

Hypertext and lost in hyperspace:
Conklin, J. (1987). Hypertext: An introduction and survey, *IEEE Computer*, 20(9), 17–41.
http://bit.ly/2yov1pt

This chapter draws on material from *Innovating Pedagogy 2014*, published under a Creative Commons Attribution Licence:
Sharples, M., Adams, A., Ferguson, R., Gaved, M., McAndrew, P., Rienties, B., Weller, M., & Whitelock, D. (2014). *Innovating Pedagogy 2014: Open University Innovation Report 3*. Milton Keynes: The Open University.

Crowd learning   **36**

Harness the local knowledge
of many people

Overview

Engaging with the crowd gives access to valuable sources of knowledge and opinion. Amateurs and experts exchange ideas, generate and discuss content, solve problems, vote for the best solutions and raise funds. A classic example of the crowd in action is Wikipedia, the online encyclopedia co-created and continually updated by the public. Other examples include citizen science activities, such as identifying birds and classifying galaxies. However, we are not yet using the wisdom of the crowd to its full potential as a resource in education and for learning. Applications of crowdsourcing in education include collecting and curating teaching resources, letting students share and discuss their work online and providing opinions and data for use in projects and research studies. Approaches to crowd learning need to consider the quality and validity of the contributions that are made by the public and how to work towards both a consensus and a diversity of views.

Crowdsourcing

Crowdsourcing involves members of the public giving and receiving information to solve problems, create content, vote for the best solutions or raise funds. Online crowdsourcing platforms, such as Wikipedia, Reddit and IdeaScale, allow amateurs to exchange ideas with experts, combining wisdom of the crowds with expert knowledge and commentary.

Wikipedia is a leading example of how people work together to produce and negotiate content for the largest encyclopedia in the world. What makes Wikipedia different from previous encyclopedias is that anyone can add or edit content. Stated like that, Wikipedia seems to be a recipe for anarchy and disinformation. But as it matured, policies were put in place by the community of Wikipedia authors to identify deliberate vandalism, stop abuse and resolve disputes. The basic principles of Wikipedia could be applied to any site for crowdsourcing:

- Anyone can edit most of the content.
- People who have registered and contributed to the site have more privileges (including moving articles, voting and undoing changes).
- People who have made substantial contributions can apply to be administrators and the community votes to accept them. Administrators can delete articles, protect them from further changes and edit protected articles.
- An arbitration committee elected by the community attempts to resolve any major disputes.
- The community sets a few general rules of good behaviour, such as requiring unbiased writing, verified content and reliable sources.

Alongside each article in Wikipedia is a discussion about what should be included and how it should be written. The history of changes is also visible. While these principles and practices are not perfect, they have enabled Wikipedia to become a huge up-to-date source of information.

Most importantly, Wikipedia and other similar sites of crowdsourced knowledge can be tools for learning. Students can learn by reading Wikipedia articles and comparing them with published reference books. Which is the more accurate, complete, up to date? Students can learn by critiquing Wikipedia articles and understanding how they are created. Does the crowdsourced process produce articles that represent a richness and diversity of views? Students can learn by editing content – *anyone* can edit most of the pages in Wikipedia (though the changes will not last long if they are badly written, inaccurate or irrelevant). Students can learn by discussing changes with other contributors. Lastly, students can learn about crowdsourcing and discuss whether or not it is a better way to create knowledge than traditional publishing.

Citizen science

Citizen science is a form of crowdsourcing for scientific or research projects. Scientists propose a project, such as spotting and counting birds, plants or insects. They set up a website for members of the public to take part in the activity and to see the results. A long-running citizen science project is the Christmas Bird Count in the United States. It started in 1900 and still continues, with thousands of volunteers counting bird species in a 15-mile circle. A similar annual project in the UK, the Big Garden Birdwatch, involves up to half a million people each year in counting bird species in their gardens.

Online citizen science sets up websites for mass participation in science activities. The Zooniverse site is a compendium of online citizen projects ranging across sciences, humanities and arts. A typical Zooniverse project is Wildwatch Kenya. A team of scientists in Kenya has set up 100 motion-activated cameras to automatically take photographs of animals as they pass by. Volunteers on the website view these photos and identify and count the animals in each one. The scientists then interpret these logs to understand animal migration.

Students taking part in a citizen science activity can learn by collecting data and making careful records and by viewing tables and charts from the thousands of contributions to understand how they change over time and location.

Crowd learning in practice

Crowd learning can be connected with school education. The investigation may form part of a worldwide citizen science initiative, such as the EarthEcho Water Challenge. Thousands of schools and individuals test their local water for acidity, oxygen, temperature and cloudiness. They share results on a world map and post stories of cleaning their local beach or river.

A project in Ethiopia and Tanzania engaged schoolgirls in proposing solutions to why many girls do not finish secondary school. It recruited girls, their families, community leaders and education officers, listened to their issues and empowered them to make changes, such as setting up safe areas for girls in schools.

A classic crowd learning project for schools was BBC Domesday. In the mid-1980s, the BBC ran a project to capture a digital snapshot of life in the United Kingdom. It recruited over one million school students, teachers and parents across the country to take photos and describe life in their local area. These were put onto the latest technology at the time – videodiscs – containing over 147,819 pages of text and 23,225 amateur photos. In 2011, the BBC managed to put much of the original content online and again asked children, and their parents who had taken part in the original project, to record local life in 2011. The archive is a fascinating comparison of local areas seen through the eyes of children at two points in time.

Conclusions

Crowd learning can serve to educate the public and let children become investigators. But it brings challenges. An expert may be needed to distinguish a valid investigation from pseudo-science. In school crowdsourcing, the teacher may be faced with the difficult task of collating and interpreting data from many students and their friends. It may be difficult to persuade others to join a project. Crowd learning is still at an early stage and more work is needed to develop good ideas and successful online environments.

Resources

Article on crowdsourcing and education, mentioning the UNESCO project in Ethiopia and Tanzania:
Edwards, J. (2017). How crowdsourcing is changing education. *InnoCentive*, December 28, 2017.
https://blog.innocentive.com/how-crowdsourcing-is-changing-education

EarthEcho Water Challenge:
www.worldwatermonitoringday.org

Zooniverse site for people-powered research:
www.zooniverse.org

Reddit crowdsource site for registered members to submit, vote on and discuss news content:
www.reddit.com

IdeaScale platform for people to submit, vote on and discuss ideas, then for teams to implement the best ideas:
ideascale.com

Christmas Bird Count:
https://www.audubon.org/conservation/science/christmas-bird-count

Big Schools Birdwatch, for schools to count birds across the UK:
https://www.rspb.org.uk/fun-and-learning/for-teachers/schools-birdwatch/

Wikipedia, crowdsourced online encyclopedia, available in 301 languages:
https://meta.wikimedia.org/wiki/List_of_Wikipedias

Handling disputes in Wikipedia:
http://bit.ly/2yTl5nc

BBC Domesday project archive:
http://bit.ly/2Pc50U2

This chapter draws on material from *Innovating Pedagogy 2016*, published under a Creative Commons Attribution Licence:
Sharples, M., de Roock, R., Ferguson, R., Gaved, M., Herodotou, C., Koh, E., Kukulska-Hulme, A., Looi, C.-K., McAndrew, P., Rienties, B., Weller, M., & Wong, L. H. (2016). *Innovating Pedagogy 2016: Open University Innovation Report 5*. Milton Keynes: The Open University.

Citizen inquiry   **37**
Fuse inquiry-based learning and citizen activism

Overview

Citizen inquiry involves members of the public in devising and running mass-participation investigations. It turns people from being consumers of scientific findings into active producers. For each investigation, people gather evidence of similar successful projects, create a plan of action, carry out an investigation along with many others, collect data with desktop and mobile technologies as research tools and validate and share results. They learn about the topic, how to be a scientist and how to collaborate.

From citizen science to citizen inquiry

Citizen science involves thousands of people in collecting data or solving problems to assist scientists in their investigations. Citizen inquiry turns this relationship around – citizens devise the investigations and scientists offer assistance.

Current citizen science projects, such as Galaxy Zoo, Foldit and iSpot, involve citizens in classifying objects, solving puzzles or observing wildlife, but scientists set the research questions and methods. Some platforms, such as Kickstarter and GoFundMe, do support members of the public to fund and organize creative projects, but they are not underpinned by a model of scientific inquiry.

The aim of citizen inquiry is to combine the creative knowledge building of inquiry-based learning, the excitement of scientific discovery and the mass civic engagement of volunteer activism. In citizen inquiry, citizens of all ages can take part in the entire process.

Learning through citizen inquiry

There is a growing desire to involve people without scientific training in practical science investigations. An editorial in *Science* magazine argues that wider personal engagement in "carefully designed, hands-on, inquiry-based exploration of the world" will inform public debate and may lead to scientific breakthroughs.

Inquiry-based learning is a powerful method for coming to understand the natural and social world through guided investigation. It is a process of exploring and then reflecting on the experience. By doing science, rather than reading about or observing it, students learn how hard it is to propose a testable question and to collect reliable results. They also experience the excitement of making discoveries and the challenge of presenting findings. The process of inquiry learning extends beyond the physical sciences – it can be a way of finding out about ourselves, our communities and our world.

Citizen inquiry extends this process to learning about how to cooperate and share. The transformative idea is to open up to citizens of all ages the process of proposing, commissioning, conducting and reporting inquiry-led scientific projects. In any citizen-inquiry project, there will be a range of expertise about the topic and knowledge of how to run a good investigation. At the start, anyone can dip into previous projects and see the data. Then each person chooses how to get involved. Some people will view the contributions of others, some will decide to analyze data and some will contribute their own data, some will set up new investigations and some with scientific training will act as guides and mentors.

Most projects are likely to be small scale and for mutual interest, involving people freely sharing a range of expertise. Some may be larger scale, involving mass participation in observation and experiment, for example to address a community issue, such as reducing plastic waste. The challenge for everyone involved is how to keep the investigation going and on the right track – so that it is carefully designed, ethical and robust.

The longest-running citizen inquiry project has been Mass Observation. It started in 1937 by three young men to create an "anthropology of ourselves". Then during the Second World War, it blossomed into a citizen study of the everyday lives of ordinary people in Britain. Volunteer observers went into public situations, ranging from pubs to churches, and recorded people's behaviour and conversations. The material they produced is a rich and varied documentary account of life during the war. Mass Observation still continues, with a panel of citizens writing their observations on topics such as changes in coffee drinking ('real coffee' stated making an appearance in Britain during Christmas 1986) or where on their bodies people carry money and credit cards. It may seem, and sometimes is, intrusive. From the outset, Mass Observers were seen as busybodies, prying into other people's lives. A challenge for citizen inquiry is how to inquire into ourselves and our communities without trespassing on privacy.

The Boston bombings of April 2013 were an outrage. They were also a salutary lesson about the dangers of citizen inquiry. On that occasion, amateur investigators analyzed photos and video that had been uploaded to public websites, then they posted accusations of suspects. These were repeated by the mass media. A consequence was that innocent people had their lives disrupted by false accusations. Citizen inquiry can be a powerful form of learning through citizen collaboration in scientific practices; it can also be a rallying point for mutual delusion.

Future developments

Citizen inquiry could be developed as extensions of current citizen science projects, offering additional opportunities for individuals and groups to devise new investigations, guiding people through the process of creating and running a study. But the area of interest has to be one that members of the public can devise.

Local wildlife and nature form one starting point for citizen inquiry. For example, a school could decide to find out which kinds of plants attract the most butterflies, design their own investigation and communicate their results. The initial motivation comes from personal curiosity about a topic, which is then maintained by forming or joining a group of investigators with similar interests and a diversity of contexts.

Although the concept seems straightforward – helping groups of like-minded people to join together in carrying out careful investigations of scientific value – there are substantial barriers to success. Devising a scientific question is a challenging task. It may not be the 'big science' of medical advances or scientific breakthroughs, but it should be personally relevant to the participants and also have wider meaning and validity, adopting methods recognized by the scientific community. For that to happen, creators of the project need guidance on choosing relevant topics, setting questions that can be answered through collective inquiry and collecting and analyzing data through rigorous and sharable methods. It isn't clear whether non-scientists in ad hoc teams can plan or adopt inquiry processes that follow the good practices of professional science.

Citizen inquiry in practice

The Family and Community Historical Research Society (FACHRS) carries out collective research into life within local communities. In a FACHRS research project, a group of people commit to carrying out a study around a central theme, exploring local and regional differences. Examples include exploring how seasons affect marriage in a community, how a community copes with crime and how local newspapers influence a community. The Society publishes a journal with a variety of papers from academics and society members.

Zooniverse and nQuire are two sites for people, schools or communities to manage citizen inquiry projects. Zooniverse projects typically involve recruiting members of the public to interpret data (usually images). Any registered user can create a project and set tasks for volunteers to do. In a typical Zooniverse project, the creator provides images or other data, then volunteers answer questions about the images or mark features. For example, the creator of a Zooniverse project may provide a large set of pictures taken by an automatic web camera in the school grounds, then volunteers identify wildlife.

The nQuire platform also allows any member of the public to start a project (which it calls a 'mission'). Rather than classifying data provided by the creator of the mission, participants in nQuire can upload their own data, which could be images, sounds, numbers or text. An example of an nQuire mission is to create a 'noise map' of a local area by recording noise levels at different locations. Linked to nQuire is the Sense-it software application (app) running on Android phones that allows people to collect data, such as noise levels, on their own phones and upload these to nQuire.

Conclusions

Creating an online community for citizen inquiry requires difficult design decisions. Should it be a place for scientific investigation, or community involvement, or learning how to be a scientist? One solution may be to create an overarching challenge that offers opportunity for open investigation. For example, the Christmas Bird Count involves thousands of people in compiling data on birds in their locality. These data-sets are available to download. Data from this and similar surveys could form the basis for local investigations into threatened species or changes in habitat, which would involve support for creating teams, maintaining interest and rewarding success. Citizen inquiry opens up scientific practices to everyone. This has the potential to be an engaging and exciting pedagogy, but there is much to be done in designing good software platforms and finding out how to support people and groups to run valid, sustainable mass investigations.

Resources

Data for download from the Christmas Bird Count:
http://netapp.audubon.org/cbcobservation/

Family and Community Historical Research Society:
www.fachrs.com

Mass Observation:
www.massobs.org.uk

How to build a project in Zooniverse:
http://bit.ly/2CwHWby

The nQuire site for citizen inquiry:
nquire.org.uk

Galaxy Zoo:
www.zooniverse.org/projects/zookeeper/galaxy-zoo

Foldit:
fold.it/portal

iSpot:
www.ispotnature.org

Kickstarter:
www.kickstarter.com

GoFundMe:
www.gofundme.com

Science editorial referring to the need for wider public engagement in science:
Alberts, B. (2011). Editorial: Science breakthroughs. *Science*, 334(6063), p. 1604.
http://bit.ly/2yvln4j

Article on the dangers of citizen inquiry into crimes:
Wadhwa, T. (2013). Lessons from crowdsourcing the Boston bombing investigation. *Forbes Online*, April 22, 2013.
http://bit.ly/2yt3JOO

A brief history of Mass Observation:
http://www.massobs.org.uk/about/history-of-mo

This chapter draws on material from *Innovating Pedagogy 2013*, published under a Creative Commons Attribution Licence:
Sharples, M., McAndrew, P., Weller, M., Ferguson, R., FitzGerald, E., Hirst, T., & Gaved, M. (2013). *Innovating Pedagogy 2013: Open University Innovation Report 2*. Milton Keynes: The Open University.

Rhizomatic learning   **38**
Self-aware learning communities that adapt to environmental conditions

Overview

A rhizome is a plant stem that sends out a tangled mass of roots to collect nutrients and help the plant to grow. By analogy, rhizomatic learning is gaining knowledge by exploring in many directions, interconnecting with others. It can involve a small or large group of people managing their own learning. Or it can be started by an educator creating the context for learning, then supporting students to grow their knowledge in a dynamic manner. The learning experience may build on social and conversational processes, as well as personal knowledge creation, linked to unbounded personal learning networks that merge formal and informal media.

Democratic education

What would happen if education were completely democratized? What if learners could choose their own curriculum and how to study? What if they could learn alongside many other like-minded people – collecting, sharing and curating resources? That's the big idea behind rhizomatic learning.

Rhizomes resist organizational structure and have no distinct beginning or end. They send out shoots in all directions, the only restrictions to growth being those that exist in the surrounding habitat. Seen as a metaphor for the construction of knowledge, rhizomatic processes suggest the interconnectedness of ideas as well as boundless exploration across many fronts from many different starting points. Dave Cormier has done most work on this as a theory and he suggests that rhizomatic learning is a means by which learners can develop problem-solving skills for complex domains.

Rhizomatic learning builds on many previous approaches to democratize education, including the liberal education espoused by John Dewey, the critical pedagogy of Paulo Freire where education becomes a struggle for freedom and deschooling society proposed by Ivan Illich. In 1971, Illich called for advanced technology to support 'learning webs', where each person indicated their interests and sought other peers for learning together.

It follows that in rhizomatic learning every learner can be a teacher and every teacher can be a learner. Political dissidents may learn together about the changing politics of their country, or citizen scientists may set up collective experiments. As Cormier puts it, "the community is the curriculum". This open curriculum is freely negotiated by all who take part. The participants also choose how to learn and what tools to use. The learning experience may build on social, conversational processes, as well as a personal knowledge-creation process. It can lead to large, unbounded learning networks that may incorporate formal and informal social media.

Learning communities

Academics who bid for and run large research multi-national research projects often engage in rhizomatic learning. They work with colleagues from many countries, many of whom they haven't met face to face. They have to decide on how to collaborate (often very rapidly to meet a deadline), what tools to use in gathering background material and how to write a joint proposal for funding. Then they carry out joint research, adapting the project to results as they emerge.

The Reddit website is a large-scale online community. It lets members submit content – such as links to other websites, text posts and images – which are voted up or down by other members. The site is split into thousands of categories, called subreddits, dedicated to topics, such as specific games, movies, sports or lifestyles. Reddit can be seen as a resource for rhizomatic learning, or alternatively as a case study of the benefits and problems of learning in open communities, including how to deal with harassment.

On a smaller scale, taking part in a group project at school or university can involve deciding on what to learn and how to go about it. What separates rhizomatic learning from peer or networked learning is that everything can be negotiated. The learners, together, establish a context for that particular episode of learning. They decide what tools to use in finding new knowledge through joint investigation and conversation. They establish the curriculum and the bounds on their studies. All these are re-shaped in response to changes in the environment, such as people joining or leaving, emerging ideas or news events.

Supporting rhizomatic learning

For an educator, supporting rhizomatic learning requires helping to create that context within which the participants build the curriculum and construct knowledge. In rhizomatic learning, as Dave Cormier says, 'Google is your friend'. So, another role for the educator is to develop students' skills in critical thinking, to look beyond the first page of a Google search, to understand which sources are more trustworthy.

Negotiating the conditions for learning can be frustrating and challenging for learners – Cormier reports that he faces a rebellion every year in his class when he adopts it. It confounds their expectations of a teacher as setter of rules and dispenser of knowledge. It is may be less robust than other ways to gain understanding, but it may ultimately lead to deeper understanding of how to learn. It is also a preparation for those workplaces where there is no teacher at hand, nor agreed ways of working, just many interacting communities.

Rhizomatic learning in practice

Rhizomatic learning has mainly been practised in higher education, particularly on postgraduate courses and in online learning where students can engage with a global network of peers and resources. At undergraduate level, Tanya Sasser describes how she runs first-year composition classes as creative writing workshops, with the main learning materials being the compositions of other students. She writes about how to balance peer and expert feedback and how to manage formal assessment where "grades haunt the act of writing, transmuting it into an act of fear and submission".

Can rhizomatic learning be successful at a younger level? Research with adolescent gamers looked at how communities of gamers developed knowledge about how to complete or modify a game. It revealed complex learning systems. The researchers concluded that there is no fixed syllabus in gaming and that participants actively blurred the boundaries of producer/consumer, teacher/learner and individual/collective. They gather around websites for specific games, such as World of Warcraft, that encourage active communities. These are self-organized rhizomatic communities, albeit under the auspices of a gaming company.

Conclusions

Rhizomatic learning is messy, unbounded and demanding. It doesn't fit comfortably into formal education. To run it fully would require not just re-thinking the role of the teacher, but also the assessment and the syllabus. Students would be encouraged to explore freely, set up new communities, respond rapidly as news happens and disrupt conventional notions of scholarship. It is the antithesis of responsible teaching. Yet this is the mode of learning in many workplaces. Perhaps there are ways to nurture communities of young learners so they are simultaneously engaged, challenged and supported.

Resources

Dave Cormier's introduction to rhizomatic learning:
http://bit.ly/2OFxsy0

And a longer paper from Cormier:
Cormier, D. (2008). Rhizomatic education: Community as curriculum. *Innovate: Journal of Online Education*, 4(5), 2.
http://bit.ly/2ECQf8E

Paper on rhizomatic learning in gaming communities:
Sanford, K., Merkel, L., & Madill, L. (2011). "There's no fixed course": Rhizomatic learning communities in adolescent videogaming, *Loading...*, 5(8), 50–70.
http://bit.ly/2OJe57r

Reddit site:
www.reddit.com

Design of Reddit:
Pardes, A. (2018). The inside story of Reddit's redesign. *Wired*, April 2, 2018.
https://www.wired.com/story/reddit-redesign/

Rhizomatic learning for first-year composition:
Sasser, A. (2012). Bring your own disruption: Rhizomatic learning in the composition class. *Hybrid Pedagogy*, December 31, 2012.
http://hybridpedagogy.org/bring-your-own-disruption-rhizomatic-learning-in-the-composition-class/

This chapter draws on material from *Innovating Pedagogy 2012*, published under a Creative Commons Attribution Licence:
Sharples, M., McAndrew, P., Weller, M., Ferguson, R., FitzGerald, E., Hirst, T., Mor, Y., Gaved, M., & Whitelock, D. (2012). *Innovating Pedagogy 2012: Open University Innovation Report 1*. Milton Keynes: The Open University.

Reputation management **39**
*Use the power of the crowd
to assess and enhance reputation*

Overview

Reputation can be seen as a currency of achievement. We gain reputation by carrying out some activity that other people rate as good or valuable. With the growth of online sharing services, such as Airbnb and Uber, reputation is also the outcome of how we rate organizations and people, by liking and promoting them. This is called reputation management. In higher education, academics already have a well-developed system of reputation through citations of their published articles. In schools, students gain reputation by passing exams, also by producing valued products such as essays or paintings and by performing acts of community service. The idea behind reputation management is to bring all these together into an online currency of reputation. People gain credit by passing an exam or carrying out an intellectual task, such as reviewing another person's creative work. They might decide to donate small amounts of reputational credit to boost another person's intellectual product or idea. This opens new possibilities for trading educational reputation. It also raises concerns about treating learning as a commodity to be bought and sold.

Educational reputation and reward

Part of the process of education is for students to demonstrate that they have learnt something, by passing exams or by producing work that the teacher rates, such as an essay or painting. Most schools have some system of reputation and reward to encourage good behaviour and incentivize students. These include gold stars, praise passports and reward stickers.

Some companies now sell to schools elaborate software to record achievements and log activities such as good attendance, taking part in extra-curricular activities and eating healthily. Students gain points and are rewarded by digital badges for other students to see.

At universities, research academics have an internationally recognized measure of reputation: the h-index. This measures how many citations their published papers receive. If an academic has an h-index of 10 it means ten of their published papers have gained ten or more citations. Since the h-index is a global measure of research reputation, it influences whether the academic gets promoted or is successful in applying for a new post. It is by no means the only factor in determining academic reputation – just the most measurable.

Some educational websites also measure and reward reputation. For example, iSpot is a site for people to record observations of nature. Anyone can upload a picture of a plant or animal and try to identify it. The site has a sophisticated method of reputation and reward. Acknowledged wildlife experts start with a high score for reputation. Newcomers have to earn reputation by posting many observations, each with a suggested identification. Others in the iSpot community help to confirm each identification. The more successful identifications a person makes, especially if those are confirmed by other people who have high reputation, the more that person's reputation increases. People with high iSpot reputation gain online badges as experts in birds, fungi, plants, etc.

Pedagogy of reputation

Now, imagine if something like the iSpot reputation system were applied more widely. Students earn reputation by passing exams, writing good essays or engaging in community service. All these acts of academic value, and the reputation they gain, are recorded for all to see.

A further step is to allow transactions, similar to currency payments, of educational reputation rather than money. One way of doing this would be to assign an initial amount of reputation to institutions and individuals, based on their status. This could be related to their standing in international league tables or to significant achievements, such as gaining a higher degree. They can then award small amounts of this reputational currency to students who graduate or colleagues whose work they value. Organizations and individuals could gain further reputation by providing recognized services to education, such as providing open courses or funding research.

Exchange of reputation is already happening in online personal services, such as eBay or Airbnb. A buyer and a seller check each other's reputation on eBay; a visitor is more likely to stay with a host of high reputation on Airbnb. Airbnb now offers experiences such as photography classes or guided tours. Anyone can set up an experience, but to be prominent on the Airbnb site they must earn reputation by running frequent events that are rated highly by visitors. Similarly, in the academic world, professors trade reputation by citing published papers from other academics and in return may get their own research cited.

Reputation management in practice

A new technology, the blockchain, is a digital system that can reliably store many kinds of educational item. Blockchain is the database for the Bitcoin currency, but the technology is more general. It offers a secure, distributed and low-cost way to store many types of records and validate any transaction that can be represented digitally.

Exam scores, degree certificates, student essays, copies of artwork, videos of dance performances can all be kept on an educational blockchain, along with information about who is permitted to view them. What makes the blockchain different from other computer databases is that it is a universal record – not held in one institution but copied across many computers. Blockchain allows people to show their own creative works and ideas to the world, staking a claim for invention and gaining recognition.

In terms of its value for pedagogy, the important aspects are that the blockchain is secure, accessible, distributed and can hold many types of educational item (or links to those items to save filling up computer memories). One use is to store exam records and degree certificates, along with the date each was registered and the organizations involved. Instead of an employer contacting the university to verify a graduate's qualifications, these can be checked using the company's copy of the blockchain. The University of Nicosia was the first higher education institution to store its exam certificates on the Bitcoin blockchain.

This method can be extended to small chunks of achievement. Learning can be recognized and rewarded at different levels, from small learning events (such as completing an online course or taking an evening class) up to a university degree that takes many years. Some organizations already use digital badges to accredit learning. These badges can now be recorded on the blockchain, strengthening the reliability and global accessibility of the badges. Individuals could add items to the blockchain, such as works of art, literary creations, academic papers or records of invention, to provide a secure record of their work and its date.

The record is public, so anyone can see how a person gained educational reputation, and the rules for adding new value are agreed by consensus.

The idea of mining and trading intellectual reputation may sound bizarre, but similar mechanisms form the basis of successful organizations such as Uber and Airbnb. The Open University is experimenting with new educational services on existing blockchains. Technologies are already in place for rating teachers and students, making donations, tracking contributions to knowledge and awarding small amounts of educational credit. The blockchain makes this process more open and visible.

Conclusions

Automated reputation management appeals to institutions that are moving towards digital operation. As with other open online approaches, there is the potential to disrupt current ways of working. Generating trust digitally means that the evidence can be distributed and there is less need for a single, central established authority. Blockchain technology could become an enabler for many innovative pedagogies.

The analogy with Bitcoin is not perfect. Part of the success of Bitcoin as a currency is that the system makes it costly to generate new coinage and the process of mining becomes more difficult over time. The incorporation of cost is useful in commerce and builds in a profit motive for being involved in running the distributed system. A system based on trust and educational reputation would need to be managed in a different way, for example with organizations and individuals gaining a level of recognition before they are able to add items to the blockchain and 'mine' new reputation. The challenge is to open up education to anyone with good ideas to share, rather than just reward existing elite institutions and a small community of scholars.

Reputation management is a new way to motivate students and reward good work. At best, it is an open meritocracy, where anyone can offer a skill, an expert service or an artefact (such as a poem or illustration) for others to enjoy and praise. It can be a way for students with low self-esteem to see how their work is valued not only by a teacher but by their peers and others. At worst, it reduces education to a commodity where students browse, buy and consume educational products with no empathy for scholarship or intellectual value and individuals boost their mutual reputation by praising each other.

The blockchain and reputational currency might reduce education to a marketplace of knowledge. Or they might extend the community of researchers and inventors to anyone with good ideas to share.

Resources

Some reward systems for schools:
www.pupilrewardpoints.co.uk
www.rewardsystem.org
www.vivoclass.com
www.epraise.co.uk

Skillshare site for experts to offer classes, earn money and gain reputation:
www.skillshare.com

Reputation as a currency:
Schlegel, H. (2014). *In Trust We Trust: Why Reputation is the Currency of the Future*. CNN, September 23, 2014.
https://edition.cnn.com/2014/09/23/opinion/in-trust-reputation-currency

Reputation management on iSpot:
http://bit.ly/2yteala

Fictional, yet plausible, future 'Uber-U' distributed university:
Teachonline.ca (2016). Uber-U is already here. Blog posting, May 6, 2016.
teachonline.ca/tools-trends/exploring-future-education/uber-u-already-here

Comprehensive introduction to the blockchain for education by Audrey Watters:
Watters, A. (2016). *The Blockchain for Education: An Introduction*. Hack Education, April 7, 2016.
hackeducation.com/2016/04/07/blockchain-education-guide

The Open University experimenting with blockchain for portfolios, badges and peer reputation:
http://blockchain.open.ac.uk/experiments/

University of Nicosia academic certificates on the blockchain:
http://bit.ly/2PNvmsr

Paper on automated reputation management:
Sharples, M., & Domingue, J. (2016). The Blockchain and Kudos: A distributed system for educational record, reputation and reward. In K. Verbert, M. Sharples & T. Klobučar (Eds.), *Adaptive and Adaptable Learning: Proceedings of 11th European Conference on Technology Enhanced Learning (EC-TEL 2015)*, Lyon, France, 13–16 September 2016. Switzerland: Springer International Publishing, 490–496.
oro.open.ac.uk/46663/

This chapter draws on material from *Innovating Pedagogy 2016*, published under a Creative Commons Attribution Licence:
Sharples, M., de Roock, R., Ferguson, R., Gaved, M., Herodotou, C., Koh, E., Kukulska-Hulme, A., Looi, C.-K., McAndrew, P., Rienties, B., Weller, M., & Wong, L. H. (2016). *Innovating Pedagogy 2016: Open University Innovation Report 5*. Milton Keynes: The Open University.

Open pedagogy   **40**
Teachers and learners create,
mix and share teaching materials

Overview

Open textbooks are published without copyright restrictions. Open pedagogy involves students, with teachers, revising and remixing material from open textbooks and other sources, such as videos and pictures, that are free of copyright. The aim is for students to learn by re-creating teaching resources in ways that make the editorial processes and creative products visible to themselves and others. Their products are continually adapting to events in the world and to new knowledge. The results can be imaginative and provocative, such as adding contemporary dialogue to an out-of-copyright movie. By recruiting their students to the open education resources movement, teachers take a stance on the value of open access to educational resources.

Open Educational Resources

Since the late 1990s, the Open Educational Resources (OER) movement has been releasing educational content with an open licence. This licence provides educational books, papers, sounds, images or videos for anyone to engage in the '5R' activities:

- **retain** copies of the content;
- **reuse** the content in a wide variety of ways;
- **revise** the content;

- **remix** the original or revised content with other material to create something new;
- **redistribute** copies of the original content, revisions or remixes.

Open textbooks are one form of open educational resource. Their open licence permits these books to be modified and adapted by educators and students. In digital format, they are usually free; the print version is sold at low cost.

An initial motivation for open textbooks was to address the high costs of these books from conventional publishers. That led to projects, including OpenStax and BCcampus, that produce books on subjects such as Introductory Statistics that attract high student numbers. The projects typically pay authors to create textbooks, which are then openly licensed.

Research comparing conventional textbooks with open ones demonstrated that student performance was as good, if not better, with open textbooks. Further studies have shown that there is no relationship between textbook cost and student performance. Combining figures on student performance and student savings has provided reliable measures for the success of OER. Such reliable measures have often been missing from past research.

These studies were important in establishing the basis for open textbooks to be adopted and removing objections on the grounds of quality. At first, most open textbooks were used in much the same way as existing ones. While there were savings for students, there was no change in pedagogy. Over time, secondary benefits related to teaching and learning have become apparent. There is some evidence that use of open textbooks has improved retention in courses. This is because, in the past, some students did not purchase a relevant textbook. This affected their confidence or even their ability to study the associated course. Educators using open textbooks have reported that they now assume all students have the textbook when they start the course and teach accordingly.

One example has been the introduction of open textbooks at Tidewater Community College, Virginia, as part of the Z-Degree program. This initiative enables students to earn a degree with zero costs for textbooks. The college redesigned its curriculum to provide course content for students. This approach is similar to a distance learning course that includes a complete set of resources, but it is delivered on campus with support. In the past, the cost of producing such material would have been prohibitively expensive for a college, but the use of OER has made this possible. The college reports gains in recruitment, retention and pass rates.

Open pedagogy

A further step has been to explore the pedagogic opportunities of openly licensed resources. Alongside more open access to education comes a commitment to pedagogy where students critique and re-shape their educational resources. David Wiley, an expert in open educational resources, argues that open pedagogy arises when educators make use of the '5Rs': retain, reuse, revise, remix, redistribute. He defines open pedagogy as "the set of teaching and learning practices only possible or practical in the context of the 5R permissions". This makes a direct link between open pedagogy and OER, although others may prefer a broader definition.

The open textbook is free to adapt. Students can edit and amend an electronic copy as part of their study. Working in a group project, students can rate the content of their textbooks, discuss with their teacher which contents are outdated or less relevant and write new material. The amended textbook can then be made freely available as a revised version. The textbook becomes a living document, updated to meet the changing world and needs of the students.

In cases where most textbooks present the perspectives of the powerful and the conquerors, interaction with open textbooks provides a means to decolonize the curriculum. Multiple authors and multiple editors can provide a greater diversity of views. This not only gives learners some ownership of the curriculum but may also shift their attitude. Knowledge is not fixed and static; it is an ongoing process involving learners. Open pedagogy emphasizes open content alongside open and distributed practices, such as working together to edit an article.

Skills for open pedagogy

A textbook written or edited by students needs to be carefully designed as a source for others to gain understanding of a topic. The art of writing a textbook is to present the essence of a topic in a clear style. Simply adding more voices is likely to produce an unreadable mess. A role for the teacher is to help students build knowledge together. They need to make informed decisions about where to get information and which sources to trust. While students may be able collectively to devise their own curriculum, they will need models to work from and guidance on how to assess and integrate perspectives.

Open pedagogy in practice

An open textbook can be edited and extended by any reader, who then makes it available for others to read online. Thus, there can be multiple versions of the book. Publishers of open textbooks, such as OpenStax, put their books through an extensive editorial process involving senior authors and peer review from a range of colleges. They function in a similar way to traditional publishing companies, with the difference that the books are available for free, funded by philanthropic donations. But OpenStax also provides a platform, CNX.org, for a wide range of original and adapted textbooks. Anyone can contribute to CNX.org and OpenStax does not edit, review or market the materials.

David Wiley is a leading promoter and practitioner of open pedagogy. One product that he developed with students at Brigham Young University is a revised version of the open textbook *Project Management for Instructional Designers*, to include video case studies, new examples, alignment with a professional exam, an expanded glossary and availability in multiple online formats.

Robin DeRosa, a professor of English, replaced a $100 textbook with an open one, put this online on a WordPress site and made students the editors. This gave them the opportunity to amend the text, excerpt longer texts, add front matter to each chapter, provide discussion questions and add interactive video. Long-time online instructor Laura Gibbs reversed this process, basing her course on the development and adaptation of an 'UnTextbook' constructed by students from openly available resources.

Conclusions

Open pedagogy is both an ideology and a practice. As an ideology, it extends the Open Educational Resources (OER) movement which is committed to making high-quality educational resources available to anyone who has a need or desire to learn. Instead of writing assignments that are graded then thrown away, students along with their teachers create works that add value to the world. As a practice, students learn by grasping the essence of a topic then teaching it to others through clear and concise text. Together, the ideology and practice may change the relation that students have with textbooks, from consumers to benefactors.

Resources

Open pedagogy and the '5Rs' from David Wiley:
http://opencontent.org/definition/

Robin DeRosa and open textbooks:
Sheriden, V. (2017). A pedagogical endeavour. *Inside Higher Ed*, August 9, 2017.

Interview with Laura Gibbs about the UnTextbook:
Gibbs, L. (2014). Anatomy of an online course. Blog posting.
http://bit.ly/2PikSUT

Open textbook produced by David Wiley and students:
Amado, M., Ashton, K., Ashton, S., Bostwick, J., Clements, G., Drysdale, J., Francis, J., Harrison, B., Nan, V., Nisse, A., Randall, D., Rino, J., Robinson, J., Snyder, A., Wiley, D., & Anonymous (2018). *Project Management for Instructional Designers*. Licensed under a Creative Commons Attribution NonCommercial ShareAlike (BY-NC-SA) license.
http://pm4id.org

How to share your educational content on OpenStax:
https://openstax.org/blog/how-share-your-own-openly-licensed-content

Tidewater Z-Degree:
https://www.tcc.edu/academics/degrees/textbook-free

Glen or Glenda – example of a movie out of copyright that could be a resource for remixing video:
https://commons.wikimedia.org/wiki/File:Glen_or_Glenda_(1953).webm

Perspectives on open pedagogy:
https://www.yearofopen.org/april-open-perspective-what-is-open-pedagogy/
http://bit.ly/2ypBi4f
http://bit.ly/2yQSKhe

This chapter draws on material from *Innovating Pedagogy 2017*, published under a Creative Commons Attribution Licence:

Ferguson, R., Barzilai, S., Ben-Zvi, D., Chinn, C. A., Herodotou, C., Hod, Y., Kali, Y., Kukulska-Hulme, A., Kupermintz, H., McAndrew, P., Rienties, B., Sagy, O., Scanlon, E., Sharples, M., Weller, M., & Whitelock, D. (2017). *Innovating Pedagogy 2017: Open University Innovation Report 6*. Milton Keynes: The Open University.

Humanistic knowledge- **41**
building communities
Learn about yourself while building knowledge with others

Overview

The goal of humanistic education is to help people become more open to experience, creative and self-directed. This is a person-centred approach. Knowledge-building communities aim to advance the collective knowledge of a community through dialogue. This is an idea-centred approach. When the two approaches are combined, they create a new one: humanistic knowledge-building communities. Students who participate in humanistic knowledge-building communities may develop their knowledge and their selves in integrated and transformative ways.

Developing the self

The humanistic movement, with its person-centred approach, emerged in full force during the American Cultural Revolution of the 1960s. Carl Rogers can be credited with articulating its key educational ideas and implications in his book *Freedom to Learn*. At its core, person-centredness is concerned with developing 'fully functioning' people – those who are open to experience, highly creative and self-directed. Such people are naturally curious about the world, but to flourish they need an environment where they feel supported to explore problems of personal relevance through practical actions. To help people onto a path of lifelong personal growth, Rogers proposed that the role of a teacher should be to facilitate students to learn, to feed their own curiosity. He set down ten principles for facilitating humanistic learning:

1. The facilitator sets the initial mood of the class or experience.
2. The facilitator elicits and clarifies the purposes of individuals as well as the entire class or group.
3. The facilitator relies on each student to motivate the learning, for purposes of personal meaning.
4. The facilitator offers a wide range of resources.
5. The facilitator is a flexible resource to be used by all.
6. In responding, the facilitator accepts both intellectual content and emotional attitudes of the students.
7. The facilitator can become a participant learner.
8. The facilitator can take initiative in sharing feelings and thoughts, in ways that do not demand or impose.
9. The facilitator is alert to expressions of deep feeling and tries to understand these from the person's point of view.
10. In functioning as a facilitator, a teacher or leader tries to recognize and accept personal limitations.

One of the major developments that came out of person-centred pedagogy is the encounter group. These groups met, often with a trained leader, to increase self-awareness and change behaviour. Variations of this idea can be seen in activities such as ice-breakers and team-building activities. Many modern organizations incorporate elements of this person-centred approach, supporting individuals to realize their talents.

Developing ideas

Idea-centredness is a more recent innovation. In the early 1990s, two educational researchers in Canada, Carl Bereiter and Marlene Scardamalia, articulated a theory of knowledge-building communities. Their motivation was to support authentic learning. They had observed that the culture of schools is often far removed from what disciplinary experts actually do. Knowledge-building communities in classrooms were developed to simulate the types of activities and practices that real knowledge workers carry out.

For example, to make scientific discoveries, researchers working on their own problems need to transcend existing ideas. So, in classrooms, ideas are at the centre of collective efforts. Using innovative technologies, such as the Knowledge Forum tool for group work, students can read and build on other students' contributions while working on problems that they find interesting. This pioneering theory and design has now spread across the globe, inspiring educational reform in countries such as Singapore.

Combining development of self and shared knowledge

When participants enter a person-centred or an idea-centred group or community, they are prompted to focus on either the self or on external knowledge. Person-centredness draws attention to the self by proposing activities that get participants to reflect on their experiences and who they are. While knowledge may be important, it is only a secondary concern in these designs. By contrast, idea-centredness focuses on advancing community knowledge as participants share the experiences of working together. The participants' selves may be important, but the idea-centred activities are not focused on the individuals.

Humanistic Knowledge-Building Communities (HKBCs) bring together these two approaches. The belief underlying HKBCs is that personal growth and shared development of ideas can co-exist and that they work together in exciting new ways. As students work with others to develop knowledge, they must also consider their own personal interests and practices as learners; as they consider themselves, they are guided by the new collective knowledge they advance.

This two-centred theory of HKBCs guides how they are applied in practice. This might occur in physical classrooms where students meet face-to-face, in online environments or in hybrid classes. For example, students in a physical classroom can divide their time between encounter group meetings (person-centred approach) and activities that advance their knowledge, such as doing independent research or having group meetings to discuss big questions (idea-centred approach). As students understand more about themselves, they are more able to explore knowledge-based questions on topics that interest them.

Humanistic knowledge-building communities in practice

The Challenges and Approaches to Technology-Enhanced Learning and Teaching (CATELT) graduate course has been run at the University of Haifa, Israel, since the mid-2000s. It combines idea-centred activities (such as writing a collaborative critique of an academic paper) to advance knowledge with person-centred experiences (such as group reflection sessions). The aim is for students to understand and practise a pattern of learning in which person-centredness (care, prizing, empathic understanding) contributes to the building of knowledge. Learners who have a positive regard for themselves and their colleagues are more likely to share their thoughts and build on the ideas of others.

Knowledge Forum is a web-based collaborative learning platform based on the ideas of Bereiter and Scardamalia. It is designed to help students advance their collective ideas, using notes that are coloured to indicate whether a person has read (and is therefore aware of) others' contributions and directional arrows that make connections between ideas.

Conclusions

Person-centredness adds a new perspective to building knowledge in the classroom or online. Students are asked to reflect on their own knowledge, limitations and strengths. They are also encouraged to be open to new experiences and to value the contributions of others. In community spaces, students discuss the challenges they face, strategies to overcome these and what makes for a good contribution. By understanding pedagogy as a blending of person- and idea-centredness, students and teachers may create new ways of learning and teaching. In the words of Carl Rogers: "The most socially useful learning in the modern world is the learning of the process of learning, a continuing openness to experience and incorporation into oneself of the process of change".

References

Seminal book by Carl Rogers on a humanistic future for education:
Rogers, C. R. (1969). *Freedom to Learn*. Ohio: Merrill Publishing Company. (Third edition published in 1994, with H. Jerome Freiberg.)

Summary of *Freedom to Learn* by C. J. Weibell:
http://bit.ly/2f9b5No

Excerpts from the book, including the quotation above:
http://www.panarchy.org/rogers/learning.html

Knowledge forum software:
http://www.knowledgeforum.com/

Knowledge-building community in Singapore:
https://www.kbsingapore.org/

Paper from Bereiter and Scardamalia on computer-supported knowledge building:
Scardamalia, M., & Bereiter, C. (1994). Computer support for knowledge-building communities. *The Journal of the Learning Sciences*, 3(3), 265–283.
http://bit.ly/2xjibsf

Paper by researchers from University of Haifa on humanistic knowledge-building communities and the CATELT course:

Hod, Y., & Ben-Zvi, D. (2018). Co-development patterns of knowledge, experience, and self in humanistic knowledge building communities. *Instructional Science*, 1–27.

This chapter draws on material from *Innovating Pedagogy 2017*, published under a Creative Commons Attribution Licence:

Ferguson, R., Barzilai, S., Ben-Zvi, D., Chinn, C. A., Herodotou, C., Hod, Y., Kali, Y., Kukulska-Hulme, A., Kupermintz, H., McAndrew, P., Rienties, B., Sagy, O., Scanlon, E., Sharples, M., Weller, M., & Whitelock, D. (2017). *Innovating Pedagogy 2017: Open University Innovation Report 6*. Milton Keynes: The Open University.

Pedagogies in practice   42

With so many new and emerging pedagogies, the obvious question for teachers and education policy makers is 'Which ones should we adopt?'. Where is the evidence that helps us decide whether to explore adaptive teaching systems, to teach science through threshold concepts or to embrace dynamic assessment? Fortunately, alongside these innovative pedagogies has come a new science of learning, where findings from neuroscience, cognitive sciences, educational and social sciences are combined to produce a deep understanding of how we learn. This has led to evaluations of pedagogy based on a combination of learning theory and empirical evidence. Recent studies have compared different methods of teaching in classrooms and online to reveal which methods increase knowledge, improve exam scores and keep learners engaged.

There is a deep, and often justified, resistance from many educational researchers to the 'medical model' of evidence that treats pedagogies as pills administered to students, tested in the same ways as a new medicine. Learning a topic is not the same as swallowing a pill – it involves a series of mental processes and often-complex social interactions with a teacher and other students. There is no educational equivalent of a 'placebo' (a similar-looking pill with no medical effect). It may take many months or years for the effects of good teaching to become apparent, as skills learned at school or in college are applied in the workplace.

Rather than relying solely on controlled experiments to evaluate new pedagogies, research is now piecing together evidence from multiple sources, rather like pieces of a jigsaw puzzle, to build up a picture of effective methods of teaching, learning and assessment. The method of design-based research has been widely adopted for educational innovation. Researchers using this approach carry out a series of trials of a new method of teaching, with each trial (or 'design experiment') leading to improvements in the method and insights into learning theory and practice.

Cooperative learning

One success has been in cooperative learning. When students work together in small groups of between four and eight people, they can deepen understanding by responding to the ideas of other students and developing a shared understanding. Over the past 40 years, hundreds of studies in labs, classrooms and online have uncovered conditions for successful cooperative learning. For groups to work well:

- All students need to know enough about the topic to be able to contribute.
- Students need to have shared goals.
- Each person should know how and when to contribute.
- Everyone should make an appropriate contribution.
- Students should share rewards such as group marks in a fair way.
- Members of a group should all have opportunities to reflect on progress and to discuss contributions.

For many students, learning in groups is not a natural process and they need to learn how to cooperate by arguing constructively and resolving conflicts. The key phrase is 'positive interdependence' – everyone sees the benefits of learning together and works to achieve the group's goals. All over the world, schools and colleges now make time for group learning activities founded on these principles of positive interdependence. Many of the pedagogies in this book rely on cooperation between learners.

Collaborative and social learning online

More recently, learning through positive interdependence has been extended to collaborative and social learning online. Here, the groups may be looser and less coherent, without shared goals. For example, the learners may be people from around the world who have signed up to study a short online course. The learning benefits come from sharing ideas and perspectives through discussions and constructive argument.

The effects of such online computer-supported collaboration are much harder to measure than for group work in a classroom. An ingenious study at The Open University compared learning benefits of 157 of its distance-learning courses.

Each course had been carefully designed according to a set of pedagogic principles, with differing mixtures of individual and collaborative learning. The university collects the exam scores for all students taking the courses, as well as results from surveys of student satisfaction with the teaching and data on how many students drop out from each course. From these data, the researchers calculated which types of course produced the most successful outcomes.

The researchers found that the design of the course had a significant effect on student satisfaction and performance. Students were more satisfied with courses that had a large element of individual reading and watching instructional videos. But students were more likely to complete courses that had more collaborative learning. Furthermore, exam scores were lower on average for the courses that were based more on individual learning by reading and watching. These findings match other studies showing that although students may not always like to take part in collaborative and social learning, they work best when they work together, pooling knowledge and sharing diverse views.

Feedback for learning

Another robust finding from studies of human psychology applied to education is the value of feedback to learning. Feedback can come from a teacher, an expert, another learner or a computer. Giving feedback is most successful when it helps a learner to improve, by finding out how to correct a misunderstanding or to build new knowledge in reaching a goal. Pedagogies that rely on constructive feedback include teachback, dynamic assessment, embodied learning and learning by making.

It is easier to study the effects of feedback than many other educational methods, so many experiments have been run into whether feedback should be immediate or delayed, positive or negative and combined with praise or punishment. In brief, giving immediate feedback works best for easy learning tasks and when the student is building knowledge. Both positive and negative feedback can help learning. Negative feedback points out shortcomings and how to correct them; positive feedback can encourage students to continue. There is good evidence that praise alone does not produce learning. Feedback must be relevant to the task and lead to specific action.

Active and constructive learning

Active and constructive learning involves students carrying out an activity that can support learning – such as commenting, critiquing, constructing – while thinking about the purpose and aim of the activity. This contrasts with instructivist learning that mainly involves listening and watching, a lecture for example. A series of studies have compared the sequencing of constructivist and instructivist approaches. They found that students who actively explore a topic (for example, by trying out a science simulation) and then receive instruction perform better on tests of knowledge than students who listen to the lecture before active exploration. The results are clear, but the explanations of why this happens are still speculative. A plausible explanation is that students who are instructed first and then explore become fixed on the specific items delivered by the lecture, whereas those who explore first gain a broader understanding of the possibilities and dimensions of the topic, which provide a framework for understanding the lecture.

Human memory and learning

The success of active, constructive and collaborative learning raises a question as to how young children learn. Around the age of 8, a typical child is learning to speak about around fifteen new words a week, without the mental effort of exploring, discussing and critiquing. How do they do it, and could that same accelerated learning be adopted or re-discovered in adulthood?

Making associations, such as 'hello – bonjour', is the basic process of learning. Studies of associative learning began over 100 years ago. They show that trying to cram lots of facts and associations into memory does not work. Instead, we need to space the practice over time, so that the learning is repeated just as the association is fading from memory, for example at 5 seconds, 25 seconds, 2 minutes, 10 minutes, 1 hour, 1 day, 5 days, 25 days, 4 months and 2 years. Rather than just viewing the association at these intervals, it is better to try and recall it. For example, learners might be asked, 'What is the French for "hello"?' while using 'flashcards' with the English word or phrase on one side and the French on the other. Many language-teaching methods are based on this method of spaced repetition. It is at the core of successful learning platforms such as Memrise and Duolingo.

Spaced repetition on flashcards is successful for making memory associations, such as learning vocabulary or multiplication tables. The 'spaced learning' pedagogy builds on findings from neuroscience that explain how humans form long-term memories. Things we remember in short-term memory fade rapidly, but if they are transferred to long-term memory they can last a lifetime. The neuroscience studies show that permanent neural connections are more likely to be made when a brain cell is stimulated at intervals than when it is constantly stimulated. Spaced learning involves 20-minute periods of learning interspersed with 10-minute practical activities. There is evidence for success in learning by spaced repetition and it is already being applied to the teaching of curriculum subjects. This is the nearest that education gets to a 'learning pill', so it has attracted media attention. This is still research in progress, though it is based on a century of research into human memory and learning.

A new science of learning

The cognitive and social processes involved in learning fundamentals of biology may be very different to those required for discussion of philosophy in an online learning environment. Research is combining observations of learning, controlled psychology experiments, investigations of human brain functioning and computational models of machine learning. Together, this work is establishing a new science of learning. Researchers piece together the evidence to form a composite picture of how people learn, individually and together, with and without the support of a teacher, at different ages and in differing cultures. This new science of learning can already help in predicting which innovative pedagogies might work in which contexts.

New pedagogies based on principles of cooperative learning are likely to be successful when the students have shared goals, similar motivations to learn and time and ability to reflect. These conditions may apply, for example, to professional development in the workplace. Findings about collaborative and social learning can inform the design of pedagogies for learning at massive scale, where the diversity of views create a 'social network effect' of vibrant discussion, but with a need to manage and contain the discussions.

Research into feedback for learning is already leading to new forms of assessment, such as dynamic and stealth assessment, and to computer-based systems for adaptive teaching. The value of active and constructive learning underpins many innovative pedagogies, such as citizen inquiry, immersive learning and computational thinking. The neuroscience of human memory may provide a basis for new pedagogies of accelerated and optimized learning.

Elements of a new science of learning

Amongst all this innovation in teaching, learning and assessment, some principles endure. The teacher still performs a central function, but that is changing from delivery of educational content to facilitating discussion and reflection. Structure is still important, perhaps even more than it was before, as we discover effective ways to initiate, embed and extend learning. Learners still need appropriate goals and support. Most importantly, learning is a collegiate process. It works best when people want to learn, enjoy the process and support each other. The next decade of innovating pedagogy may focus less on the individual elements of instruction and more on how to merge the new pedagogies into an effective process of lifelong learning.

Resources

Introduction to design-based research

Wang, F. & Hannafin, M. J. (2005). Design-based research and technology-enhanced learning environments. *Educational Technology Research and Development*, 53(4), 5–23. https://bit.ly/2op08f6

Cooperative learning

Overview of cooperative learning:
http://www.co-operation.org/what-is-cooperative-learning/

Survey of successful methods and procedures of cooperative learning:
Johnson, D. W., & Johnson, R. T. (2009). An educational psychology success story: Social interdependence theory and cooperative learning. *Educational Researcher*, 38(5), 365–379.

Collaborative and social learning online

Comparison of group activity in online courses showing that assessing group activity does not improve participation, but that well-structured and appropriate tasks can make groups more effective:
Brindley, J. E., Walti, C., & Blaschke, L. M. (2009). Creating effective collaborative learning groups in an online environment. *The International Review of Research in Open and Distributed Learning*, 10(3).
www.irrodl.org/index.php/irrodl/article/view/675/1313

Comparison of courses with individual and collaborative learning:
Rienties, B., & Toetenel, L. (2016). The impact of learning design on student behaviour, satisfaction and performance: A cross-institutional comparison across 151 modules. *Computers in Human Behavior*, 60, 333–341.
oro.open.ac.uk/45383/
Toetenel, L. & Rienties, B. (2016). Analysing 157 learning designs using learning analytic approaches as a means to evaluate the impact of pedagogical decision-making. *British Journal of Educational Technology*, 47(5), 981–992.
oro.open.ac.uk/45016/

Constructive feedback

Review of research on feedback, with advice on how to design effective feedback:
Shute, V. J. (2008). Focus on formative feedback. *Review of Educational Research*, 78(1), 153–189.
https://fla.st/2NWm3op

Active and constructive learning

Research on transfer of knowledge from one task to another:
Bransford, J. D., & Schwartz, D. L. (1999). Rethinking transfer: A simple proposal with multiple implications. *Review of Research in Education*, 24, 61–100.
http://bit.ly/2EBXei0

Paper on a framework for active learning:
Chi, M. T. H., & Wylie, R. (2014). The ICAP framework: Linking cognitive engagement to active learning outcomes. *Educational Psychologist*. 49(4), 219–243.

Overview of 'productive failure' – learning by exploring first:
www.manukapur.com/research/productive-failure/

Human memory and learning

Early paper on 'graduated interval recall' for foreign-language learning:
Pimsleur, P. (February 1967). A memory schedule. *The Modern Language Journal*. Blackwell Publishing, 51(2), 73–75.
files.eric.ed.gov/fulltext/ED012150.pdf

Spaced learning

Kelley, P., & Whatson, T. (2013). Making long-term memories in minutes: A spaced learning pattern from memory research in education. *Frontiers in Human Neuroscience*, 7, 589.
http://bit.ly/2CCfsgy

Duolingo:
www.duolingo.com

Memrise:
www.memrise.com

A new science of learning

Koedinger, K., Booth, J. L., & Klahr, D. (2013). Instructional complexity and the science to constrain it. *Science*, 342(6161), 935–937.
http://bit.ly/2AmZHcc

Meltzoff, A. N., Kuhl, P. K., Movellan, J., Sejnowski, T. J. (2009). Foundations for a new science of learning. *Science*, 325(5938), 284–288.
www.ncbi.nlm.nih.gov/pmc/articles/PMC2776823/

This chapter draws on material from *Innovating Pedagogy 2016*, published under a Creative Commons Attribution Licence:

Sharples, M., de Roock, R., Ferguson, R., Gaved, M., Herodotou, C., Koh, E., Kukulska-Hulme, A., Looi, C.-K., McAndrew, P., Rienties, B., Weller, M., & Wong, L. H. (2016). *Innovating Pedagogy 2016: Open University Innovation Report 5*. Milton Keynes: The Open University.

Index

Note: Page numbers in italics indicate figures. Page numbers in bold indicate tables.

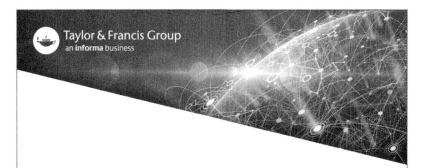

Printed in Great Britain
by Amazon

15180332R00154